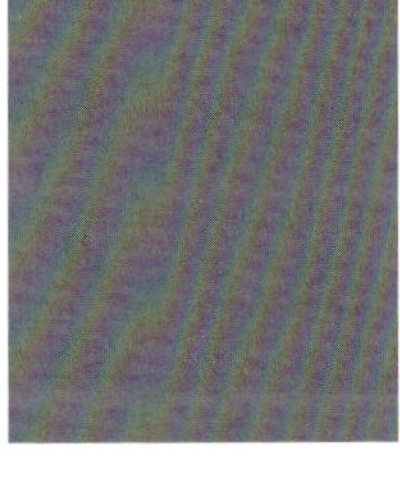
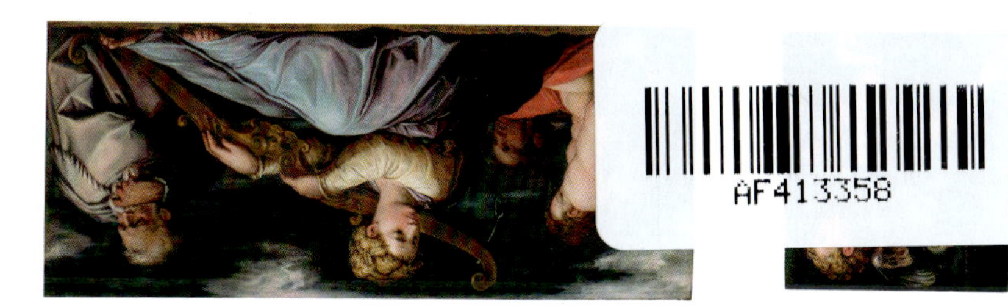

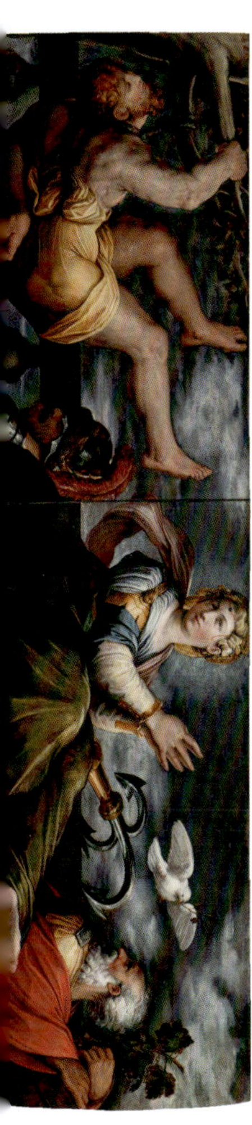
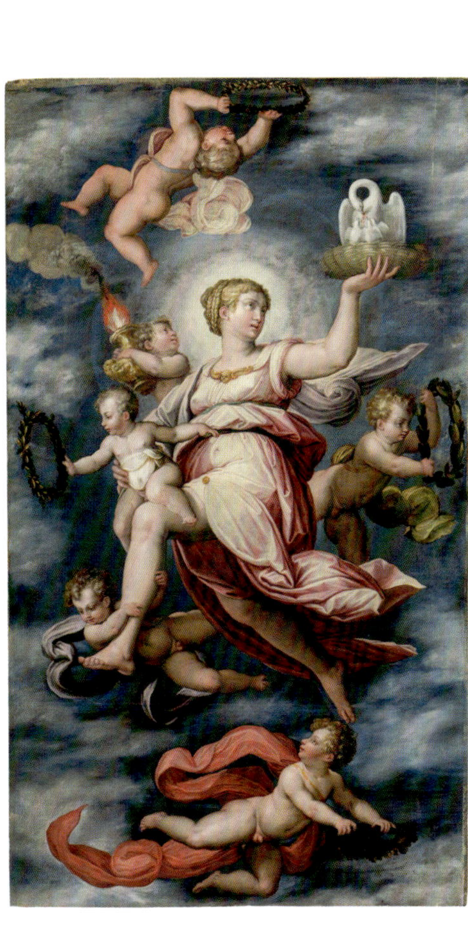
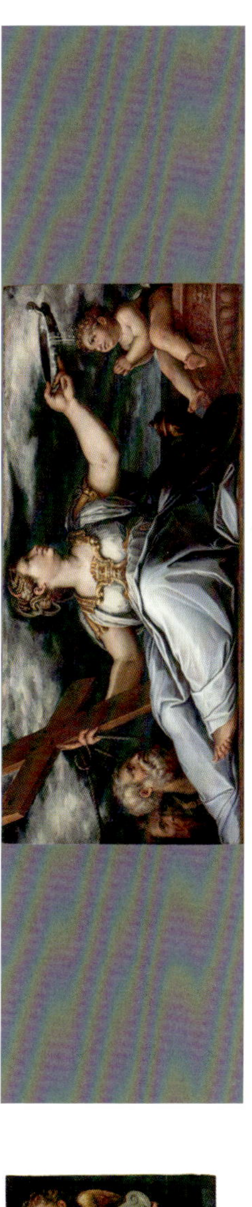
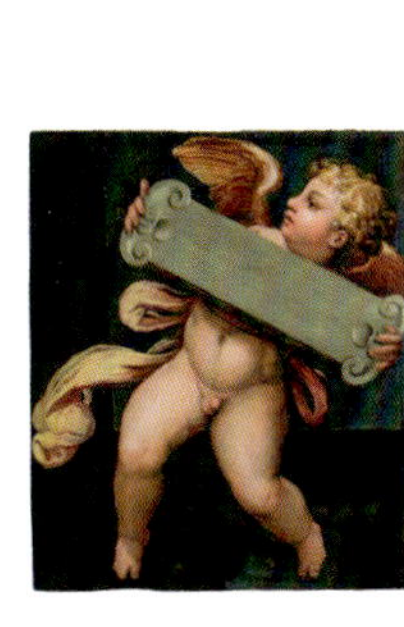
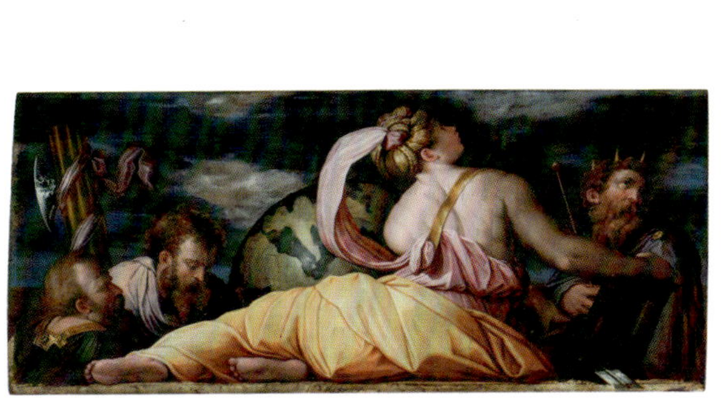
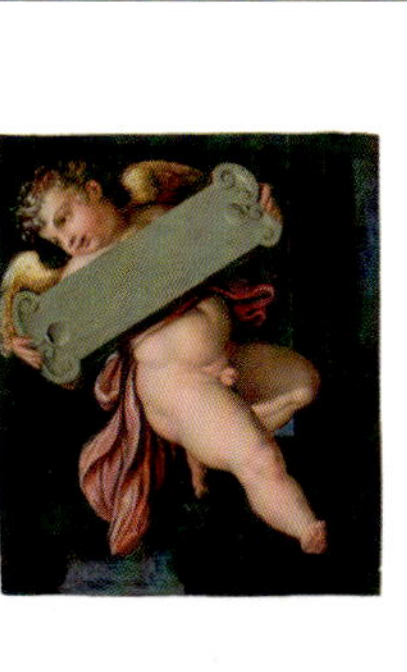

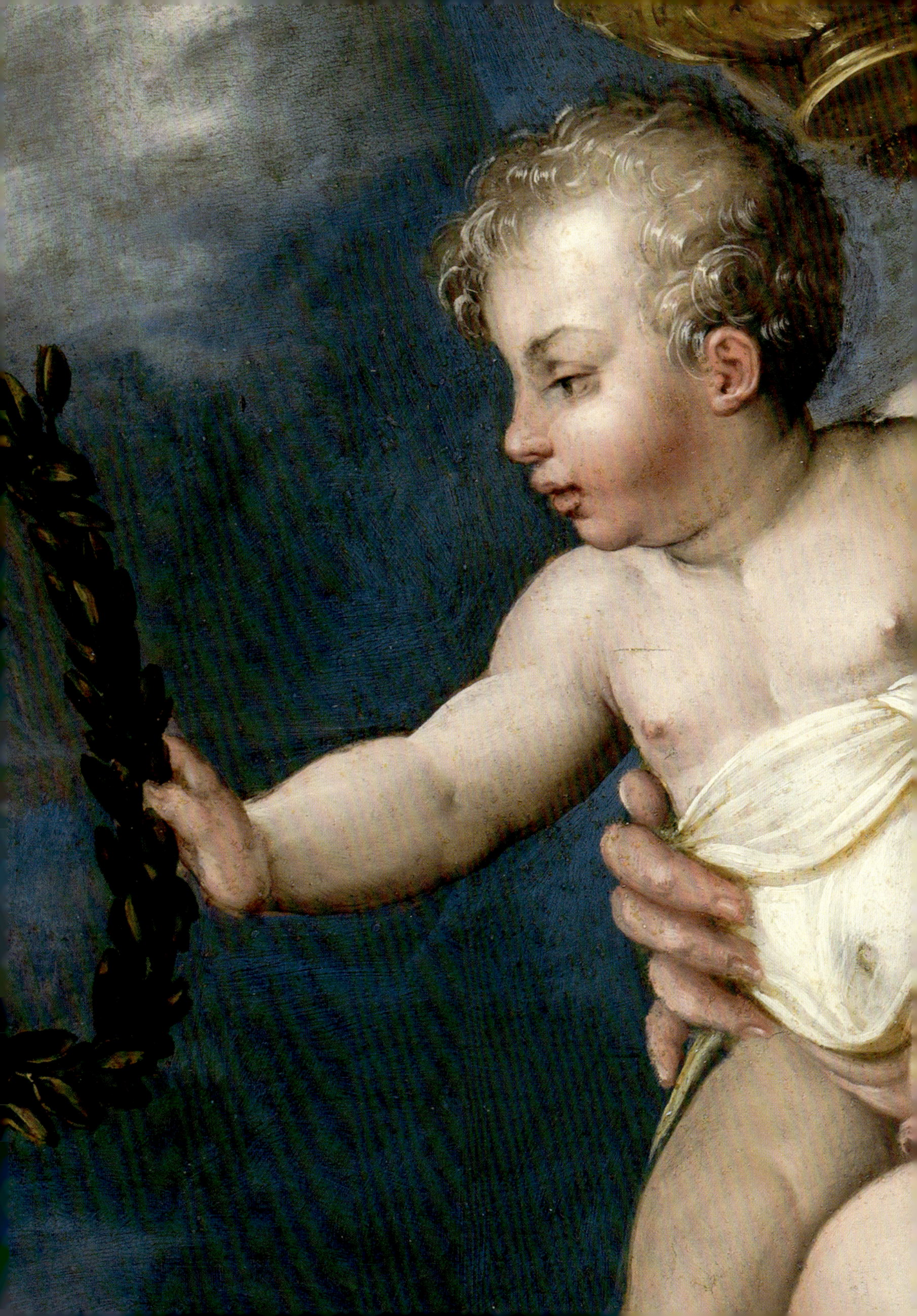

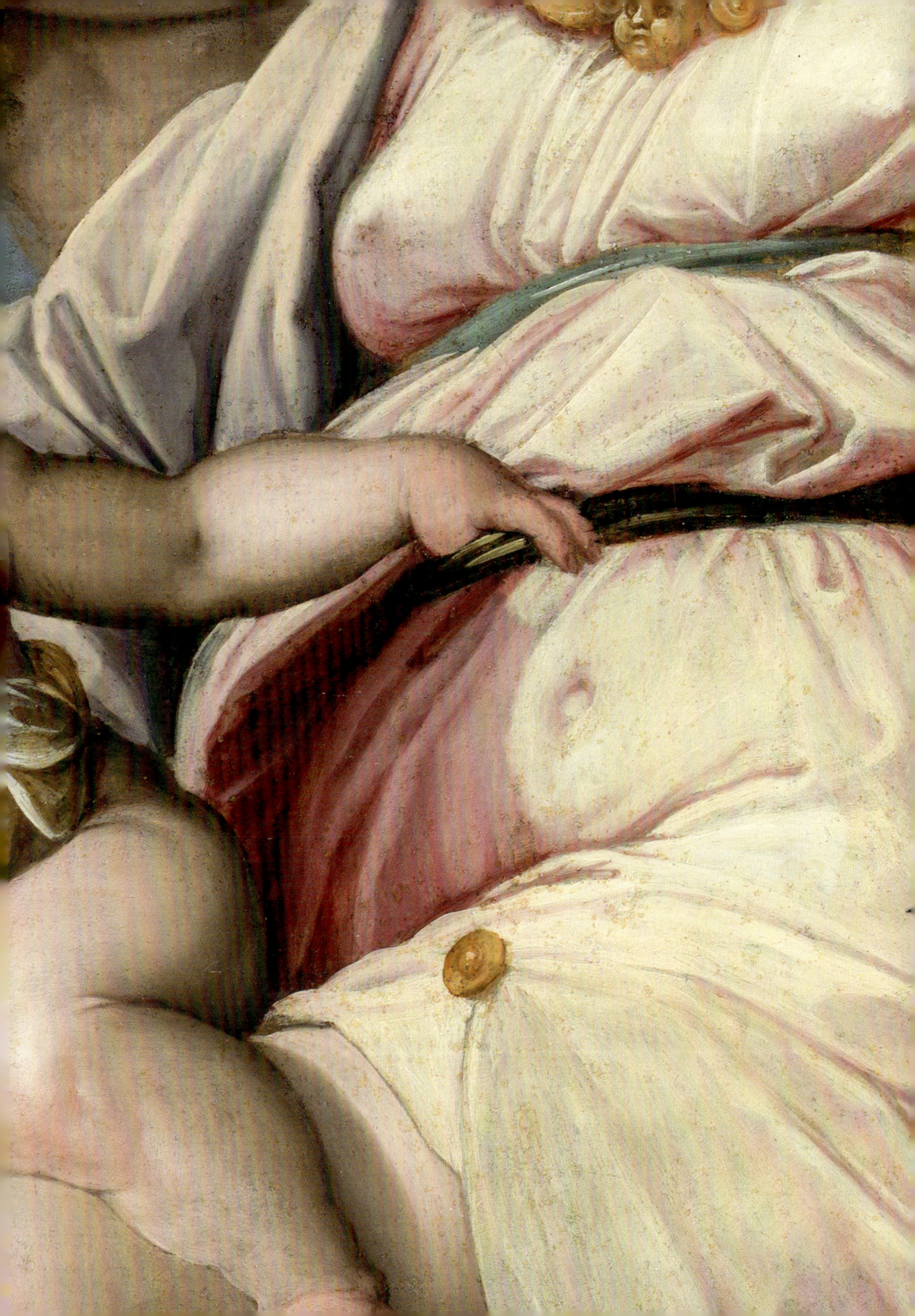

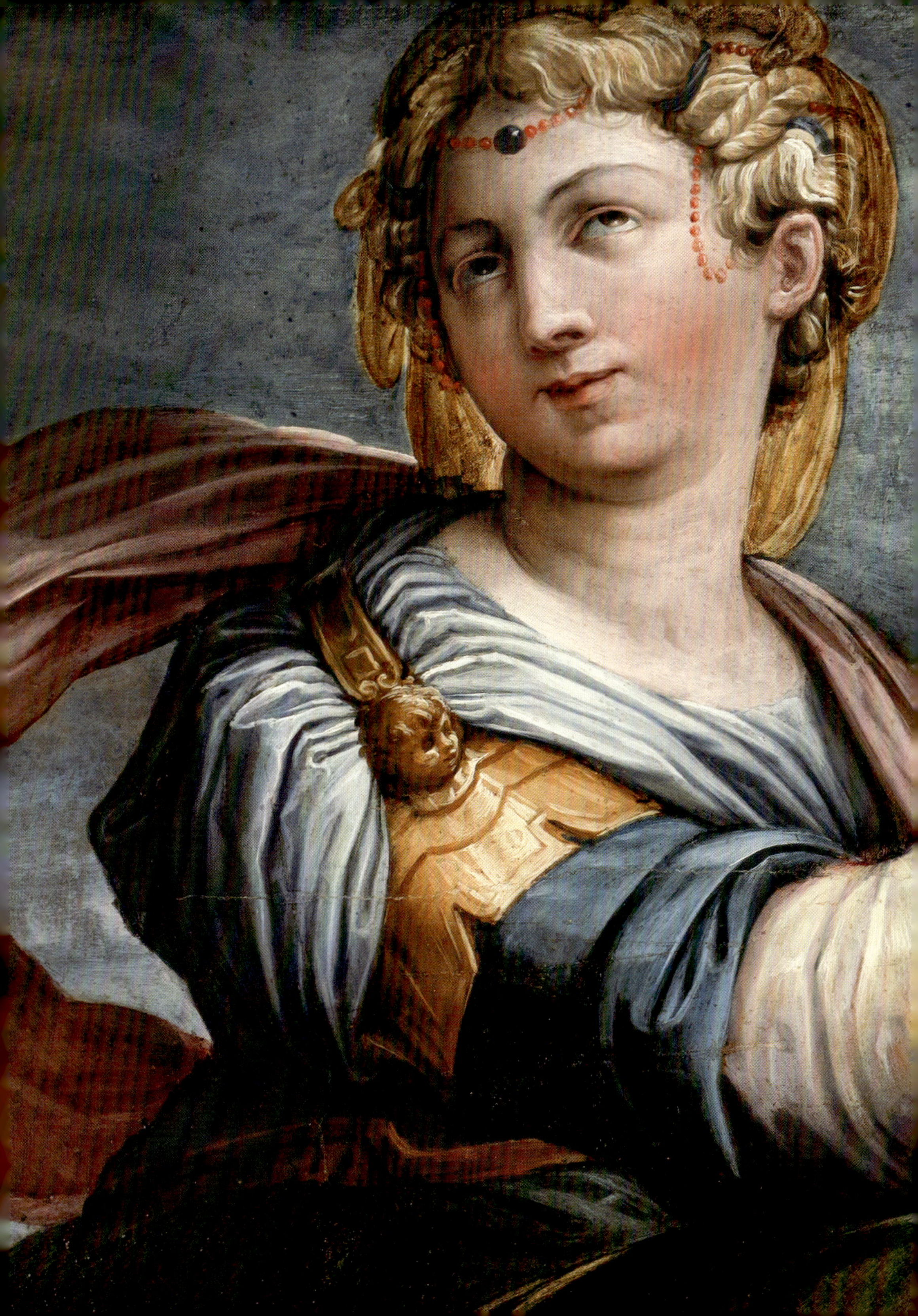

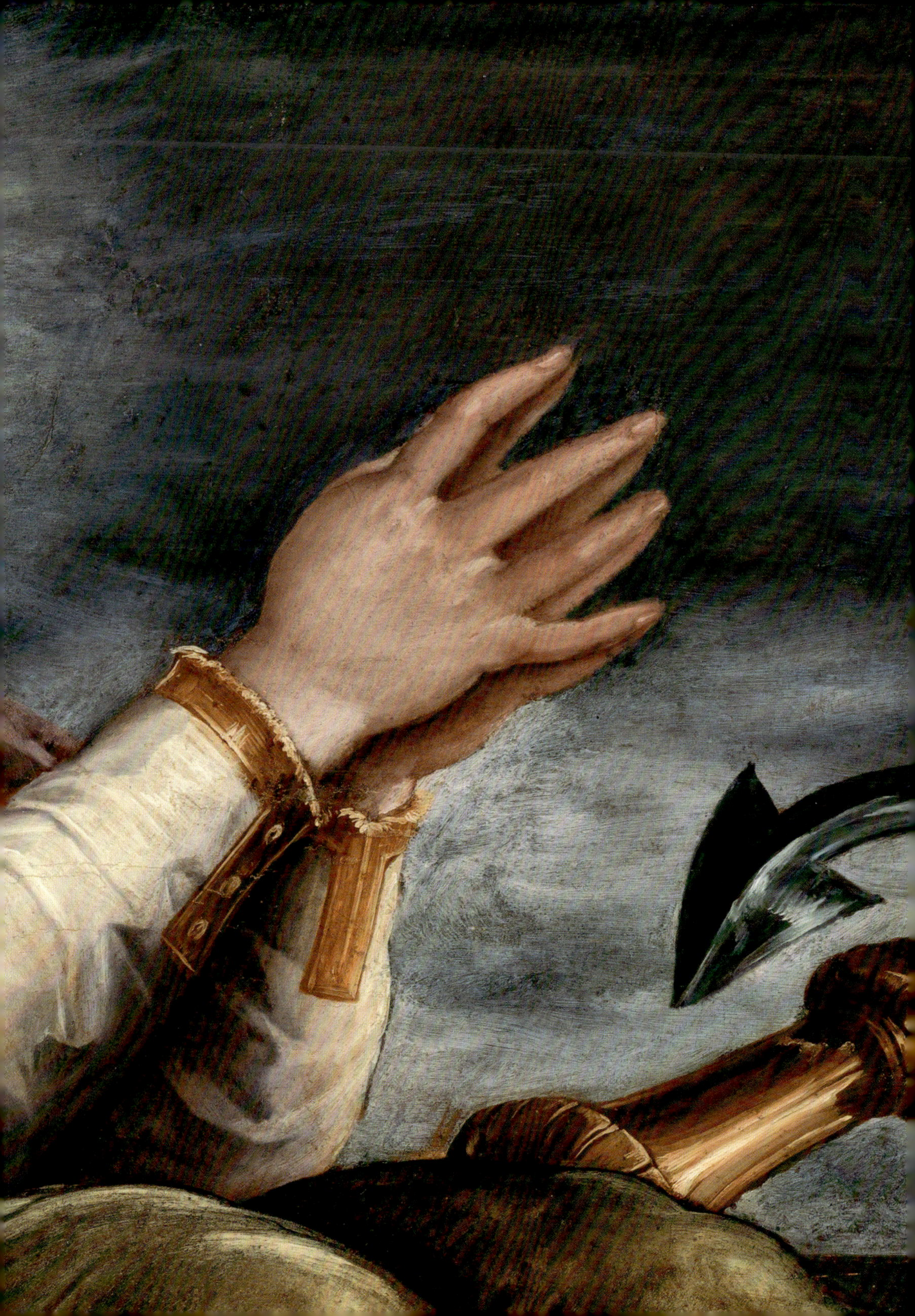

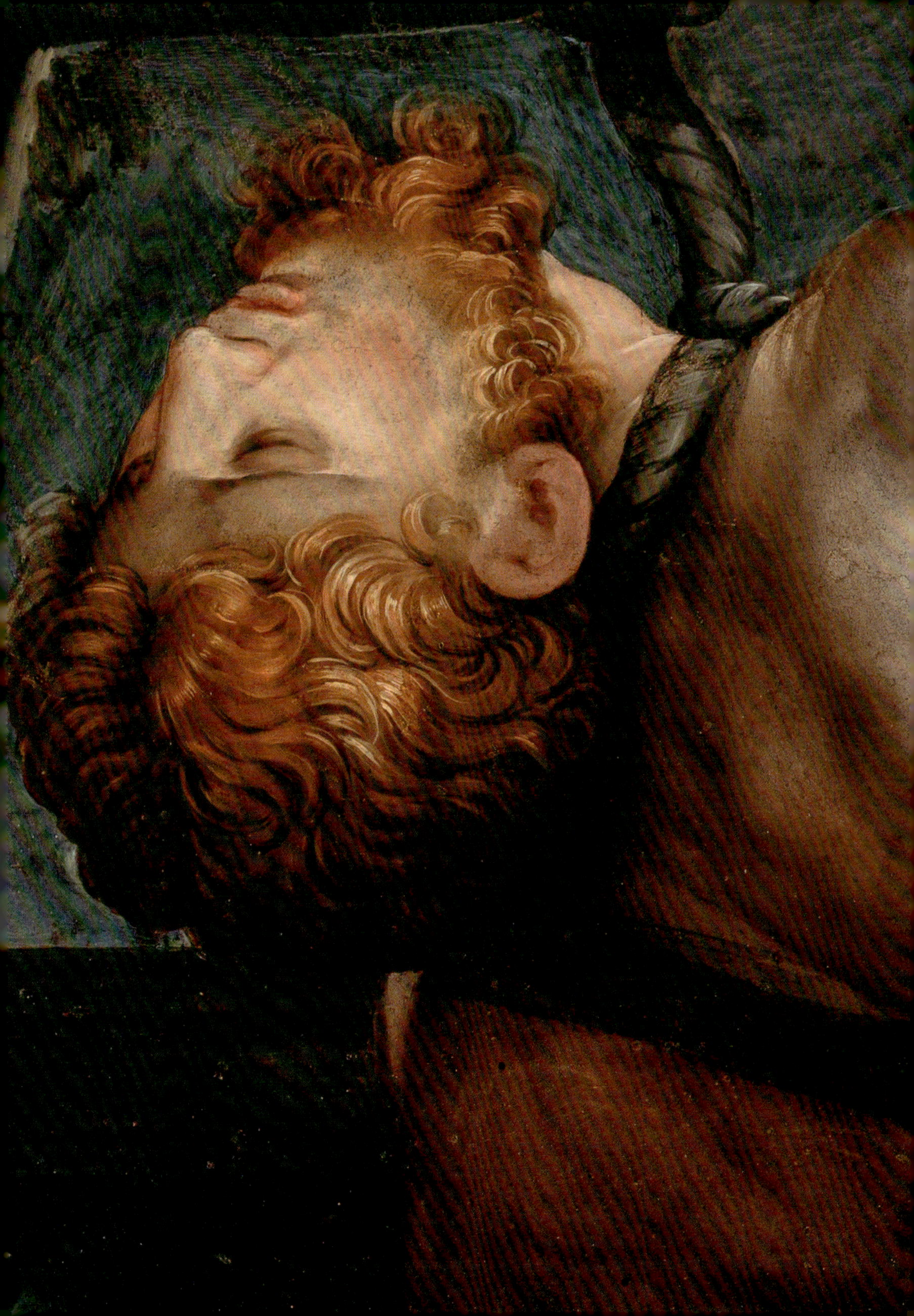

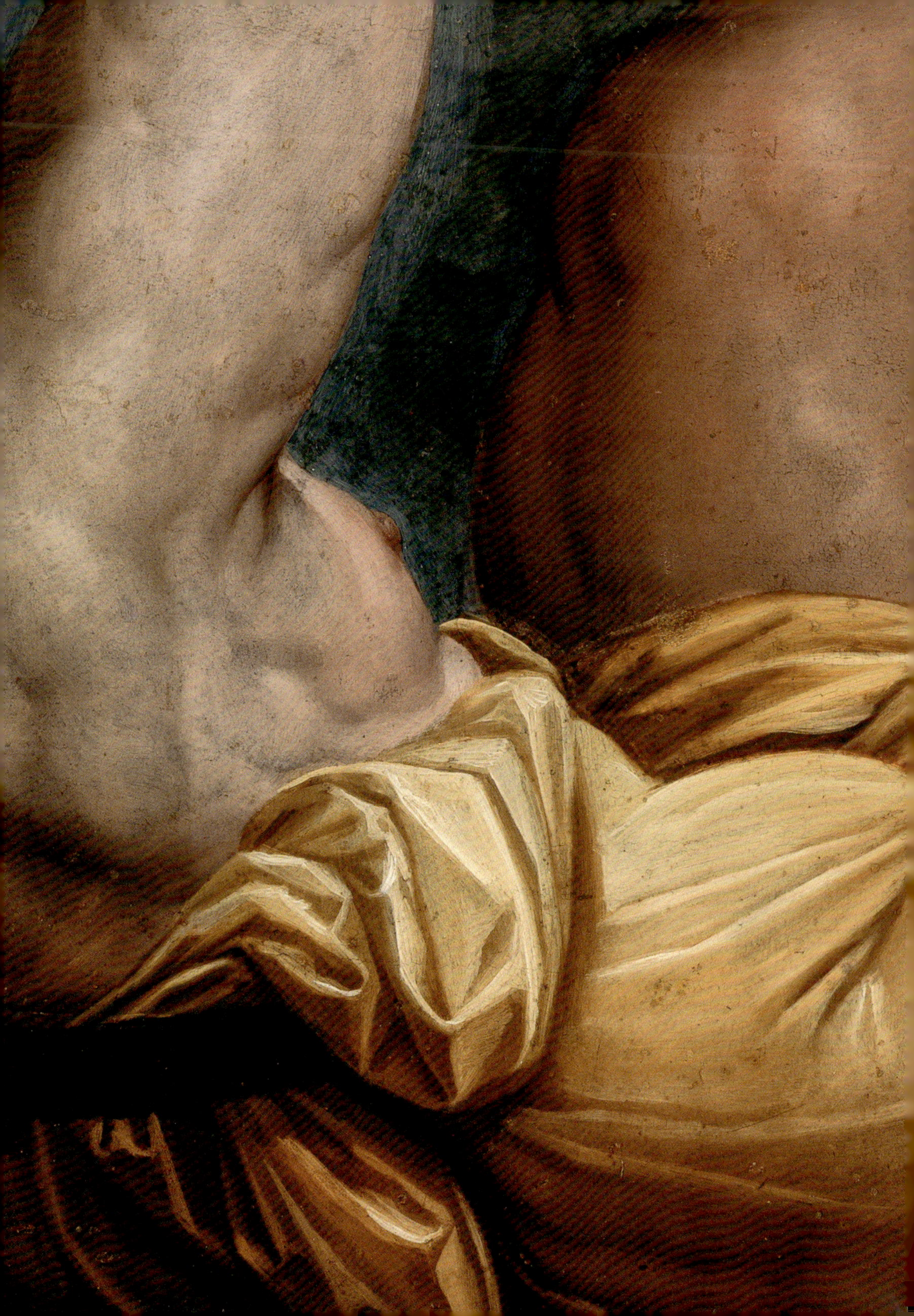

The publication of this volume has been financed by

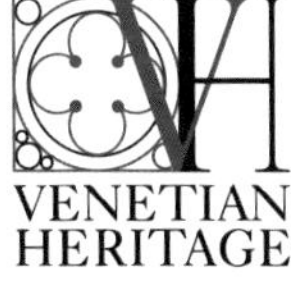

thanks to the support of Luca Marzotto and Roger Thomas

The Venetian Masterpiece by Giorgio Vasari

A re-assembled Renaissance ceiling

edited by Giulio Manieri Elia

Marsilio Arte

Giulio Manieri Elia

Director, Gallerie dell'Accademia in Venice

The present volume celebrates an exceptional event: the return to Venice and reassembling of an entire painted Renaissance ceiling, a masterpiece created by Giorgio Vasari in 1542. A work that few museums in the world can boast of, the final result of a long process of acquisition, restoration, preliminary study and planning, culminating in the final reassembly of the panels. More than two centuries ago, Venice witnessed the start of the gradual dispersal of the panels of the Corner ceiling, one of its foremost art works. Forty years ago, the Italian State, via what was then the Venetian Historical and Artistic Superintendence, in efficient collaboration with the Ministry of Culture, launched a great project aimed at finding and recovering the lost fragments of this precious artifact, which, like a jigsaw puzzle, was gradually reassembled.

An exemplary case of virtuous coordinated planning and persistent action that has led to this extraordinary result. The hunt for the lost fragments began in 1980 with the purchase of the so-called *Suicide of Judas*, which because of its theme had been initially judged an unlikely candidate, and ended in 2017 with the recovery of the *Allegory of Hope*, laying the ground for the reconstruction of the whole that we celebrate today. For the Italian State, the acquisitions were promoted by: Anna Maria Maetzke, Francesco Valcanover, Giovanna Nepi Sciré, Giovanna Damiani, and Paola Marini while Caterina Bon Valsassina and Stefano Casciu have contributed by offering in deposit the *Allegory of Charity* and the *Suicide of Judas*. I personally have contributed to all the phases of the project since 2002. Rossella Cavigli, our colleague from Arezzo, restored all the panels in view of their reassembling into a whole, while Roberto Saccuman restored the wooden supports.

The initiative has been an extremely significant and virtuous example of public-private collaboration, especially in two moments: the recovery from abroad of the last two panels and the restoration of the whole. Venitian Heritage distinguished itself by providing an essential contribution both financially and in terms of organization, and the Italian Embassy and Consulate in London very hospitably provided logistical support. In the purchase of the *Allegory of Faith*, ministerial funds were integrated by a league of contributors that included Venetian Heritage, Venice in Peril Fund, Pro Venezia Sweden, Fondazione di Venezia, Vela SpA, MSC cruises, SAVE SpA, Consorzio Venezia Nuova and Fondazione Veneto Banca. In the purchase of the *Allegory of Hope* the amount allocated by the Ministry was integrated by the contributions of Venetian Heritage and Venice in Peril Fund. There was great participation around this initiative, and all worked passionately and effectively to achieve the common goal, a coordinated joint action leading to an outstanding result.

Valentina Marini Clarelli Nasi

President, Fondazione Venetian Heritage Onlus, Venice

Peter Marino

Chairman and President, Venetian Heritage Inc., New York

Since 1999, Venetian Heritage has been promoting Venetian culture through an enormous campaign of restoration projects carried out not only in Venice but throughout the territories that were once part of the Venetian Republic.

This vast and ambitious program has received the support of Italian and international institutions, foundations, and patrons, united by the desire to preserve the incredible artistic heritage that the Venetian Republic spread across the eastern Mediterranean from the Middle Ages to the end of the eighteenth century.

In 2015, Venetian Heritage began a fruitful collaboration with the Gallerie dell'Accademia by funding, in partnership with Samsung, the permanent installation of the first four rooms of the new exhibition space on the museum's ground floor. Building on this project, Venetian Heritage financed the permanent installation works of the Saloni Selva-Lazzari, which houses some never-before-exhibited paintings by influential 17th and 18th-century artists. This new wing, inaugurated in September 2021, has made it possible to enjoy an uninterrupted exhibition space through the museum's ground floor.

Venetian Heritage has supported the restoration of multiple masterpieces of Venetian painting for the Gallerie dell'Accademia, such as the *The Fortune-Teller* by Giovanni Battista Piazzetta, the *The Descent from the Cross* by the Neapolitan artist Luca Giordano, the scene of *Erminia and Vafrino Find the Wounded Tancredi* by Gianantonio Guardi, the *Scourge of the Serpents* by Giambattista Tiepolo, whose restoration was dedicated to the memory of Lawrence D. Lovett, the founder of Venetian Heritage. To promote Venetian art and culture, Venetian Heritage has cofinanced many important exhibitions at the Gallerie dell'Accademia, such as *Aldo Manuzio. Renaissance in Venice* and *Canova, Hayez, Cicognara: The Last Glory of Venice.*

We are particularly proud to present this volume dedicated to the incredible recomposition of the Giorgio Vasari ceiling in Palazzo Corner Spinelli, which was achieved thanks to Venetian Heritage's support for acquiring the two panels depicting *Faith* and *Hope.* We wish to thank all those who generously contributed to the success of these significant acquisitions. Moreover, thanks to the generous donations of Simon R. Low, Venetian Heritage was able to fund the complex conservation work on the wooden supports of all the panels that make up the ceiling, essential for its reconstruction in the room XIIIA found in the Palladian corridor on the first floor of the museum.

We want to extend our gratitude to all those who, over the years, have dedicated themselves to the study, recovery, and restoration of Giorgio Vasari's Venetian masterpiece, especially to the authors of this volume: Giulio Manieri Elia, Rossella Cavigli, and Luisa Caporossi. We would also like to thank Roberto Saccuman, Serena Bidorini, Silvia Salvini, and Ornella Salvadori for their valuable technical-scientific contributions. The publication of the catalog was financed thanks to the generosity of Luca Marzotto and Roger Thomas, Vice President and Board Member of Venetian Heritage Foundation respectively, to whom we extend our sincerest gratitude for their constant and faithful support.

There could not have been a better occasion to celebrate the 450th anniversary of the death of this great artist from Arezzo than through the recomposition of his extraordinary ceiling that inspired Titian, Veronese, and Tintoretto. This project is another example of a successful collaboration between the public and private sectors.

Photo credits
Su concessione del Ministero della Cultura – Gallerie
dell'Accademia. Foto Matteo De Fina

Beinecke Rare Book and Manuscript Library, Yale University
Rossella Cavigli
A. Dagli Orti/Scala, Firenze
Foto Fine Art Images / Heritage Images / Scala, Firenze
Foto Scala, Firenze
Su concessione del Ministero della Cultura – Biblioteca
Nazionale Marciana
Su concessione del Ministero della Cultura – Direzione
regionale Musei della Toscana – Firenze
Su concessione Ministero della Cultura – Gallerie degli Uffizi.
Foto Scala, Firenze
Teylers Museum, Haarlem, the Netherlands

Cover
Giorgio Vasari, *Allegory
of Faith*, 1542, detail

Design and layout
Livio Cassese

Translation
Gabriele Poole

©2024 by Marsilio Arte s.r.l.,
Venice

First Edition August 2024

ISBN 979-12-546-3257-4
www.marsilioeditori.it

Printed by
Grafiche Veneziane s.c.r.l.,
Venice
for Marsilio Arte s.r.l., Venice

contents

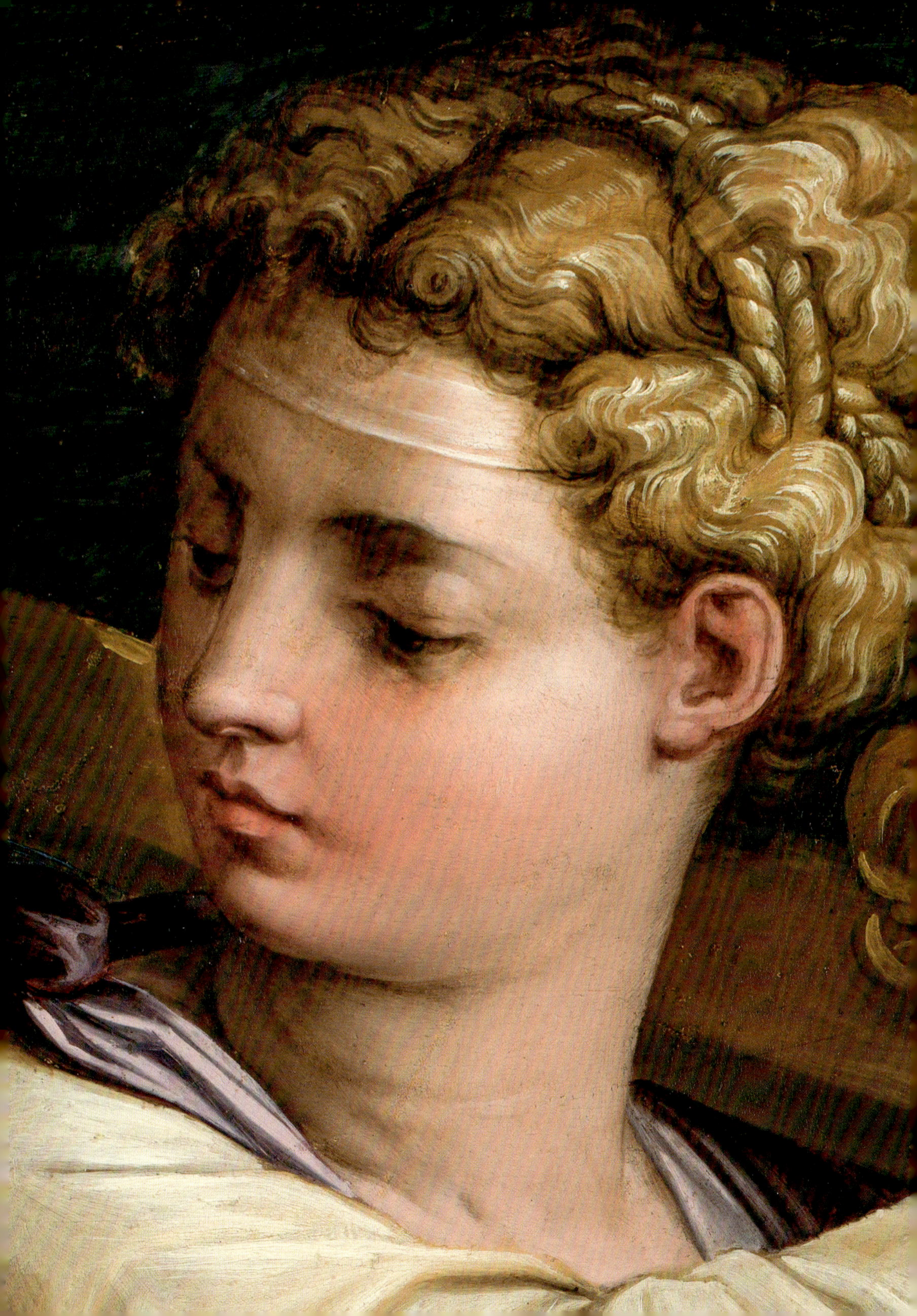

Re-Assembling the Puzzle

Toto Bergamo Rossi, Giulio Manieri Elia

A long adventure that lasted almost forty years, with an acceleration in the last twenty; we are talking about the reassembling of the panels that composed the coffered ceiling of the "Camera nova" in the Corner Spinelli palace, a project that involved a great number of people who understood the importance and passionately contributed to this incredible enterprise: individual actions coordinated for a single great purpose: bringing back home to Venice one of the most extraordinary pictorial ensembles ever created, the Venetian masterpiece by Giorgio Vasari. An entire Renaissance ceiling is now reassembled: a goal that when the first panels began arrive we scarcely deemed possible. A great success for the offices of the Ministry of Culture and other public and private entities who contributed to it. These pages, written together with Toto Bergamo Rossi, director of Venetian Heritage Onlus Foundation, with whom we have shared much of this adventure, are therefore dedicated to the many people who participated in this long and successful project.

Giulio Manieri Elia   For more than twenty years I have been working on the reassembling of the ceiling of Casa Corner Spinelli and for at least ten I have been passionately and effectively supported by Venetian Heritage and in particular by Toto Bergamo Rossi. The year 2002 was crucial for the events we are narrating: with Giovanna Nepi Scirè, then Superintendent for the historical and artistic heritage of Venice, we succeeded in acquiring, with funds from the Ministry, a *Putto with Table*, from a private Milanese collector, represented by Galleria Carlo Orsi. In the same year we obtained on deposit, thanks to the ready collaboration of Superintendent Caterina Bon Valsassina and of Matteo Ceriana, the central compartment with the *Allegory of Charity*, which belonged to the Braidense collection and had been kept in the museum of the Società di Storia Patria in Gallarate. In that same year, however, we also met with an initial failure. We attempted with dedication and much effort to purchase the *Allegory of Faith* owned by Lord Kennet, but the complexity of administrative procedures caused the deal to bog down. However, we did not lose faith and, in 2011, after almost ten years, having obtained the backing of Venetian Heritage, we resumed the struggle to obtain the panel. The clock was ticking since preparations were being made to auction the work . This time, with Superintendent Giovanna Damiani, we decided to attempt a private negotiation. To obtain the necessary financial resources, we launched a fundraising that would combine public and private economic support. Then, along with Toto Bergamo Rossi, and accompanied by Nicola Todaro Marescotti of the Italian embassy in London Embassy, which had intervened in our support, we visited Lord Kennet's house. There we discovered, to our great amazement and some concern, that the panel—so invaluable to us—was casually positioned above a working fireplace in the living room, where we were greeted by the entire family. However, despite the placement it proved to be in good condition, as we were able to promptly determine.

Toto Bergamo Rossi The relationship between the Gallerie dell'Accademia and Venetian Heritage began in 1999, when the then Superintendent for the Artistic and Historical Heritage of Venice and director of the Gallerie dell'Accademia, Giovanna Nepi Scirè, requested a grant for the acquisition of a special device for producing high-resolution thermographic images of the museum's paintings. From that moment began a productive collaboration, which is still ongoing. In 2011 we adhered enthusiastically to the "treasure hunt" launched by Giovanna Damiani for Vasari's lost masterpiece.

GME A speech by Paolo Costa, former Mayor of Venice, at the annual meeting of the International Private Committees for the Preservation of Venice sparked the initiative to buy back the Kennet panel. It was then that the project for recovering the dispersed sections of the ceiling, promoted by the Venetian Superintendency, became public. *La Nuova Venezia* on October 22, 2011 published an article entitled "Costa launches hunt for Ca' Corner Vasari," and on March 28, 2012 Gian Antonio Stella, to whom we were introduced by Salvatore Settis during a conference, declared his support for the project and reported on it in the pages of *Corriere della Sera*. Although the fundraising proved to be long and complex process, neither we nor Venetian Heritage lost heart. We were also lucky to be able to count on the kind understadning of the owners in relation to both the timing and economic demands, which were considerably reduced. Thus, on June 18, 2013, the contract of sale was signed by Giovanna Damiani and Lady Kennet at the Consulate of Italy in London. The joint funds, raised over two years, came from the Ministry of Culture, the Soprintendenza Speciale per il Patrimonio Storico Artistico ed Etnoantropologico e per il Polo Museale della città di Venezia e della Gronda lagunare, Venetian Heritage and Venice in Peril Fund.

TBR The fundraiser organized by Venetian Heritage dedicated to the acquisition of the panel depicting the *Allegory of Faith* was supported by the Fondazione di Venezia, MSC, Venezia Marketing Spa, GRUPPO SAVE Spa, Consorzio Venezia Nuova and Fondazione Veneto Banca. In addition, some supporting members and friends of Venetian Heritage also contributed generously to the fundraising campaign, including Princess Firyal of Jordan, Marta Coin, Valentina Marini Clarelli Nasi, Lady Monika del Campo Bacardi, Alvise di Canossa, Luca Marzotto, Carla Bossi Comelli, and Lydia Salmon Fasoli. We also managed to obtain a technical sponsorship for the transportation of the work from London to Venice, thanks to the valuable and constant collaboration with the Arterìa company. I fondly remember our visit to the home of Lady Kennet, who lived in the house that was once the home of the writer Sir James Matthew Barrie, the creator of the legendary Peter Pan.

GME   In 2016, with Paola Marini, Director of the Gallerie dell'Accademia, we resumed the project, trying to obtain what scholars at the time believed to be the entire last missing piece. The title of the work, the *Allegory of Hope*, was auspicious. The Weidenfeld family, owners of the work, had often informally suggested that they would be willing to part with the work. It was finally offered for sale, through Christie's London, in July 2016. I was able to travel to London and see it thanks to the support of Nicolas Penny, former director of the National Gallery in London, who helped me enter the Weidenfeld home, along with some London museum workers who had come to move the work. Placed in the studio of the well-known publisher George Wiedenfeld (Austrian by birth, exiled in England and naturalized British), it was accompanied on the wall by an array of portraits of Roman pontiffs of the sixteenth and seventeenth centuries, a rather surprising choice for a person of Jewish origin. The negotiation, which had on this occasion an exceptional supported in the person of Oscar winning director James Ivory, was concluded in July 2017, thanks to a larger contribution by the Ministry of Culture and the ready financial availability of Venetian Heritage and Venice in Peril Fund.

TBR   Once again, the public-private synergy has born fruit. It was Venetian Heritage with Venice in Peril Fund that raised the missing funds needed to acquire the painting depicting the *Allegory of Hope*. We organized with the then director of the Gallerie dell'Accademia, Paola Marini, a press conference at the Galleries' restoration laboratory at the Scuola della Misericordia, where the Corner Spinelli ceiling panels were being restored. Director James Ivory, a longtime supporter and honorary member of Venetian Heritage, made an appeal to the press for the raising of the missing funds and also contributed a major donation. He was followed by Pierre d'Arenberg, Maria Audi Catafago, Jean-Marc Droulers, Alexis Gregory, Enrico and Claudia Moretti Polegato, Tom and Alice Tisch, and the Swedish pro-Venetia Committee. Once again the Artería company took on the role of technical sponsor by transporting the *Hope* panel from London to Venice free of charge. Venetian Heritage starting in 2013 financed the travel expenses of restorer Rossella Cavigli, who was in charge of the restoration of all compartments of the Vasari ceiling at the Laboratorio della Misericordia. In addition, the conservation work on the wooden supports of the eight panels performed by Roberto Saccuman was funded through the generous contribution of Simon R. Low.

GME The year 2016 was important for the acquiring of new information on the work. The material study of the panels during the restoration work, a preliminary step in the reassembling of the ceiling, allowed Rossella Cavigli, Conservation Restoration Officer of the Regional Directorate Museums of Tuscany, who directed the restoration, to propose, together with her colleague Luisa Caporossi, a final disposition of the panels in the ensemble that differed from the one hypothesized in previous studies. In particular, the colleagues from the Regional Museums Directorate of Tuscany were able to confirm that the so-called *Suicide of Judas*, on display at the Casa Vasari Museum, was indeed part of the ensemble—a hypothesis already advanced in the past—and more specifically—a hypothesis never advanced before—that it was actually a missing section of the *Allegory of Hope*. This discovery led us to a different estimate of the size of the original panel and of the entire ceiling. After a series of coordinated initiatives between Venice and Arezzo to explain the importance of re-assembling the ceiling, in 2018, thanks to the collaboration and willingness of Director Stefano Casciu, we were granted on loan of the so-called *Suicide of Judas* and were able to recompose the two sections. As it turned out, this was not the last piece of the puzzzle. As we were able to ascertain, we are still missing two sections that were cut out respectively from the *Allegory of Faith* and the *Putto with Table*. While these are certainly significant parts of the whole that we hope to add to the other paintings sooner or later, their absence does not detract from the extraordinariness of the result we are celebrating today.

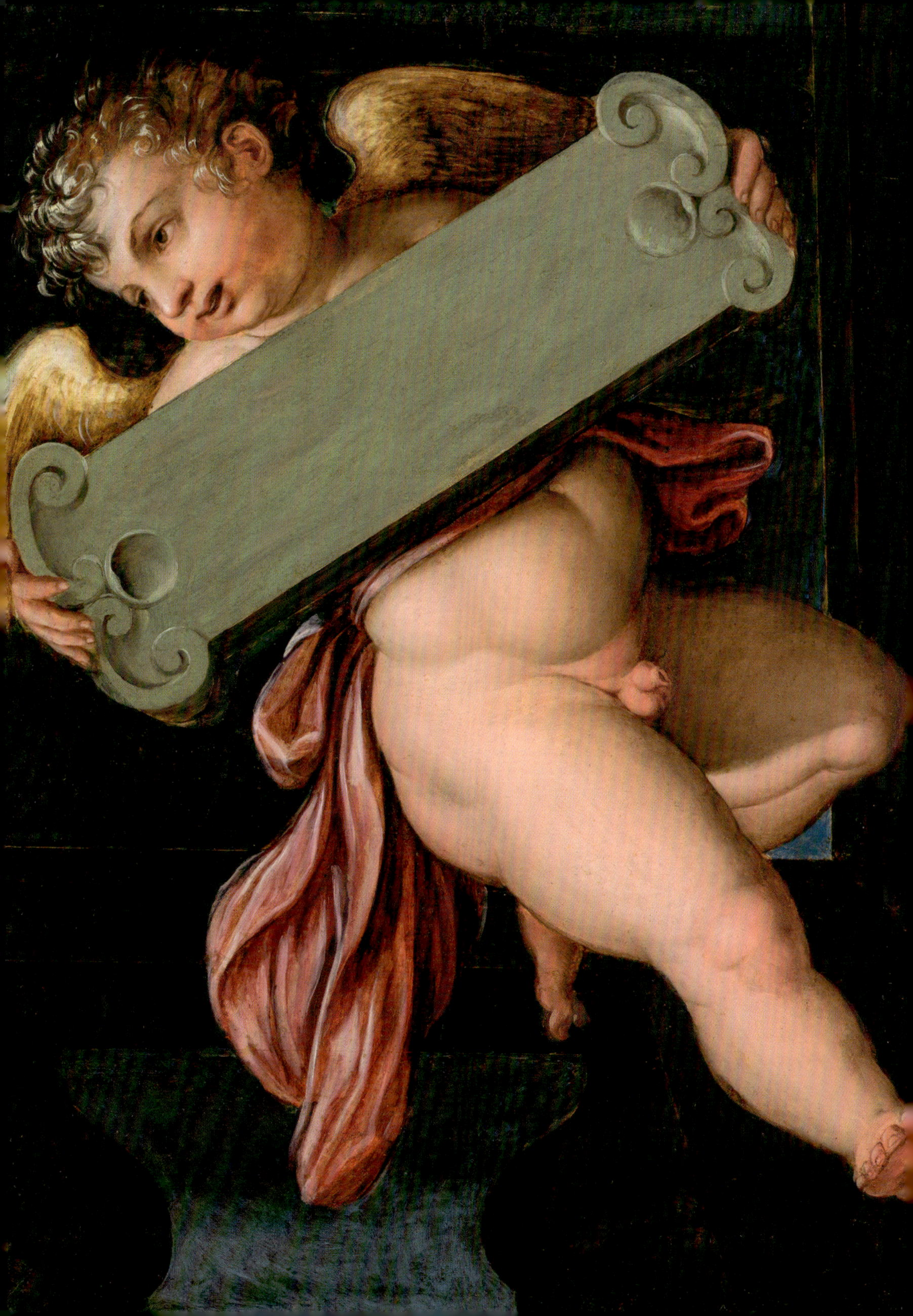

"They Stayed in Venice . . . Painting for the Magnificent Giovanni Cornaro the Roof or Ceiling of a Room."
Genesis, Loss and Recovery of Giorgio Vasari's Venetian Masterpiece

Giulio Manieri Elia

On December 1, 1541, Giorgio Vasari arrived in Venice following an invitation by Pietro Aretino, who had been residing there since 1527, for the purpose of designing the scenes of the comedy la *Talanta*, which was to be staged during the Carnival of the following year by an association of young patricians devoted to the theater called the Sempiterni.[1] Vasari's intention for coming might also been from the start that of consolidating his relationship with Aretino, who was from Arezzo like himself, and gain access through him to the court of Cosimo I.[2] Be as it may, his friendship with Aretino certainly helped him come into contact with the circle of the wealthy Venetian patrons. The young Vasari, however, had also his own cards to play: ambitious and eager to establish himself in the city, he could present himself as a representative and connoisseur of the art culture of Raphael and Michelangelo in Central Italy. Such knowledge certainly has an effect on families such as the Corner, who because of their ties to the Catholic hierarchy looked towards Rome for guidance in their taste for art. It was from this family that Vasari obtained an important commission, thanks also to the mediation of the Veronese architect Michele Sanmicheli (to whom, in gratitude, he donated a drawing depicting *St. Michael defeating the rebellious angels*).[3] He was asked to paint the coffered ceiling of a room in the palace that Giovanni Corner had recently purchased from the Lando family on the Grand Canal, after the family residence in Campo San Polo had caught fire and burned to the ground.[4]

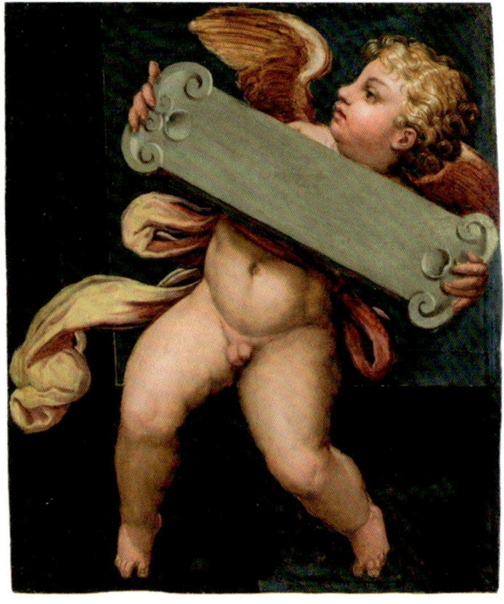

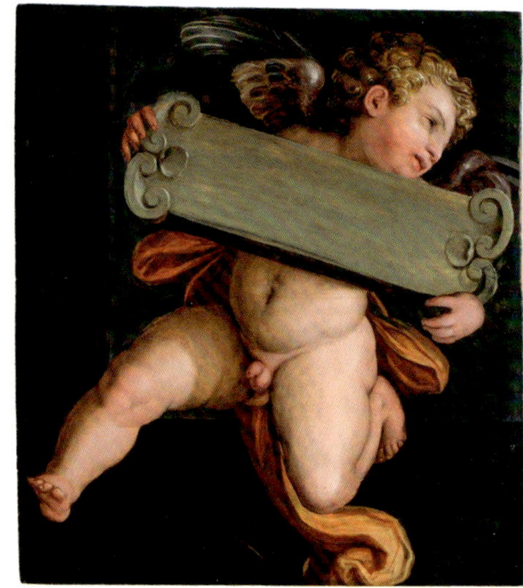

2
Giorgio Vasari, *Putto with plaque*,
1542, panel, 77,2 × 65,4 cm,
cat. 1372

3
Giorgio Vasari, *Putto with plaque*, 1542,
panel, 69,4 × 61,8 cm, cat. 2015

previous page
1
Giorgio Vasari, *Putto with plaque*,
1542, panel, 77,3 × 67,9 cm,
cat. 1373

Giovanni Corner,of the San Polo branch, was a notable figure in the Venice of those years, the Corner being one of the city's most influential, wealthy and noble families. His aunt was Queen Catherine of Cyprus, his grandmother a niece of John IV Comnenus, Emperor of Trebizond, and his palace at the corte dell'Albero where Vasari painted the ceiling and where Giovanni Corner established his residence after the renovation, was frequented by intellectuals and writers such as Giovanni Grimani, Giangiorgio Trissino, Diego Hurtado de Mendoza, ambassador of Charles V, and Aretino himself, who indeed may have been invited to Venice by the Corner family. Also, his nephew was one the members of the Sempiterni council, who participated in the organization of the Carnival celebrations.[5]

Returning to the commission, we do not know for sure in which room of the palace the ceiling was located. The most recent hypothesis refers to a modest sized room in the southeast corner of the inner courtyard, whose specific function we do not know, but which at the time must have been recently completed since it is referred to in documents as the "new room".[6]

The ceiling consists of nine painted elements totaling about 12 square meters of panels, with a subject that could be described as a *Triumph of the Virtues*. As Vasari himself noted, the Virtues are distributed in five of the panels while in the other four in the corners there are four *Putti with tables*: "in a middle one Charity ... in four squares Faith, Hope and Justice and Patience ... and another 4 paintings with inside four putti in the corners."[7] *Faith, Hope* and *Charity,* the latter larger than the others and placed in the center, are three theological virtues. They are accompanied by *Justice*, a cardinal Virtue, and *Patience*, a lesser Virtue. Although the general subject, suggestive of divine love and moral qualities, would have been well suited to a bridal chamber,[8] the hypothesis seems actually unlikely given that the documents indicate that, the year after the ceiling was made, Giovanni Corner's bedroom was one of the two large rooms facing the Grand Canal.[9]

As Luisa Caporossi argues in her essay in the present volume, it is possible to identify the Virtues thanks to their symbolic attributes, with other figures placed as corollaries evoking concepts associated or contrasting with the main theme:[10] *Patience* calmly bears the weight of a yoke, her head bowed as a sign of obedience and docility;[11] beside her, an elderly man, perhaps inspired by Michelangelo's *Jeremiah* in the Sistine Chapel, is identifiable as Job.[12] The figure of *Justice* is depicted with her back to the viewer, suggesting impartiality, and with two traditional attributes: a law code and sword. She is accompanied by two figures bearing fasces, symbolizing civil and military justice, and a crowned figure, identifiable as Solomon[13] or Trajan.[14]

The Virtues are depicted with bold foreshortenings, and complex and refined postures, and arranged—all except *Charity*—around the perimeter of the room, with a perspective from below projecting onto an open sky, with a rather somber coloration. The impression is that of a space with an open roof and the effect must certainly have been one of surprise and disorientation for those entering the room.

As he himself recalls, Vasari enlisted the help of Cristoforo Gherardi[15] and an apprentice named Battista.[16] The painting technique appears careful but executed with rapid, vibrant and rather free brushstrokes, probably

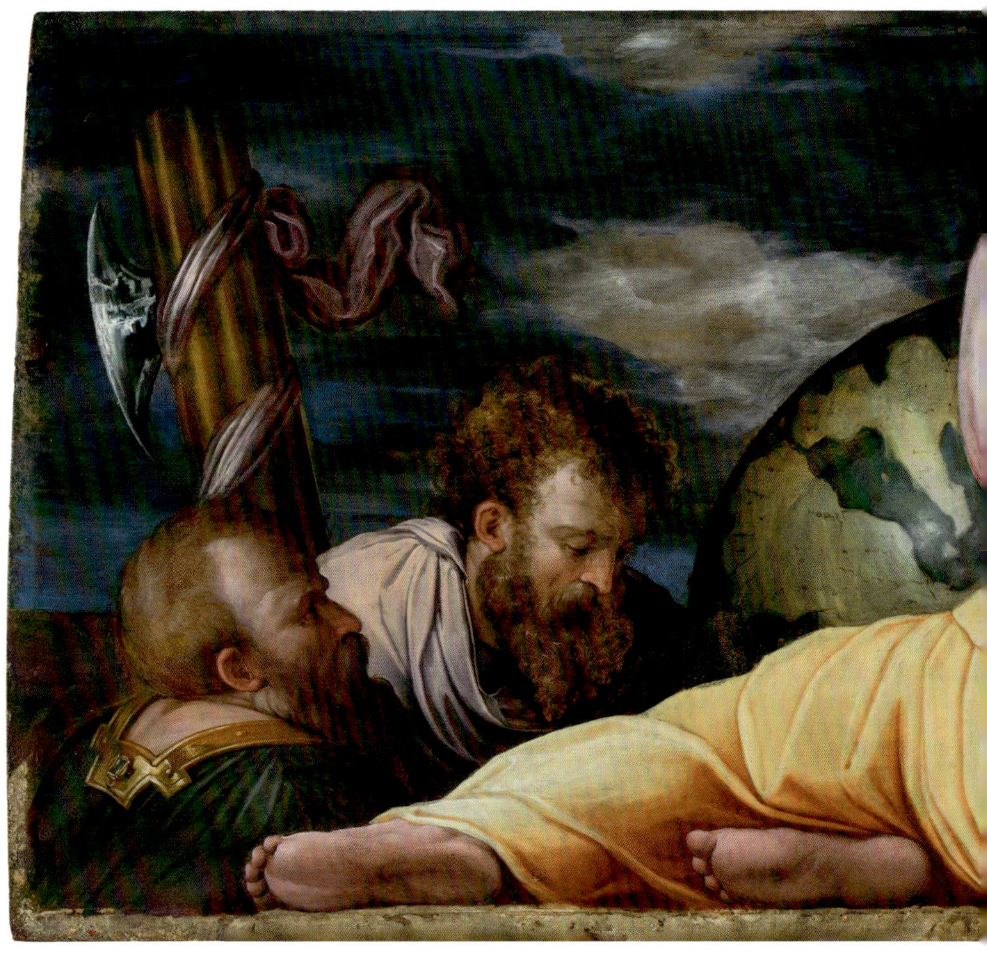

4
Giorgio Vasari, *Allegory of Justice*,
1542, panel, 77,7 × 181,5 cm, cat. 1371

because the works were meant to be viewed from a distance. The panels were originally separated by beams that framed them, enhancing the individual scenes, and dividing them into isolated narrative sections. To increase the sense of unity of the whole, Vasari resorted to a tromp-l'oeil effect, painting a continuous architectural element, a balustrade running behind all the subjects in the outside panels (Virtues and Putti), creating the effect of a single environment opening towards the sky, and projecting the Virtues into the shared space intended for the spectators and especially for the owner of the house, whom the allegories are symbolically convened to celebrate.

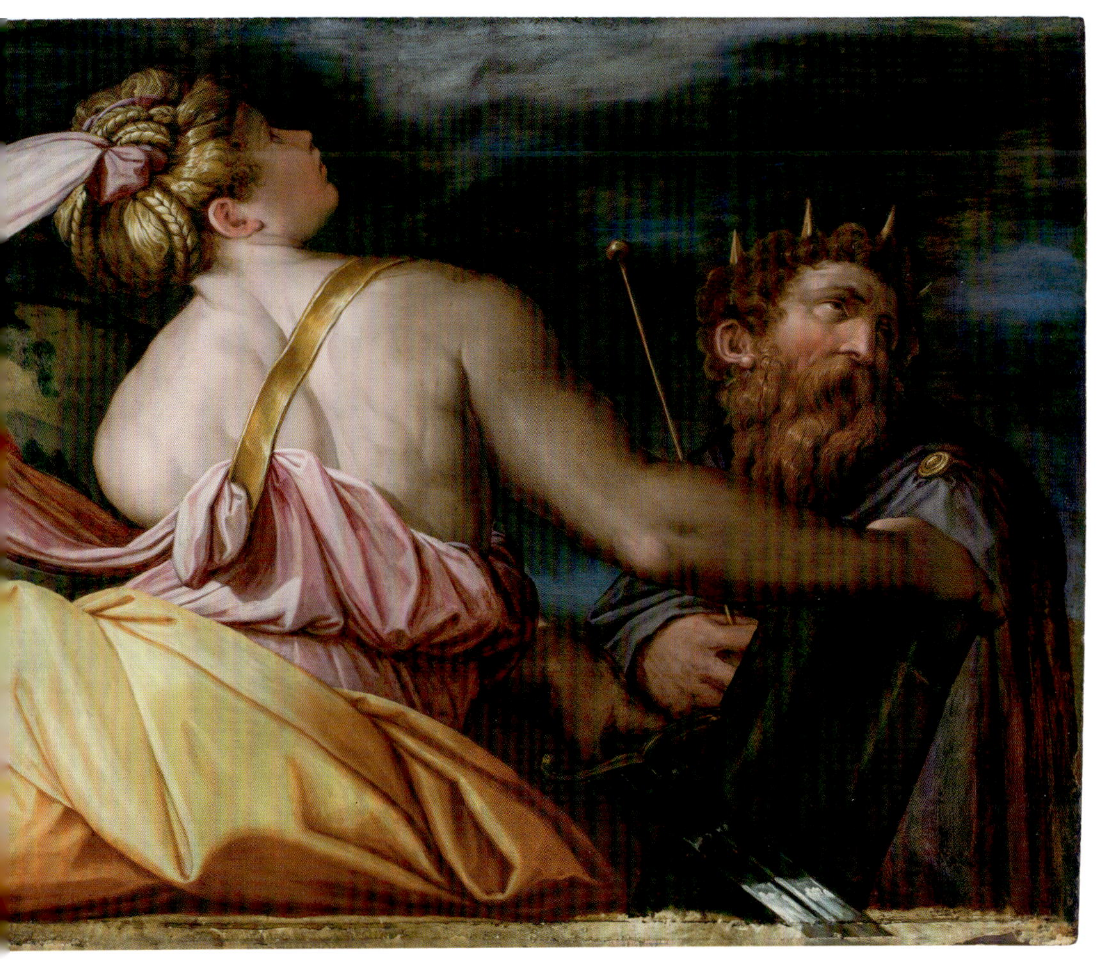

The surprise caused by the room was certainly increased by the sense of richness and opulence created by the techniques and expensive materials used by the master: the wooden beams, carved with "balls and leaves", were covered with gold leaf, supplied by "Messer Iseppo", goldsmith in San Lio,[17] and the sky, as well as some of the blue layers, were made with lapis lazuli or "fine ultramarine azure," a particularly bright and expensive pigment supplied by the miniaturist Francesco Giallo.[18]

The work was admired by Vasari's contemporaries, as evidenced by the reception by Venetian artists, who were certainly struck by the unified

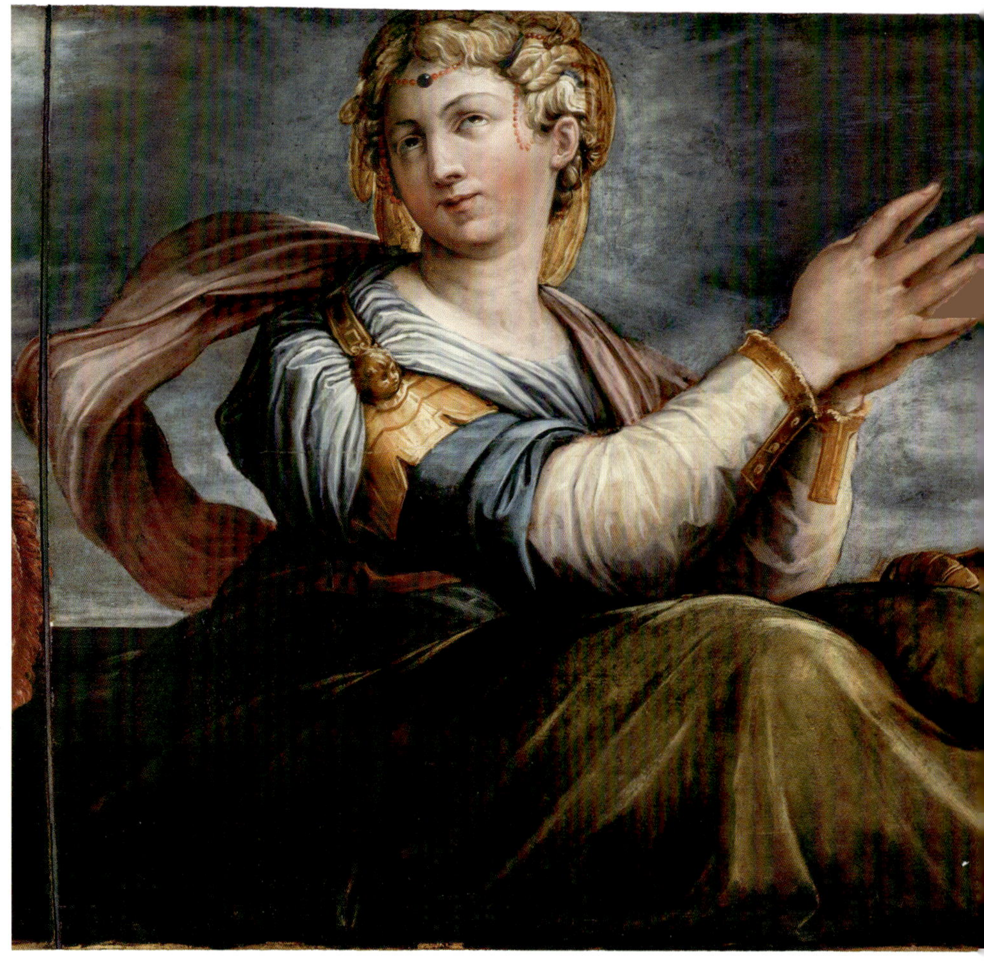

5
Giorgio Vasari, *Allegory of Hope*, 1542,
panel, 76 × 169 cm, cat. 2049

composition, foreshortened vision, effective perspectival arrangement from below, and sophisticated and complex postures of the subjects, as well as their monumental size, which combined into a masterpiece the likes of which had never been seen in Venice. In general, Venetians were very receptive to the fashion for ceilings painted with illusionistic narrative compositions, sparked by works such as Giulio Romano's frescoes in Mantua. Tintoretto, for example, painted the ceiling of a room in the palace of Vettor Pisani with scenes from Ovid's *Metamorphoses*, at the same

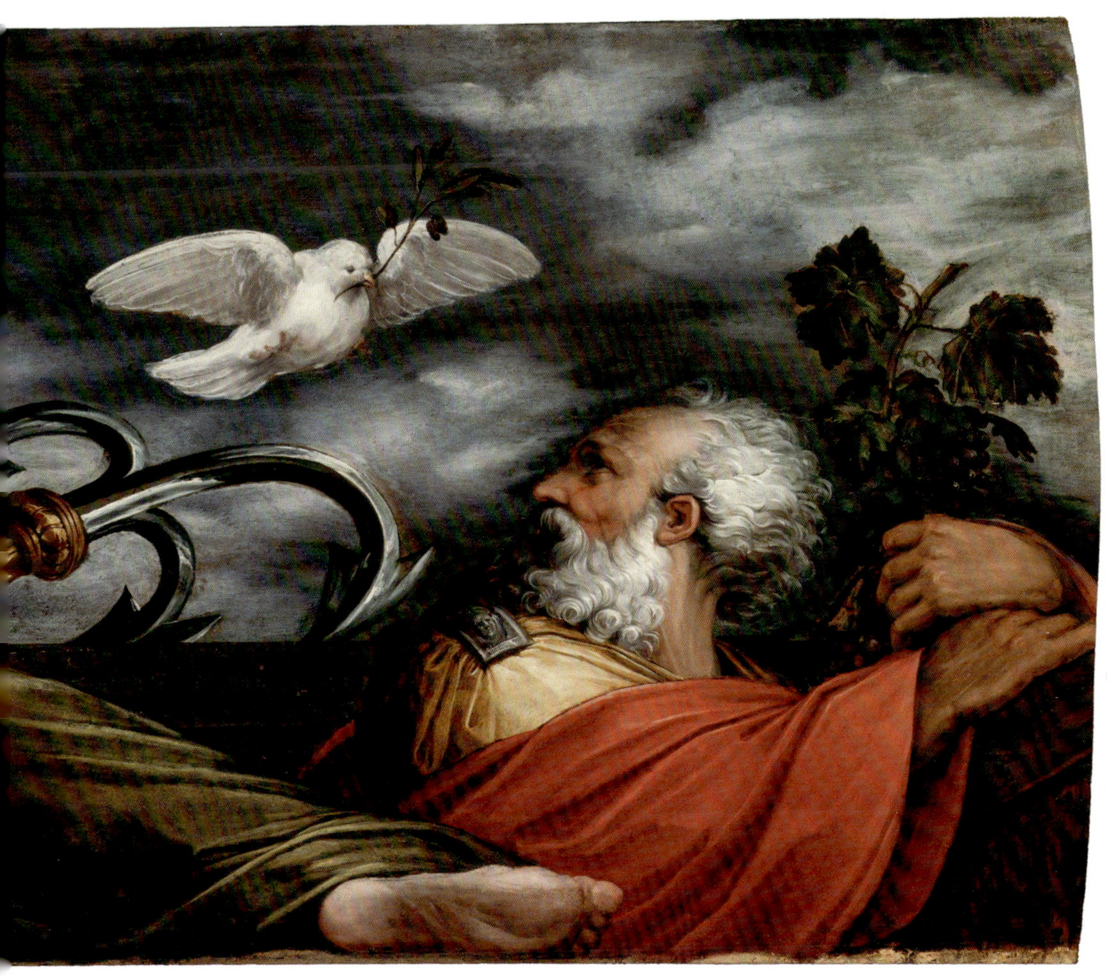

time or a few months later after Vasari's painted the Corner residence ceiling,[19] while Titian, a few years later, created a number of powerfully foreshortened subjects in his paintings for the sacristy of the church of Santo Spirito in Isola (originally commissioned to Giorgio Vasari) and in the central panel of a ceiling in the Scuola Grande di San Giovanni Evangelista.[20] Vasari's painted ceiling, in short, became a milestone that needed to be taken take into account by all discerning local artists. Tintoretto, in particular, cited the figure of Judas, featured in the panel of

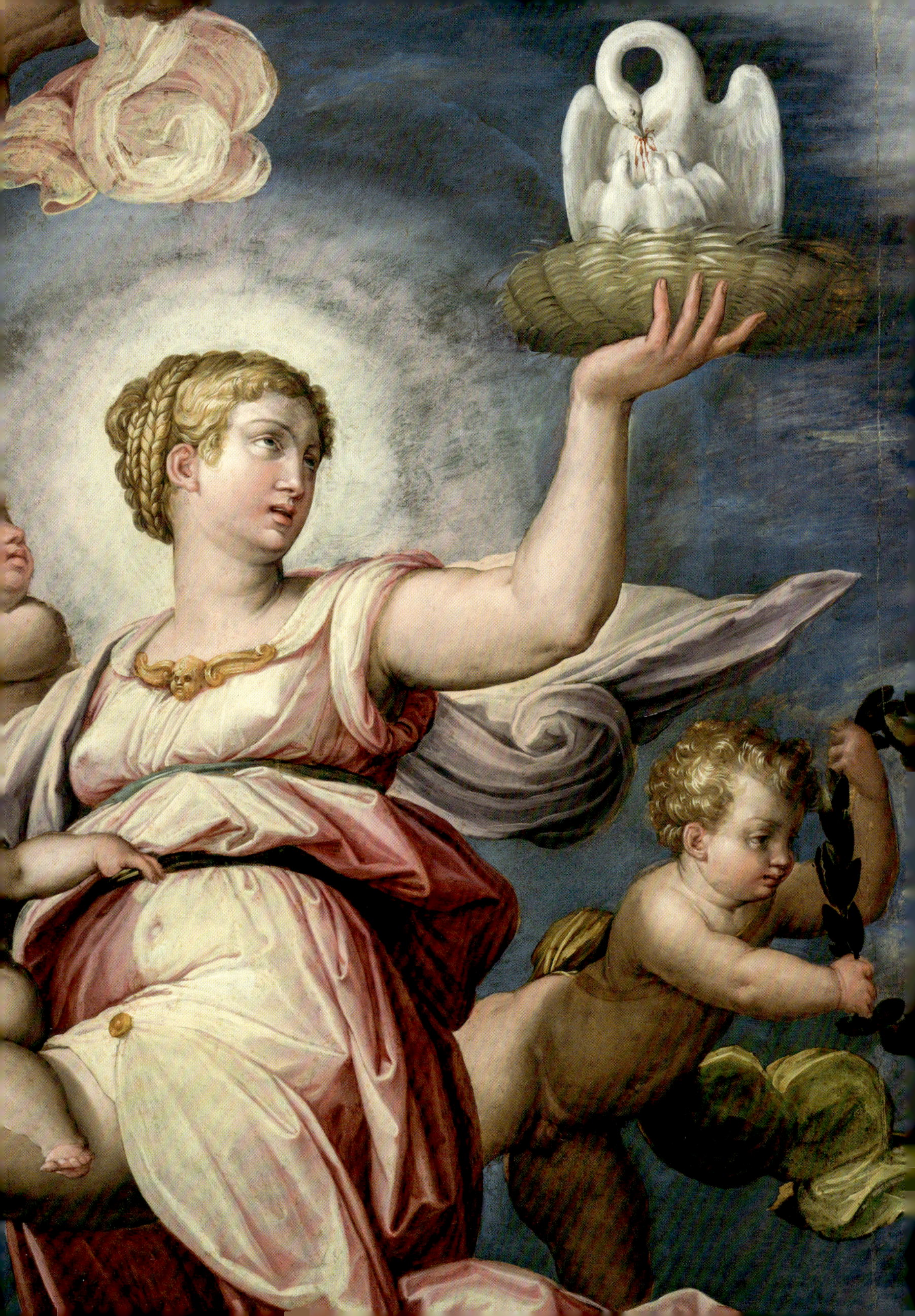

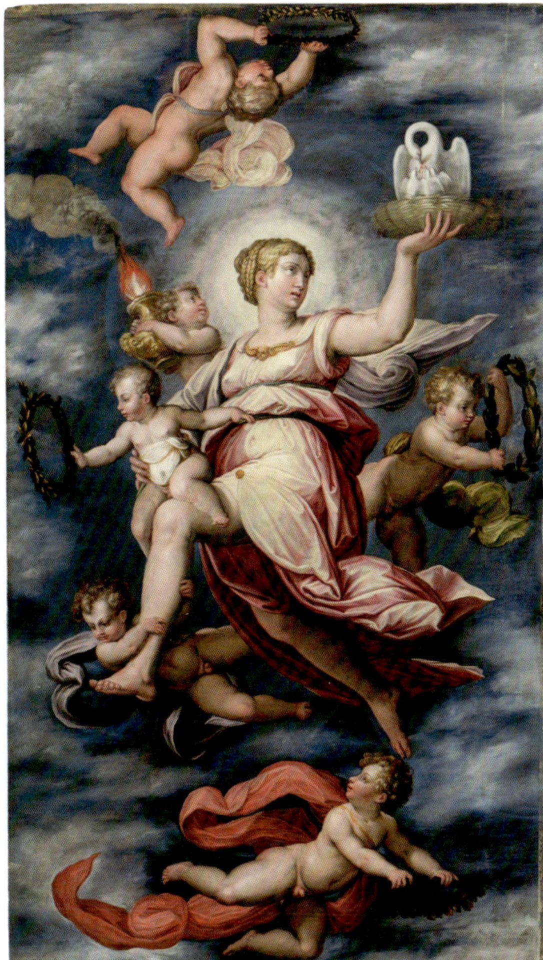

6
Giorgio Vasari, *Allegory of Charity*,
1542, panel, 262,7 × 150,4 cm
Milan, Pinacoteca di Brera

the *Allegory of Hope*, in his *Primavera,* originally located in the ceiling he painted in Ca' Barbaro a San Pantalon,[21] while Veronese replicated, almost verbatim, the composition of Vasari's *Allegory of Faith* in the *Allegory of Peace* made for a ceiling in Palazzo Porto in Vicenza, now in the Pinacoteca Capitolina.

In his works in Venice, Vasari used compositions already painted elsewhere and replicated them elsewhere later: his *Patience*, for example, is found both in the Palazzo della Cancelleria in Rome and in the Sala del Camino of his own house in Arezzo (as an *Allegory of Fatigue*) and finally in the Hall of the Gualdrada in Palazzo Vecchio in Florence.

Vasari's description of the Corner ensemble was of fundamental importance: it ensured the almost unanimous attribution of the work,[22] facilitated the identification of the individual panels, which were re-emerging from oblivion on the antiquarian market, and guided the reconstruction of the whole that gradually, thanks to the discovery of the fragments and the progress in the studies, got closer and closer to the original. After this phase, the next step was the analysis of the individual panels, following the recent restoration of all the panels described by Rossella Cavigli in the present volume, which made it possible to assign the so-called *Judas* to the panel with *Hope* and guided the current and final reconstructive hypothesis.[23] Incidentally, the first to discuss the issue of the original composition had been Jürgen Schulz in 1961,[24] followed by Florian Härb in 1998,[25] who was able to benefit from the identification of the central panel, and, finally, by Liana De Girolami Cheney,[26] who proposes two different possible arrangements of the Virtues on the sides of the *Charity*.

As for the history of the work, for about two centuries since it was made we have no record of it, and can only assume that it remained in the Corner palace at the Corte dell'Albero in its original location. Things, however, changed in the course the 18th century, driven by changes in ownership, as well as possible changes in fashion, economic problems, and commercial interests. The date of the removal of the panels from their original location is not yet known, but it is possible that it occurred around 1740 when the palace, still owned by the Corner, was rented to the Spinelli family.[27] We know for certain, however, that two decades later, the ceiling had been dismantled and was no longer in the room, as attested by a 1762 inventory, which suggests that the panels were hanging—as paintings and no longer as ceiling panels—on the walls of the second room on the second floor of the Corner palace in San Polo.[28] The subjects are correctly identified as *Faith, Charity, Hope* and *Patience,* and so are the four *Putti.* Vasari's autography, on the other hand, seems to have been lost along with the panels generically described as "in the old manner". Also missing in the description, but this may have been a mere oversight, is the *Allegory of Justice.*[29]

A few years later, the disappearance of the ceiling as a unified work was finally sealed by the diaspora of subdivisions. This is incidentally an eloquent example of how complex and difficult to reconstruct, can be the history of our national artistic heritage, given the vagaries that can affect even architectural works like the present one, which would seem less subject to collector and merchant attractiveness. Going back to Vasari's ceiling, an estimate by Giovanni Sasso, dated 1799, records the start of alienations beginning with *Faith* and *Hope,*[30] the very two panels that, so many years later, were brought back to Italy from abroad. It is conceivable that it is at this juncture that the two panels, the longest of the whole, were curtailed into a format better suited to wall display.[31] With a fragment of the *Hope*, as mentioned, a totally autonomous subject was created: the so-called *Suicide of Judas.*[32] In the 1799 estimate made for Palazzo Corner in San Polo, three Virtues are thus mentioned: *Patience* and *Justice*, described as friezes, and a "panel ceiling painting representing a Deity, of the Salviati school" and "four panel ceiling painting of little putti authored by Salviati"[33] . Sasso's annotations are important because they demonstrate, on the one hand, a sharper critical attributive understanding, assigning the panels more reasonably to Giuseppe Salviati, and dividing the subjects into ceiling works, which included *Justice* and the putti, and wall works, which included the other *Virtues*.

Although the first two fragments of the ensemble were on the market as early as the end of the 18th century, it was only in the 20th century that we are able to follow the work's peregrinations: *Hope*, curtailed as already reported, ended up in the collection of the well-known Austrian publisher, naturalized British, Georg Weidenfeld in London, around 1950.[34] Exhibited in 1952 in Naples along with *Patience* and *Justice*,[35] it was purchased for the Gallerie dell'Accademia in 2017, after the death of the owner.[36] *Faith*, on the other hand, followed a tortuous and perilous mercantile route: in 1910, we find it in Germany, at in Frankfurt am Main, at the Rudolf Bangel auction house; then in 1930 in Berlin, at the Internationale Kunst auction house;[37] around 1940, in Hamburg, in the Robert Scholz-Forni collection,[38] in 1953 in Cologne, at the Kunsthaus Lampertz auction house. It then moved to Switzerland, resurfacing in Zurich, in the hands of antiquarian H. Trainé;[39] it was then sold in London in 1966[40] to Wayland Young, Lord Kennet, British writer and politician, and remained in his possession until 2013, when it was put for sale by his wife after the death of her husband, and finally purchased by the Gallerie dell'Accademia.[41]

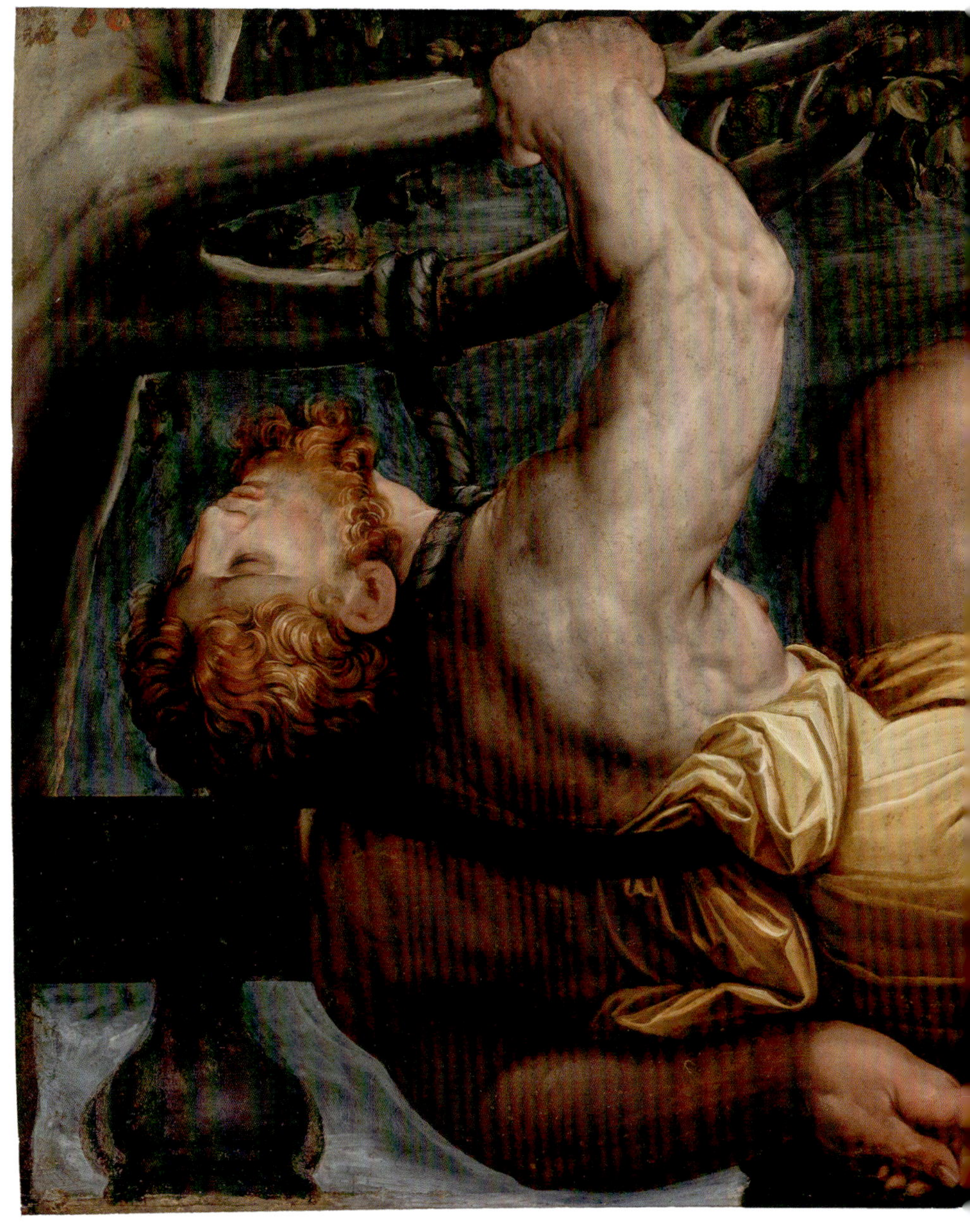

7
Giorgio Vasari, *The Suicide of Judas*, 1542,
panel, 77 × 130,5 cm
Arezzo, Casa Vasari

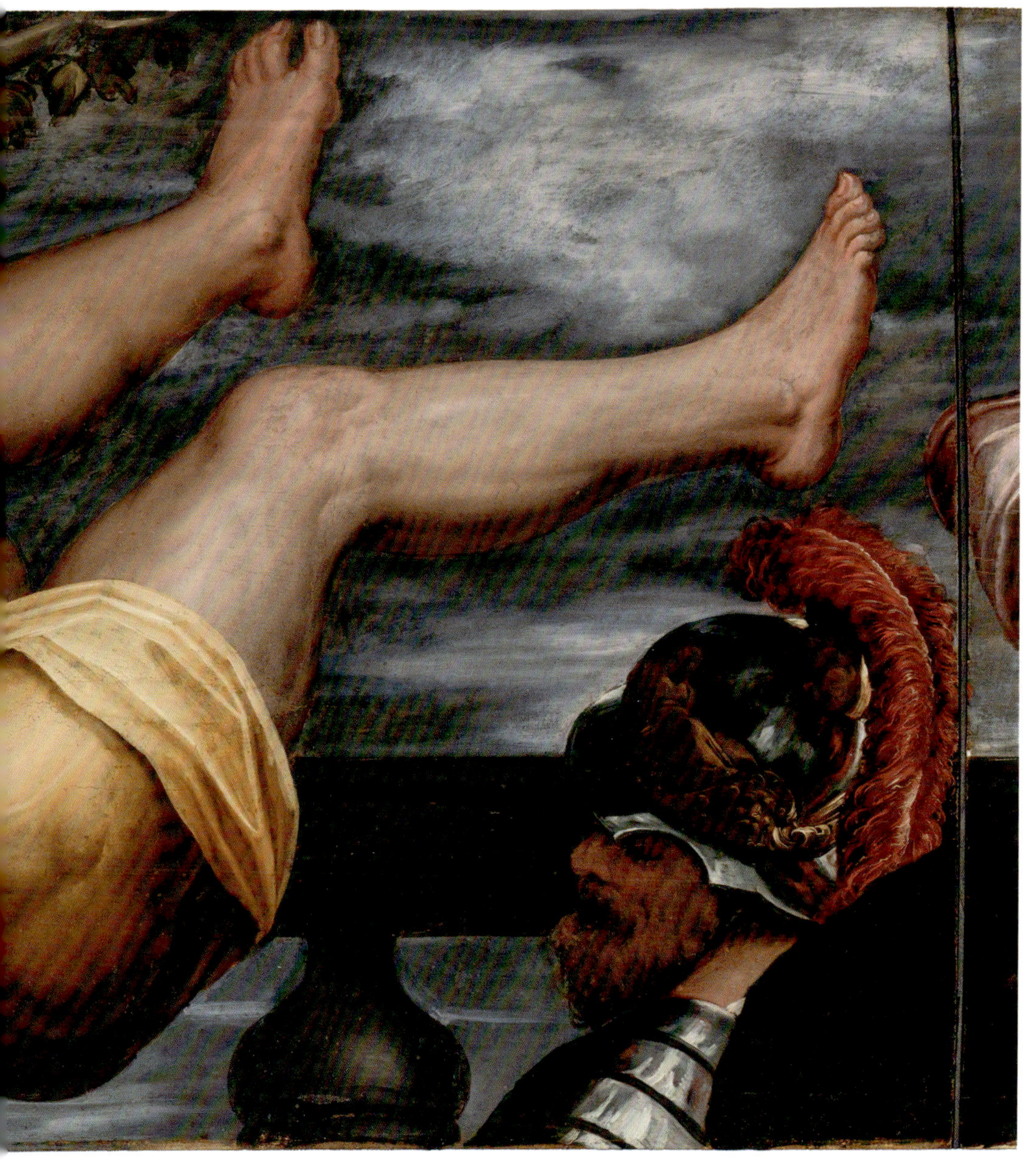

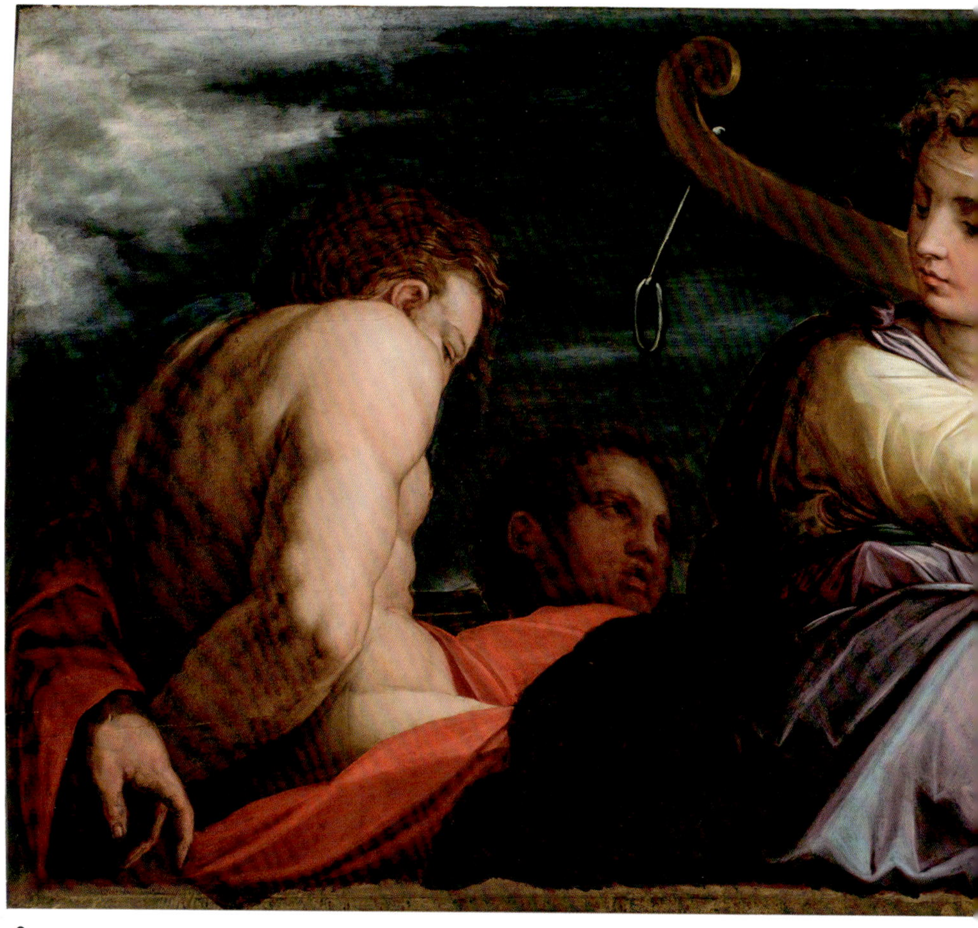

8
Giorgio Vasari, *Allegory of Patience*,
1542, panel, 77,3 × 184,7 cm, cat. 1370

The other panels, instead, followed mainly Italian mercantile routes. When Giovanni di Francesco, the last representative of the Corner di San Polo family, died on October 27, 1798, the panels were divided into two groups, to be inherited by his two daughters. To Elisabetta, wife of Almorò Grimani, went *Charity*—the largest panel in the series—and two *Putti*, while Laura, wife of Alvise Mocenigo I di San Stae, got *Patience* and *Justice* and the other two *Putti*.[42] *Charity* soon drifted away from Elisabetta's group, re-emerging in Milan in the hands of antiquarian Fedele Bozzoli, who gave it, as early as 1819, to the Pinacoteca di Brera in exchange for other works. From the Pinacoteca di Brera it went on deposit, in 1973, to the Museo Civico della Società

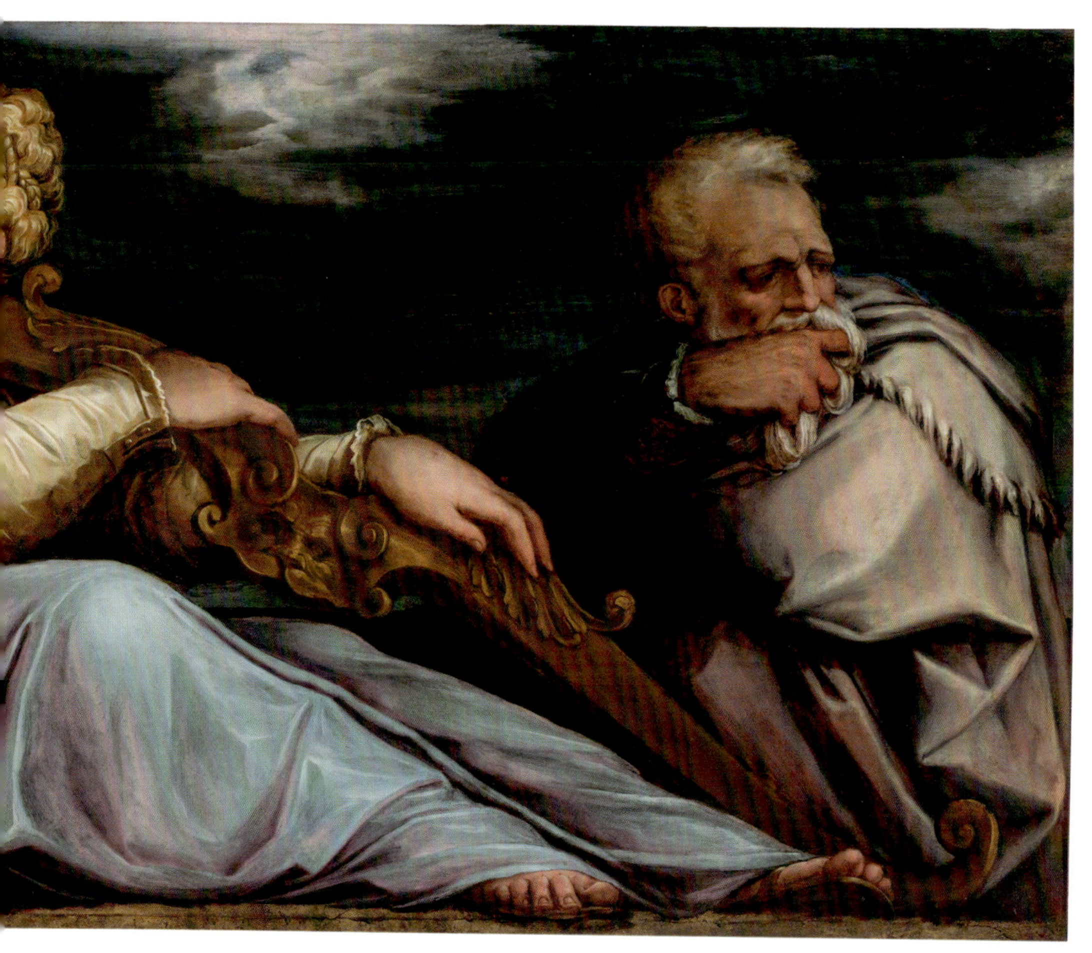

di Storia Patria di Gallarate,[43] and from there it was passed on, in 2002, to the Gallerie dell'Accademia in Venice. While traces of one *Putto con tavola* have been lost, the other transited in a Grüneisen (possibly Wladimir de Grüneisen) and a Jacque Radicati collection in Brozolo,[44] only to resurface in a collection in Terni, in 1998. Thanks to a photograph published in *AD Architectural Digest*,[45] the panel was identified by Luisa Vertova, who published it assigning it to the Venetian ceiling.[46] It later went to a collection in Milan and was finally purchased by the Italian State in 2002.[47]

The Laura Corner group, unlike the previous one, remained together and was the last to leave the family. In 1842, the four panels are still attested

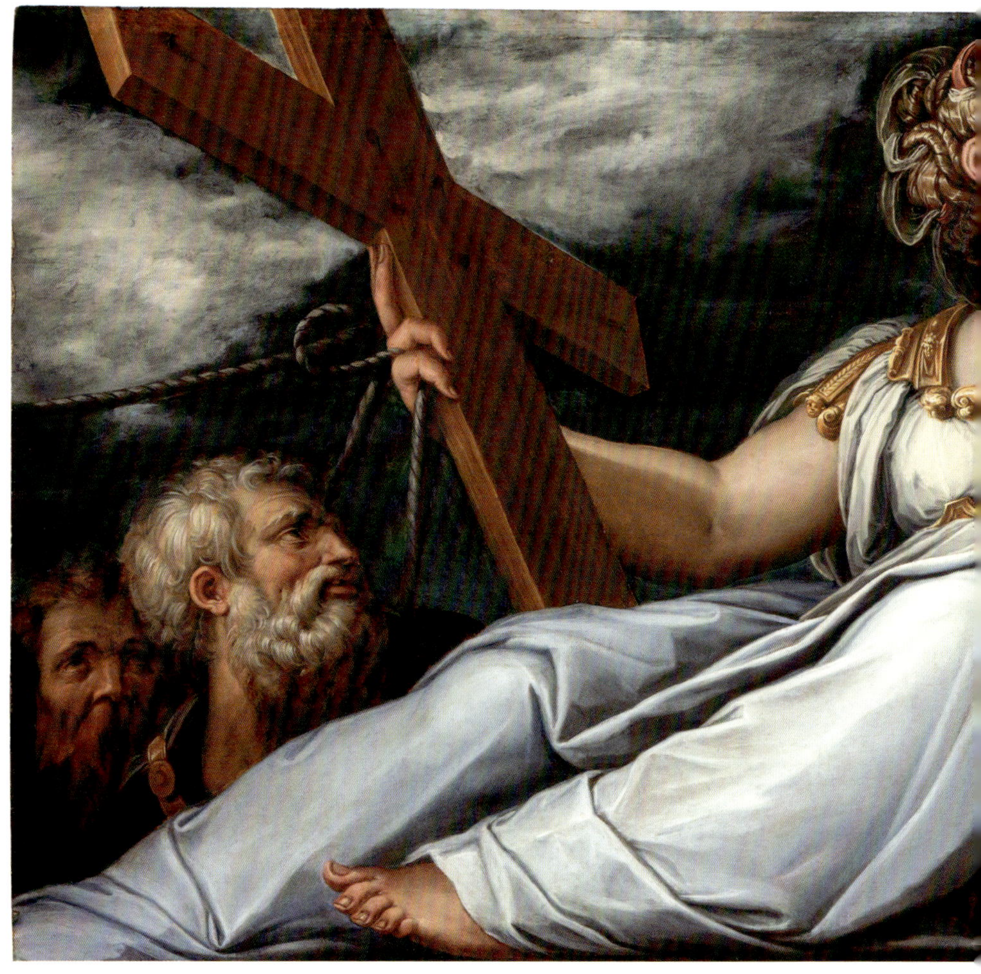

9
Giorgio Vasari, *Allegory of Faith*, 1542,
tavola, 77 × 171 cm, cat. 2042

in Palazzo Mocenigo,[48] although misidentified as *Liberty* and *Strength* and assigned to the "Roman school," while the *Putti* were assigned to "Domen-ichino instead of Vasari." In 1865, the four panels were in Palazzo Contarini da Mula in San Beneto, owned by the Mocenigo, then were sold and entered the Venetian collection of Prince Giovannelli where they are documented with certainty from 1908[49] to 1928.[50] Sold again they arrived at the Di Cap-ua collection in Rome in 1932.[51] They achieved a certain visibility and no-toriety by being included in the famous exhibition on Mannerism in Venice in 1981.[52] Finally, in 1987, they were sold by Giovanna di Capua Sestrieri to

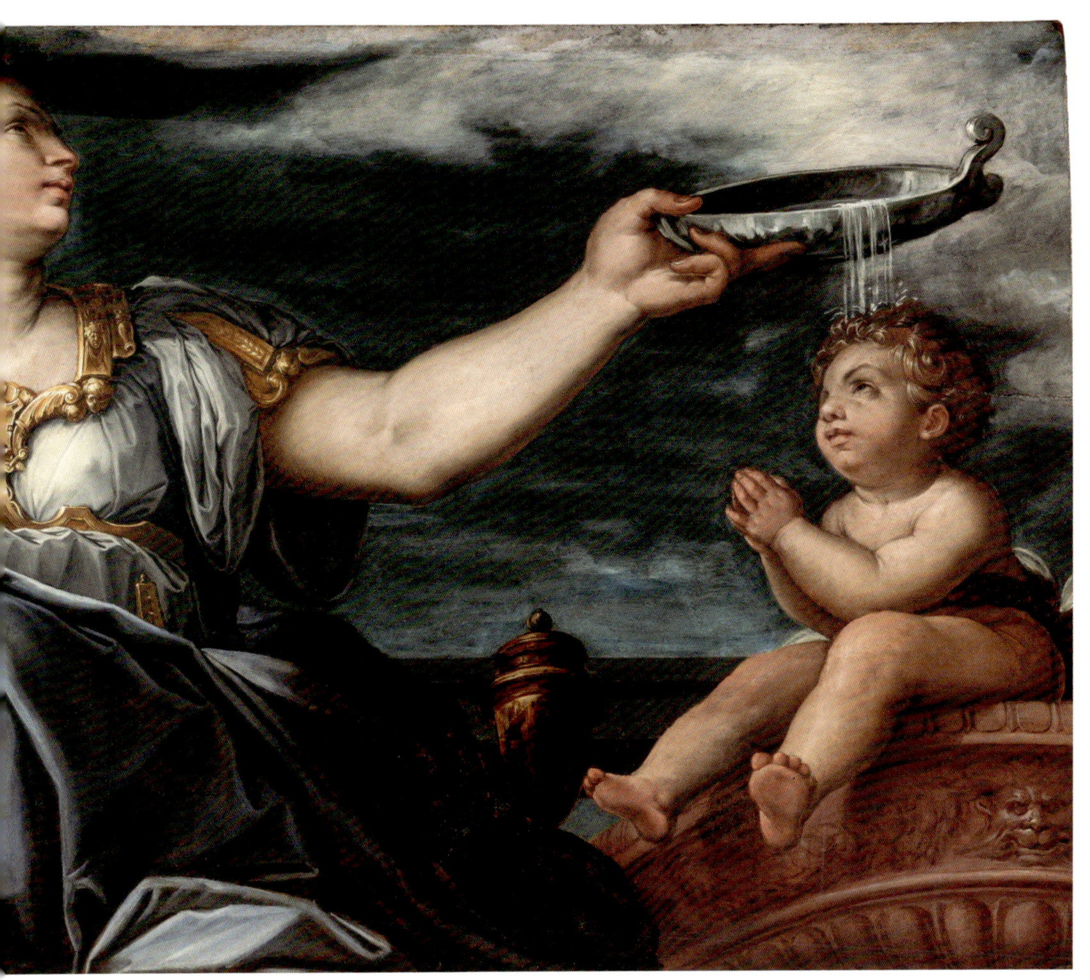

the Italian State, which allocated them to the Gallerie dell'Accademia in Venice. This was the first fundamental step in the long and commendable process pursued by the State and, first and foremost, by Venetian institutions, which led to the gradual reacquisition of the scattered panels, in what appeared as an impossible dream: the reassembling of the original ensemble in the city where the masterpiece was originally born. On the four hundred and fiftieth anniversary of his death, Giorgio Vasari finally returns to Venice.

1 "Being then Giorgio, through messer Pietro Aretino, called to Venice to order and make for the gentlemen and gentlewomen of the Compagnia della Calza the apparatus of a most sumptuous and very magnificent feast, and the scene of a comedy made by the said messer Pietro Aretino for the said gentlemen," G. Vasari, *Le Vite de' più eccellenti pittori, scultori ed architetti*, edited by G. Milanesi, Florence 1871, vol. VI, p. 223.

2 B. Agosti, *Giorgio Vasari. Luoghi e tempi delle Vite*, Milan 2013 p. 52.

3 Munich, Staatliche Graphishen Sammlung, inv. 2272. Also believed to be an ancient copy by Vasari. F. Härbs, "Prospero Fontana alias Giorgio Vasari: Collaboration and the Limits of Autorship," in *Francesco Salviati e la Bella Maniera*, Proceedings of the conference (Rome, Villa Medici, March 5–7, May 14–16, 1998), edited by C. Monbeig Goguel, Ph. Costamagna, M. Hochmann, Paris 2001, pp. 578–79.

4 "I remember how on the eighth of April 1542 the Magnificant Messer Giovanni Cornaro, a Venetian gentleman, commissioned me, by order of Messer Michele da San Michele, Veronese architect in St. mMark, a ceiling or soffit in wood to paint in oil with nine large squares," *Il Libro della Ricordanze di Giorgio Vasari*, edited by A. Del Vita, Arezzo 1929, p. 39. See also https://www.memofonte.it/home/files/pdf/ vasari_ricordanze.pdf. The text is based on previous contributions: G. Manieri Elia, "Allegory of Patience," in *Giorgio Vasari and the Allegory of Patience*, exhibition catalog (Florence, Palazzo Pitti–Galleria Palatina, November 26, 2013–January 5, 2014), edited by A. Bisceglia, Livorno 2013, pp. 54–57; G. Manieri Elia, "Giorgio Vasari's Faith and the ceiling of the 'Camera nova' in Palazzo Corner Spinelli," in *Ricche Minere*, I, 2014, pp. 71–77; G. Manieri Elia, in *Il giovane Tintoretto*, exhibition catalog (Venice, Gallerie dell'Accademia, September 7, 2018–January 6, 2019), edited by R. Battaglia, P. Marini and V. Romani, Marsilio–Electa, Venice–Milan 2018, p. 129.

5 M. Hochman, "Between Venice and Rome: Cardinal Francesco Corner," in *Saggi e memorie di Storia dell'arte*, 18, 1992, pp. 97–110, 203–06. Ibid., p. 101.

6 Cf. J.C. Röesler, The "Camera nova" by Michele Sanmicheli and Giorgio Vasari, Palazzo Corner Spinelli, in "Ricche Minere," I, 2014, pp. 63–69. Ibid., p. 67.

7 *Il Libro delle Ricordanze* cit., p. 39 and https://www.memofonte.it/home/files/pdf/ vasari_ ricordanze.pdf cit.

8 L. De Girolami Cheney, *Giorgio Vasari. Artistic and Emblematic Manifestations*, Washington 2012, p. 101.

9 G. Romanelli, "Giorgio Vasari a Venezia," in *Studi in Onore di Egidio Martini*, edited by G. M. Pilo, Venice 1999, pp. 48–53, doc. B, p. 53.

10 See also L. Caporossi, R. Cavigli, "Vasari at Venice. The "Suicide of Judas" at Arezzo, Another Addendum to the Corner Ceiling," in *The Burlington Magazine*, CLVIII, 1354, 2016, pp. 10–12. Ibid., p. 11.

11 The identifying symbols of Patience are cited by Vasari in *Lo Zibaldone di Giorgio Vasari*, edited by A. Del Vita, Rome 1938, p. 23.

12 L. Vertova, "Vasari at Venice , an Addendum," in *The Burlington Magazine*, CXLI, 1151, 1999, pp. 105–06. Ibid., p. 106. See also A. M. Maetzke, C. Davis, *Giorgio Vasari. Principi, letterati e artisti nelle carte di Giorgio Vasari*, exhibition catalog (Arezzo, Casa Vasari and Sottochiesa di San Francesco, September 26–November 29, 1981), Florence 1981, p. 130.

13 L. Vertova, "Vasari at Venice" cit., pp. 105–06.

14 L. De Girolami Cheney, *Giorgio Vasari* cit., p. 106.

15 "In Venice, Vasari and Cristofono stayed for a few months, painting for the magnificent sir Giovanni Cornaro," G. Vasari, *Le Vite* cit., vol. VI, pp. 225–26.

16 G. Romanelli, "Giorgio Vasari a Venezia" cit., doc. A, p. 53.

17 Ibid.

18 Ibid.

19 V. Romani, in *Il giovane Tintoretto* cit., p. 159.

20 Ibid, p. 141.

21 The ceiling can be dated around 1546–48; the *Primavera* is at the Chrysler Museum of Art today in Norfolk. R. Echols and F. Ilchman, in *Il giovane Tintoretto* cit. pp. 221–22.

22 An exception is Adolfo Venturi, who assigns the work to Giovanni Battista Ponchini, A. Venturi, *Storia dell'arte italiana: La pittura del Cinquecento*, vol. IX, t. 4, Milan 1936, p. 1058.

23 The restoration was conducted by Rossella Cavigli under the direction of the author, assisted by the technical direction of Chiara Maida and then Francesca Bartolomeoli. The restoration of the support was carried out by Roberto Saccuman. See L. Caporossi, R. Cavigli, "Vasari at Venice" cit.

24 J. Schulz, "Vasari at Venice," in *The Burlington Magazine*, CIII, 705, 1961, pp. 500–11.

25 F. Härb, "Modes and Models in Vasari's Early Drawing Oeuvre," in *Vasari's Florence. Artists and Literati at the Medicean Court*, edited by P. Jacks, Cambridge 1998, pp. 83–110. Ibid., p. 104.

26 L. De Girolami Cheney, *Giorgio Vasari* cit., p. 129, fig. 12.

27 L. Olivato, L. Puppi, *Mauro Codussi*, Milan 1977, p. 205.

28 M. Favilla, R. Rugolo, "Gli apparati decorativi di Palazzo Corner dal Seicento all'Ottocento," in *Palazzo Corner Mocenigo a Venezia, sede della Guardia di Finanza*, edited by B. Buratti, M. Favilla, G. Guidarelli, R. Rugolo, Rome–Venice 2019, p. 157 and appendix doc. 1.1, p. 187. Other works from ceilings are mentioned in the document as evidence of the extensive procedure of disassembly from their original locations.

29 Ibid.

30 Ibid.

31 The discovery of the curtailment is the result of the panel analyses that were part of the recent restoration (see Rossella Cavigli's essay in the present volume).

32 The work, auctioned in Rome in 1980, was purchased by the State for Casa Vasari in Arezzo. Christie's Rome, *Paintings, drawings and prints,* October 20, 1980, lot 292. The panel is on loan to the Gallerie dell'Accademia in Venice, granted, thanks to the collaboration of director Stefano Casciu of the then Polo Museale della Toscana (Regional Directorate National Museums Tuscany), to allow it to be reunited with the rest of the panel and the ceiling panels. We take this opportunity here to also mention, along with the authors of the essays in the volume, that this year marks the 20th anniversary of the passing of Anna Maria Maetzke. It was she, together with Margherita Lenzini Moriondo, who strongly advocated the purchase of the *Judas*.

33 M. Favilla, R. Rugolo, "Gli apparati decorativi di Palazzo Corner" cit., p. 157 and doc. 3.1, nos. 340–46, p. 205.

34 B. Nicolson, "Mannerism at the Arcade Gallery," in *The Burlington Magazine*, XCII, 562, 1950, pp. 203–05.

35 R. Causa, F. Bologna, *Fontainbleau e la Maniera italiana,* exhibition catalog (Naples, Mostra d'oltremare e del lavoro italiano nel mondo, July 26–October 12, 1952), Florence 1952, p. 35, pl. 56.

36 Funding for the purchase was obtained through a public-private partnership: the Ministry of Culture (Mibact at the time) and two private committees for the preservation of Venice: Venetian Heritage and The Venice in Peril.

37 *Antiquitäten Tapisserien Gemälde alter und neuer Meister,* auction catalog, Internationales Kunst, Berlin 1930, lot 455.

38 M. Goering, P. Gazzola, "Giorgio Vasari," in U. Thieme, F. Becker, *Allgemeines Lexikon der Bildenden* Künstler, XXXIV, 1940, pp. 119–128. Ibid, p. 122.

39 J. Schultz, "Vasari at Venice" cit., 1961, pp. 500–11. Ibid., p. 507.

40 Catalog *of Old Master Paintings*, auction catalog, Sotheby's, February 23, 1966, lot 28.

41 Again a public-private collaboration with funds from the Ministry, Venetian Heritage Foundation of Venice, Vela SpA, The Venice in Peril Fund, MSC Crociere, SAVE SpA, Consorzio Venezia Nuova and Fondazione Veneto Banca.

42 M. Favilla, R. Rugolo, "Gli apparati decorativi di Palazzo Corner" cit., p. 159–60 .

43 A. Giovannetti, entry, in *Pinacoteca di Brera. Scuole dell'Italia centrale e meridionale*, Milan 1992, pp. 39–40.

44 Information can be obtained from the labels on the back of the painting. For the work see C. Orsi, *Vasari a Venezia: un dipinto proveniente da palazzo Corner-Spinelli*, Milan 2002.

45 *AD Architectural Digest*, March 1998, p. 127.

46 L. Vertova, "Vasari at Venice" cit.

47 It is by following this purchasing process, thus since 2002, that my long activity aimed at the recovery of this masterpiece began, and which the present reassembling now concludes with great satisfaction.

48 R. Lauber, "Nuovi contributi per i dipinti del 'Camerino Cornaro'. Gioielli di famiglia, del nome di *gens* Cornelia," in *Caterina Cornaro: illusione del regno*, proceedings of the conference (Asolo, October 9, 2010), edited by D. Perocco, Sommacampagna 2011, pp. 73–96. Ibid, p. 86 with document references.

49 W. Kallab, V*asaristudien. Mit einem Lebensbilde des Verfassers aus dessen Nachlasse herausgegeben von Julius v. Schlosser*, Wien-Leipzig 1908, p. 71.

50 A. Venturi, *Storia dell'arte italiana* cit., p. 1058.

51 Historical Archives Regional Museums Directorate of Veneto, letter from Giovanna di Capua to Francesco Valcanover, March 18, 1987, prot. 1882.

52 D. Mc Tavish, entry, in *Da Tiziano a El Greco. Per la storia del Manierismo a Venezia*, exhibition catalog (Venice, Palazzo Ducale, September 1–December 28, 1981), Milan 1981, p. 86, pl. p. 87.

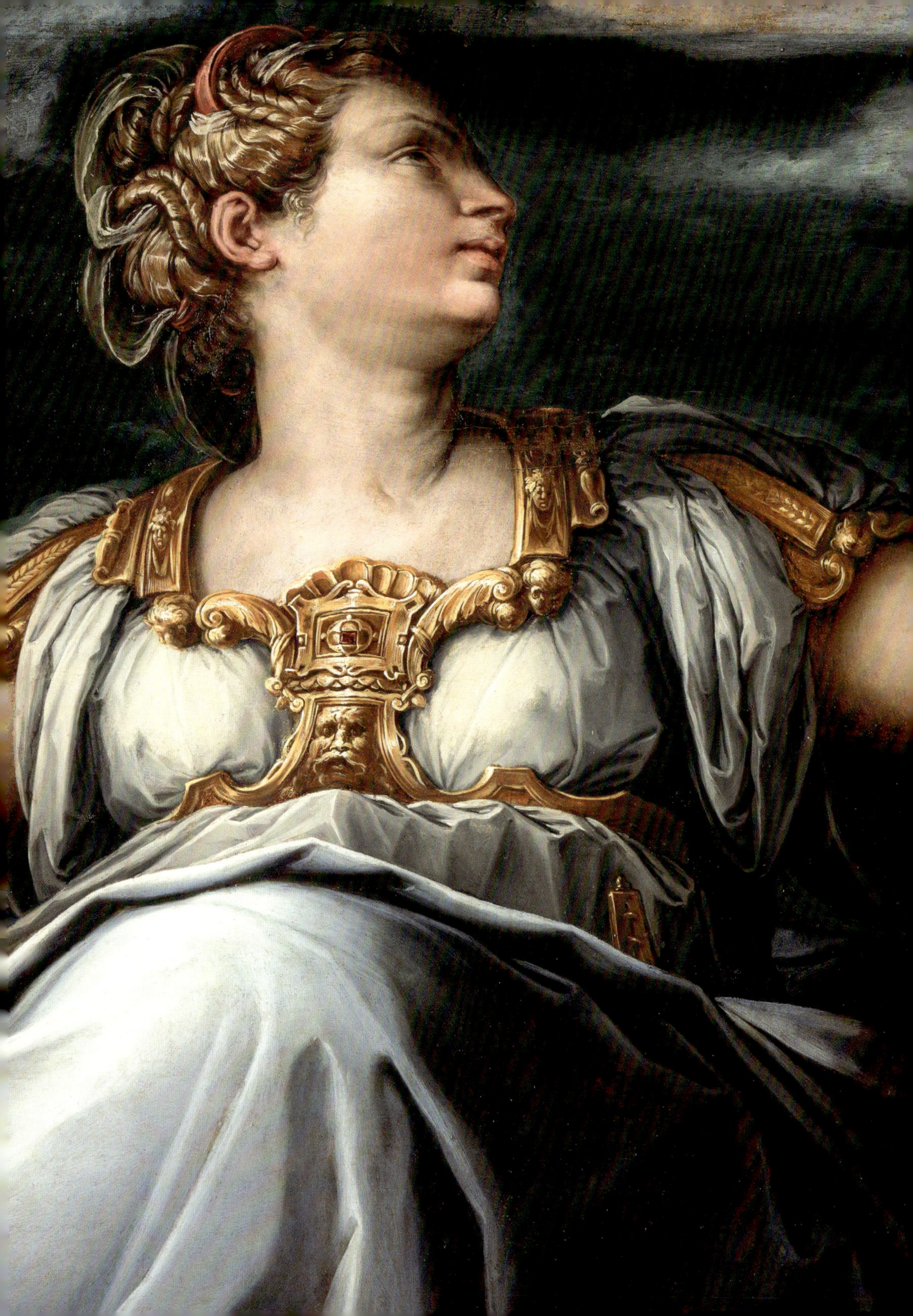

Between Cuts and Silences.
Hypotheses for the Iconographic Program
of Vasari's Corner Ceiling.
The *Sacrifice of Christ* and the *Virtues*
Instrument of Salvation

Luisa Caporossi

When in his *Ricordanze* Vasari describes the work carried out in the spring of 1542 at Palazzo Corner in Venice, he describes only some of the subjects he painted, namely *Charity, Faith, Hope, Justice* and *Patience*, adding only in passing that the Virtues "all accompanied by various figures according to a purposefully made drawing" without, however, adding anything on these characters, which must have had a precise function, having been inserted inside a "drawing" specifically prepared for Giovanni Corner's "new room." Even bearing in mind the brevity characteristic of a volume of recollections with "expense notes," this silence of Vasari, a painter much concerned with the "inventions" for his paintings, is somewhat surprising. Whatever the reason for this omission, it should be noted from the start that these figures flanking the main personifications are in fact essential to a correct reading of the ceiling and distinguish it from other more traditional depictions of Virtues.

In a short essay written a few years ago,[1] we had the opportunity to evidence how a painting purchased by the Italian state in 1980 for the Vasari House in Arezzo,[2] had to be precisely one of these "mysterious" figures mentioned by Vasari as designed specifically for the Corner ceiling, given the many similarities with other panels of the Corner ceiling. The Arezzo panel depicted a man hanging himself and was long believed to have been originally part of a second unknown Venetian composition by Vasari,[3] insofar as it was not considered compatible with the *Carità che incorona le*

Virtù of the Corner ceiling.[4] The belief was reinforced by the fact that the known sources for the work spoke about a coffered ceiling only nine panels, which fit with Vasari's mention of the painting of five panels of the Virtues, plus four other panels with Putti intended for the corners.[5]

Yet that beautiful bearded Judas, wrapped only in a thin yellow robe, which did not qualify him as a historical figure, seemed to continue telling us that something was off, and, upon further reflection, both arguments that had that led to the exclusion of *Judas* from the Corner decoration, the incompatibility of the subject and the number of panels, turned out to be incorrect. First of all the figure was not, or not merely, Judas, but rather a personification of the concept of *Despair*, and therefore thematically connected to the *Hope* panel, at the time still in a private collection in London.[6] More specific evidence was the traces of Hope's robe remaining in the *Despair* panel, and, conversely, the missing part of the red plume of the helmet of the soldier looking at "Judas" in *Despair* that could still be detected in the *Hope* panel. *Despair* had in other words once been part of the *Hope* panel [fig. 5, pp. 28–29; fig. 7, pp. 34–35].

Once the enigma of the *Despair* panel was solved, a number of things became clear. In terms of composition, the Virtues were meant to be accompanied by the depiction of their opposite Vice. In material terms, given the size of the reassembled panel, it became evident that the wooden frame, which for decades critics had believed to have been basically square in shape,[7] had been in fact rectangular. Secondly, the panel with *Faith*, located opposite *Hope* on the other longer side of the room, had to originally have been the same size of the reassembled panel with *Hope*, and must therefore also have been cut. On the basis of this new data, despite Vasari's silences and the parts still missing in the panels, an attempt was made to review the overall meaning of the ceiling,[8] and reflect on what subjects could possibly have been removed and hopefully could be found on the market.

The concept of *Despair* could indeed be personified through Judas, an exemplary case of "desperation," as it often happens in the *Triumph of Virtues*, where he figures as a "prisoner" of Hope, crushed under her feet (as in the Visconti Tarot card, Yale, Beinecke Library, fig. 1),[9] or also by another subject intent on killing himself, as in the *Disperacio* that Vasari

1

Bonifacio Bembo, *The Triumph of Hope*, Tarocchi Visconti Modrone, c. 1445, Cary Collection of Playing Cards, Beinecke Rare Book and Manuscript Library, Yale University

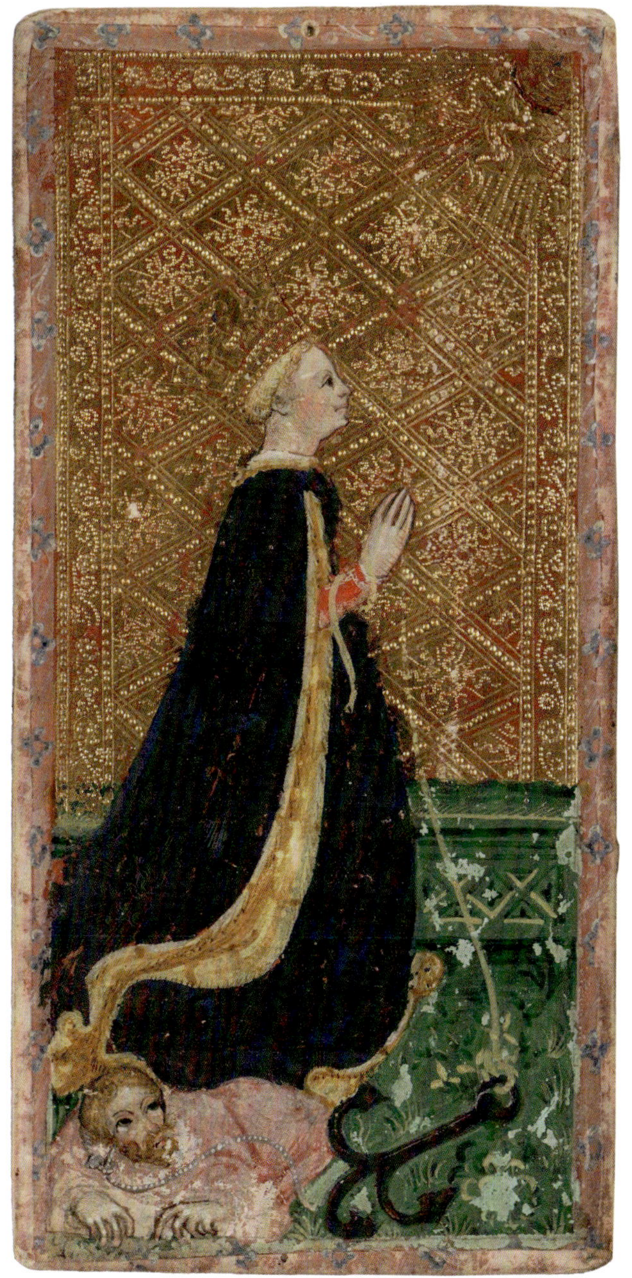

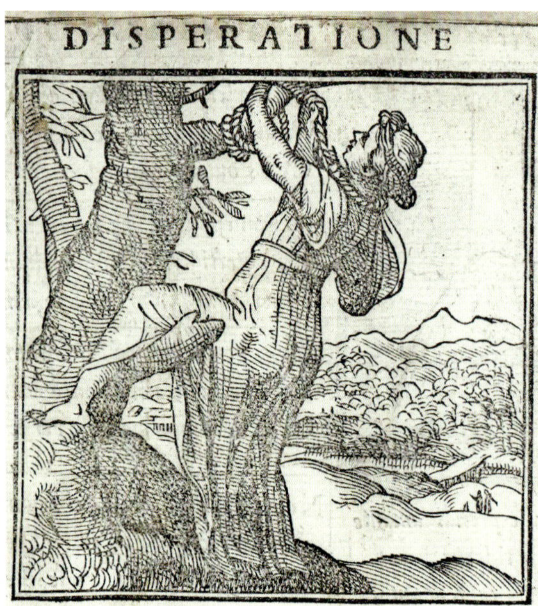

2
Lambert Sustris, *Desperation*, in
*Le ingegnose Sorti, composte per
Francesco Marcolini*, Venice 1550,
p. 41

could see on the capital of the Doge's Palace in Venice, where a woman stabs herself in the throat while tearing out her hair, or again like the *Disperatione* in the newly printed volume of the *Sorti,* in which a young woman is fastening a rope to a tree [fig. 2].[10] In the Corner ceiling, Vasari decided to depict a man about to make his choice, a suspended moment where the suicide has not yet been committed. The man is grasping the branch of a fig tree, and seems on the verge of throwing himself over the balustrade, with the expression on his face seems almost peaceful not that he has arrived at his decision. His other arm is held behind his back, as if bound, restrained by a mysterious force. This detail is being studied by a soldier with his head slightly bowed, his shiny helmet reflecting the scene. The suicide's eyes are closed and illuminated by *Charity*'s light filtering through the branches but leaving the man's forehead in the shadow, while he is reached by the smoke from the flame held by one of *Charity*'s putti [fig. 3].

The figure of the suicide stands not only as the opposite of Hope but also of the possibility of salvation offered by divine *Charity*, that is, by the blood of

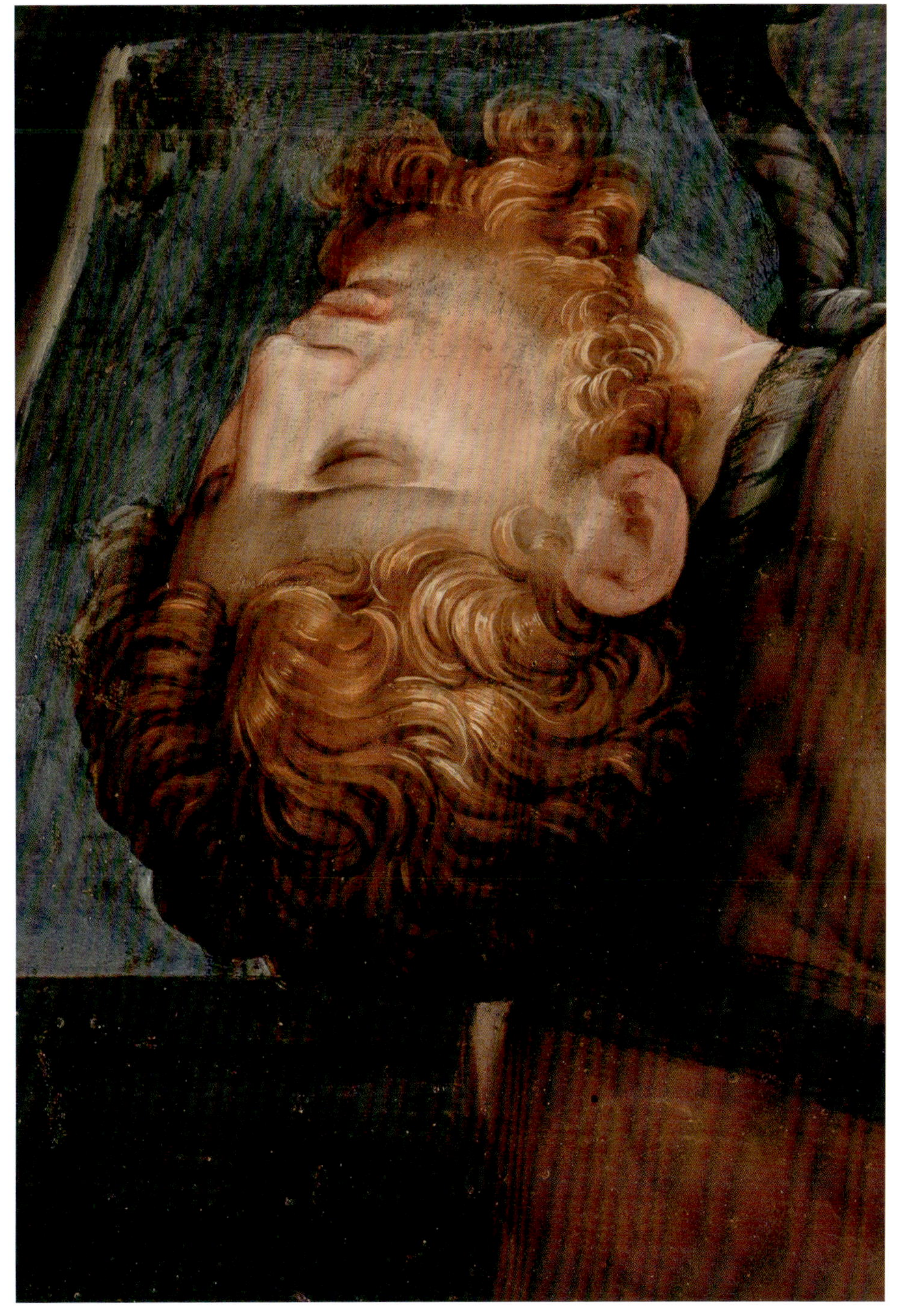

3
Giorgio Vasari, *Desperation*, detail of
the eyes

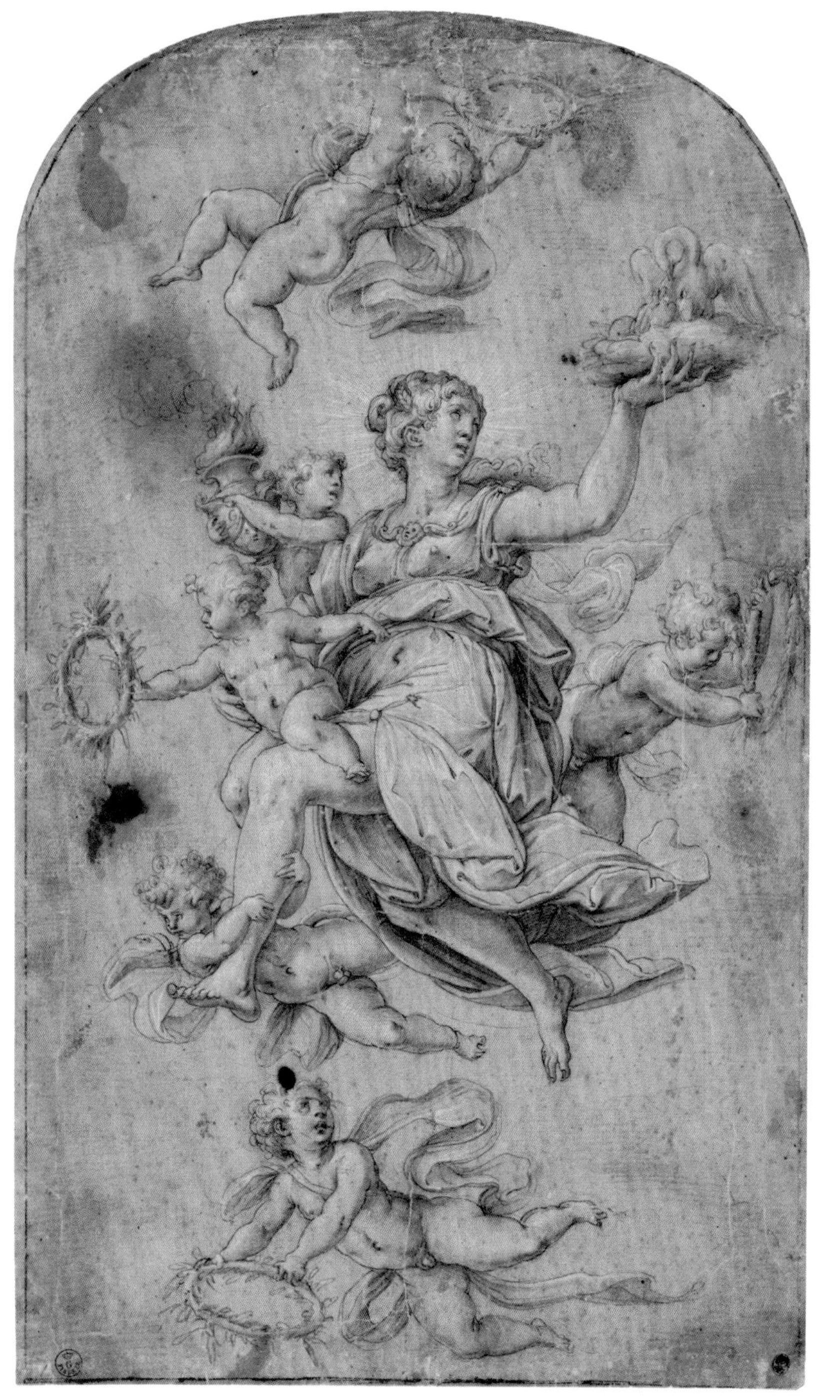

4
Giorgio Vasari, *Charity*,
Florence, Uffizi, Gabinetto disegni e
stampe, inv. 1071s

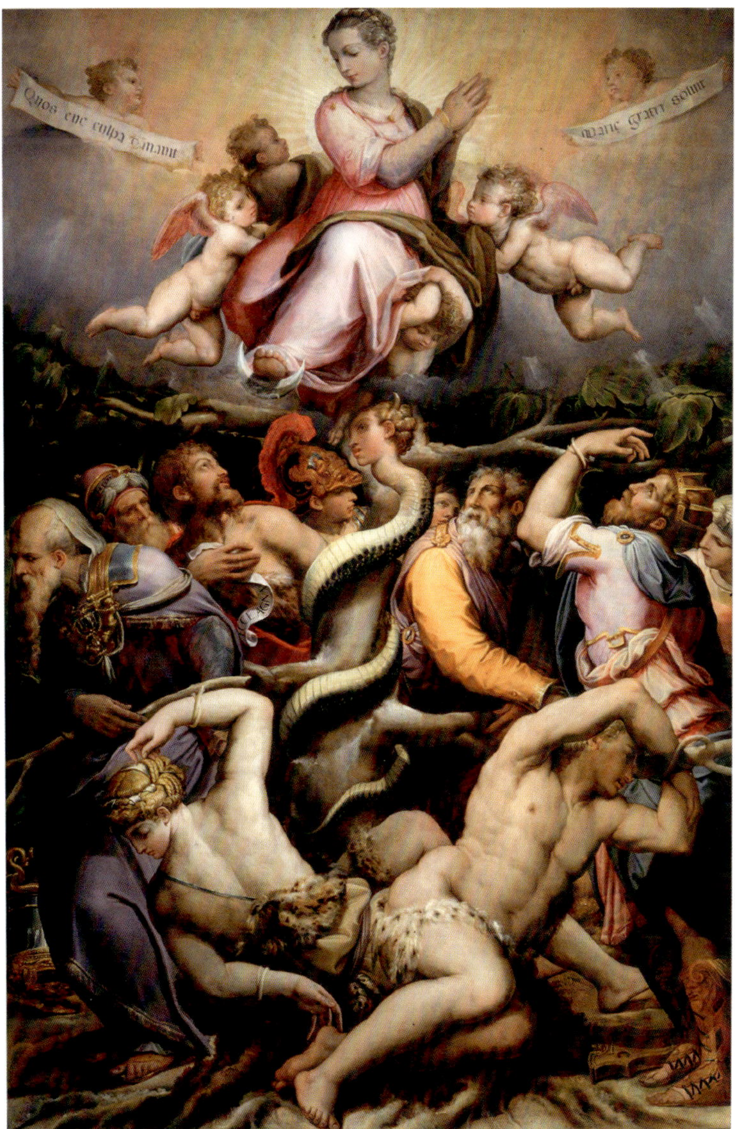

5
Giorgio Vasari, *The Immaculate
Conception*, 1543, Lucca, Museo nazionale
di Villa Guinigi, MIC – Direzione Regionale
Musei della Toscana

Christ who redeemed all humanity from original sin. For this reason, *Charity*
is not depicted giving breast to indicate love for one's neighbor, as in other
portraits, but raising a pelican tearing open her breast to feed her little ones
with her blood, a symbol of Christ's sacrifice and of God's love [fig. 4].[11]

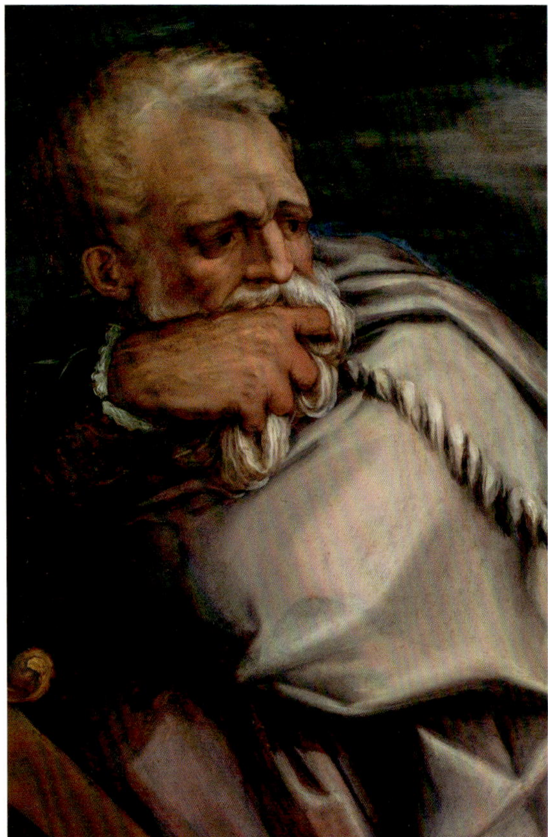

6
Giorgio Vasari, Job, detail in *Patience*

It is likely that in Venice Vasari was inspired by ideas that he had already put into painting in the *Immaculate Conception*, painted for Bindo Altoviti in 1540. In that painting, Adam and Eve and other Old Testament characters had been depicted bound to the tree of good and evil as they were "loosened" from sin by the divine light filtering through the branches of the tree. In his autobiography, Vasari explained his invention with these words "rays, likewise passing through the leaves of the tree, shed light on the bound and seem to go about loosening their bonds with the virtue and grace they derive from her from whom they proceed."[12] Upon his return from Venice in 1543, Vasari re-elaborated the subject for a new patron, Biagio Mei from Lucca,[13] and among the variations was the replacement of Judas with Eve, similarly depicted with her arm behind her back, suggesting her being bond by sin.[14] [fig. 5]

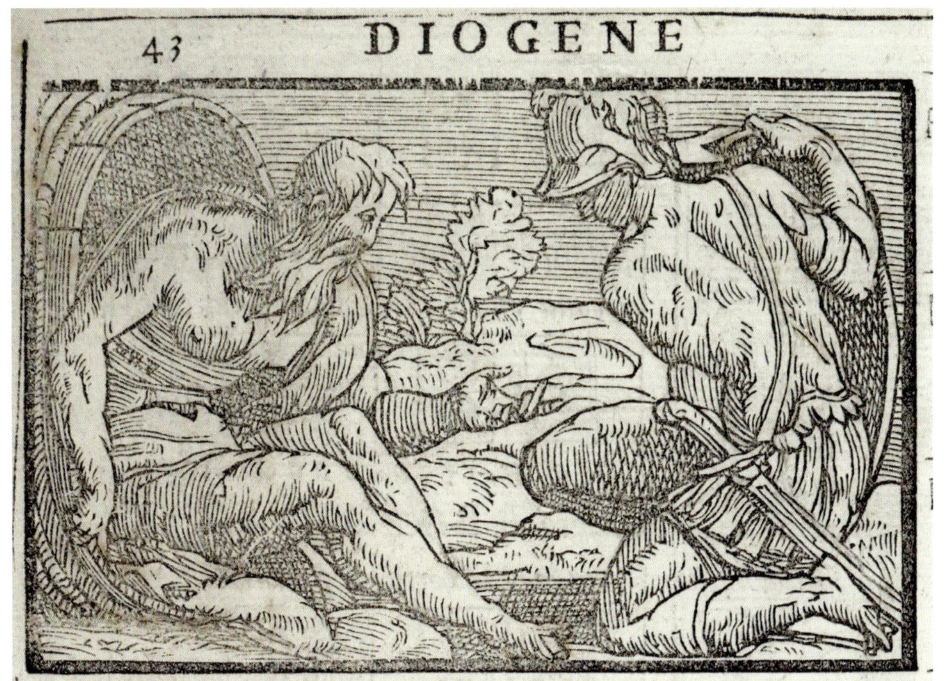

7
Giuseppe Porta, *Diogenes and Alexander the Great*, in *Le ingegnose Sorti, composte per Francesco Marcolini*, Venice 1550

Once the ceiling is reassembled, it becomes clear that it is meant to be interpreted as a single scene centered on the appearance of Charity on a cloudy sky above a terrace, which all the painted figures witness and to some extent participate in.[15] Among these, *Despair* has an important role, not only as a pendant to *Hope*, but also as the object of the reflections of the pensive helmeted soldier painted just below Hope and of the white-bearded man in the *Patience* panel, long identified with Job [fig. 6].[16] The patriarch, who in the biblical account patiently endures all the misfortunes unjustly inflicted on him and resists his wife urging to commit suicide, seems to be meditating on the opposite choice made by Judas. He is absorbed in his thoughts, combing his beard according to a coded gesture expressing suffering and doubt,[17] as if he too were still in process of making his choice and not already the paragon of virtue known to all.

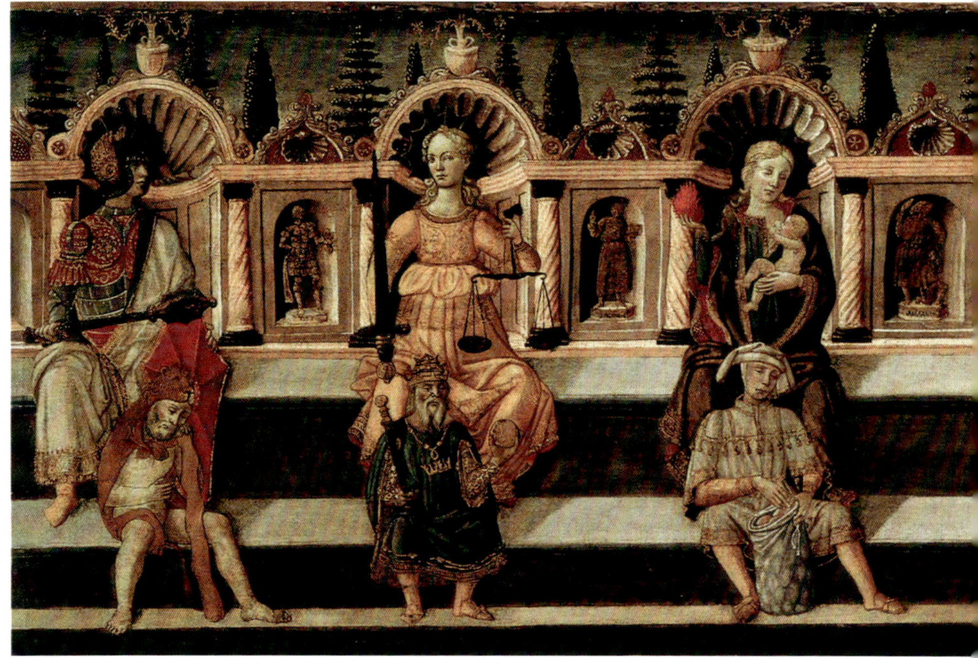

8
Giovanni di Ser Giovanni, known as
Scheggia, painted chest picturing the
seven Virtues, c. 1467–1469,
Barcelona, Museu Nacional d'Art de
Catalunya, inv. 64967

Incidentally, the traditional iconography for Job depicted him almost naked and covered with sores, whereas here he seems more like a philoso-
pher in meditation. St. Augustine writes that Judas's sin in killing himself
was first of all that of not having trusted in divine salvation (*De Civitate Dei*,
Book I, ch. 17). Such behavior is contrasted by Augustine with the virtuous
choice made by Job, who was severely tempted by suicide but remained
steadfast in his faith (*De Civitate Dei*, book I, chapters 10–12; ch. 24).

The soldier with his head lowered in front of the suicide in progress also
recalls the depiction of Alexander the Great, as pictured in the company of
Diogenes in the *Sorti* volume [fig. 7].[18] The Macedonian emperor was often
used as an example of Hope, on the strength of a passage from Plutarch's
Parallel Lives,[19] though not as frequently as Noah, figuring on the opposite
side of the panel. The Noah / Alexander the Great pairing can also be found,
incidentally, in a caisson panel with the *Virtues* by Ser Giovanni known as lo

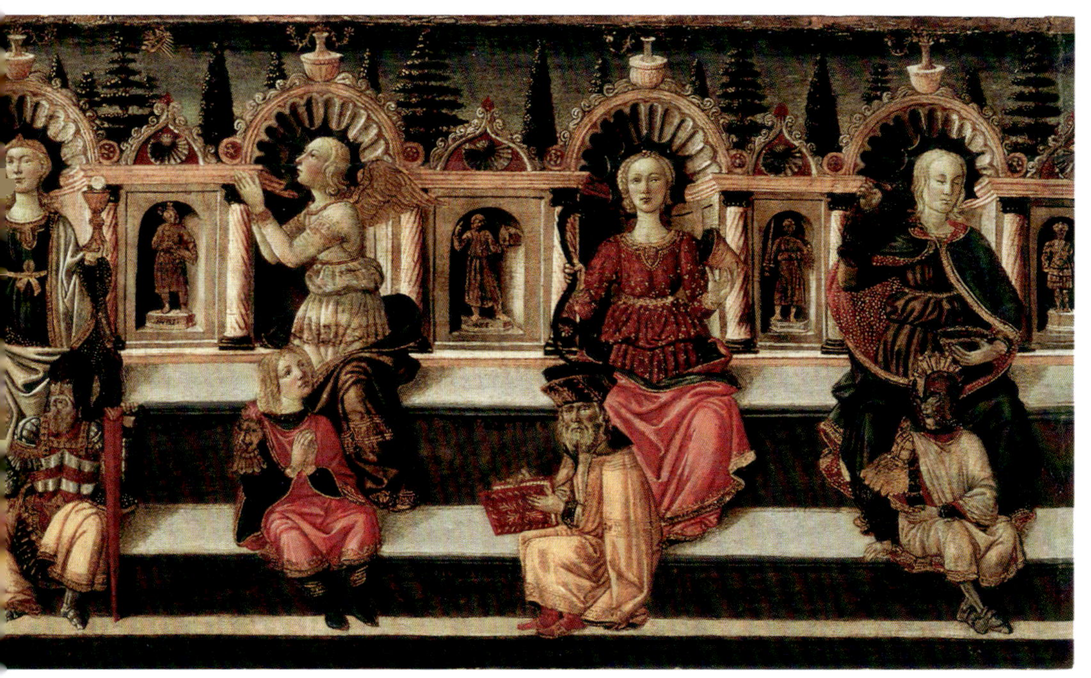

Scheggia (Barcelona, Museu Nacional d'Art de Catalunya, fig. 8),[20] although generally Alexander was depicted beardless, as also in the engraving of the *Sorti* mentioned above.[21] In the *Hope* panel, Noah is shown on a barrel clutching a fragile vine shoot, in the act of turning suddenly toward the dove heralding the end of the flood.[22] In the biblical account the bird bears an olive branch in its beak, but in the painting it is a clover, a plant befitting *Hope*, as clarified by Augustin, who specifies that clover is "the first thing that comes out of the sown wheat, and this is what we call the green of hope."[23]

As we can see, the reassembled panel of *Hope* helps us understand the plays of meanings that must have characterized the entire ceiling, via cross-references between the various painted details, which the patron must have certainly enjoyed illustrating to his guests. Thus, the anchor of Hope firmly fixed to the balustrade, a sign of salvation and stability, is contrasted with the impending leap of Judas over the same balustrade. The slender vine to which Noah holds himself is contrasted with the sturdy fig tree from which tradition says Judas hanged himself. The sturdiness of the tree is of course counterproductive for the salvation of the "desperate" person, who should instead open his eyes toward the infinite divine mercy, as Noah does as he turns toward Hope and the dove. The details of the cask and vine associated with the patriarch obviously refer back to the episode of Noah's drunkenness, a consequence of the first harvest and thus the first sign of rebirth following the flood, and could also be a reference to the Eucharist wine, the source of salvation and redemption from sin.

On the other long side of the room is *Faith* who, while looking at the pelican, imparts the sacrament of baptism to a child [fig. 9, pp. 38–39]. In this panel, too, the figure personifying the Vice opposite to the Virtue in the panel must have been cut off; there remains on the edge of the panel a flap of a black robe that must have belonged to the figure, who must also have been tied to the rope held by Faith. The unusual presence of a rope serves also as an iconographic pendant to the rope with which the man in *Desperation* is about to hang himself, on the opposite side. It also echoes the image of the two Vices tied to a rope, painted by Giotto in the Scrovegni Chapel in Padua, contrasting them in fact with *Fides* and *Spes*.[24] Giotto's *Desperatio* was a woman hanging herself, while *Infedelitas* was a figure tied with a rope to a small idol [figs. 9–10].

Compared to the Scrovegni chapel, here the function of the rope is reversed: it does not bind a Vice to an idol, rather it is Faith that is binding to herself what was most likely a personification of Heresy or Unfaithfulness, unfortunately cut away at an unspecified date and at the moment considered lost. The motif may be an adaptation of a theme known as the "Gallic Hercules" derived from Lucian, illustrating the persuasive power of speech through the depiction of Hercules dragging men by their ears with ropes or chains tied to his tongue. The subject had been used by Holbein in 1520, possibly at the suggestion of Erasmus of Rotterdam, to express the arrogance of the "Germanic" religion over the Catholic one.[25] The motif in the Corner ceiling may be intended to illustrate the powers of persuasion of Faith; Alciati too, in his *Libro degli emblemi,* had associated the Gallic Hercules to the emblem of persuasion, writing that "he who has mighty

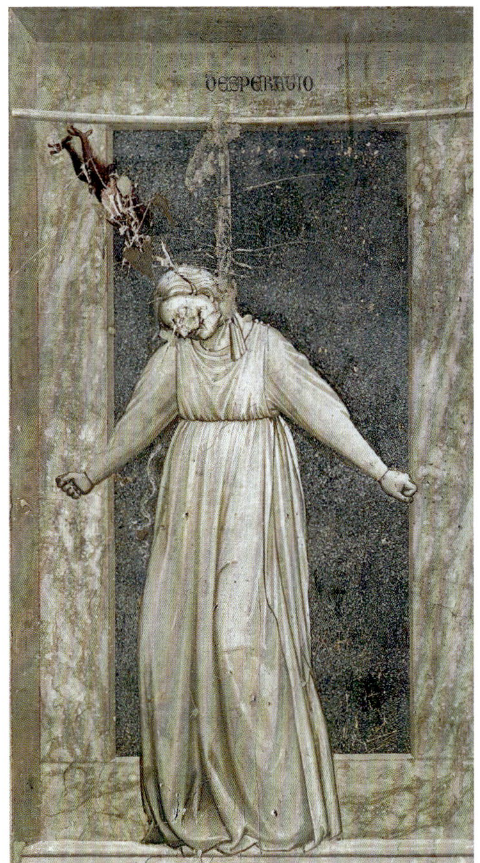

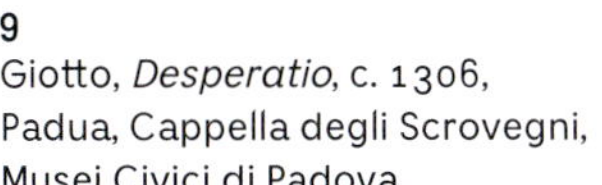

9
Giotto, *Desperatio*, c. 1306,
Padua, Cappella degli Scrovegni,
Musei Civici di Padova

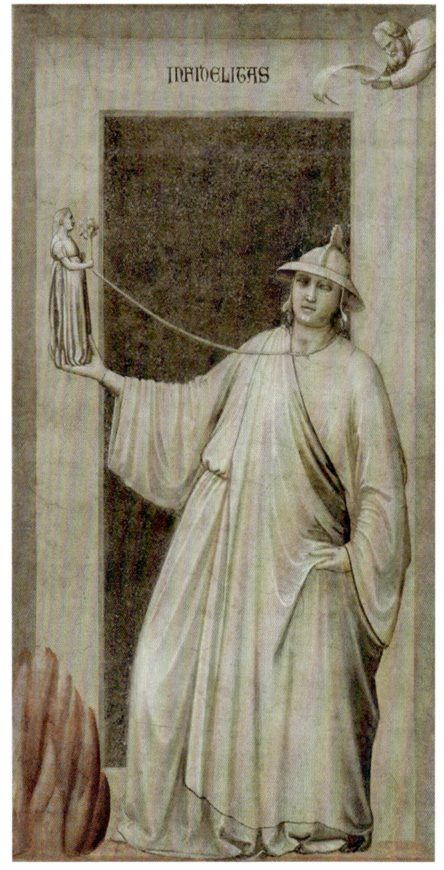

10
Giotto, *Infidelitas*, c. 1306,
Padua, Cappella degli Scrovegni, Musei
Civici di Padova

eloquence makes even the hardest hearts follow his desires."[26] One should also keep in mind that in 1541, the year before the painting of the ceiling, an attempt had been made to recompose the disputes with the Lutherans in Regensburg under the leadership of the Venetian Gaspare Contarini[27] and, although no agreement had been reached, the efforts to find a peaceful solution at the imminent next council were continuing.[28] In this particular context, Venice could be seen as a place of *charitas* and harmony.[29]

The *Faith* panel had evidently been cut also on the other side, probably to separate another example of Virtue. As suggested by the *Hope* panel, each panel had two figures associated to the, one Christian and one pagan. It

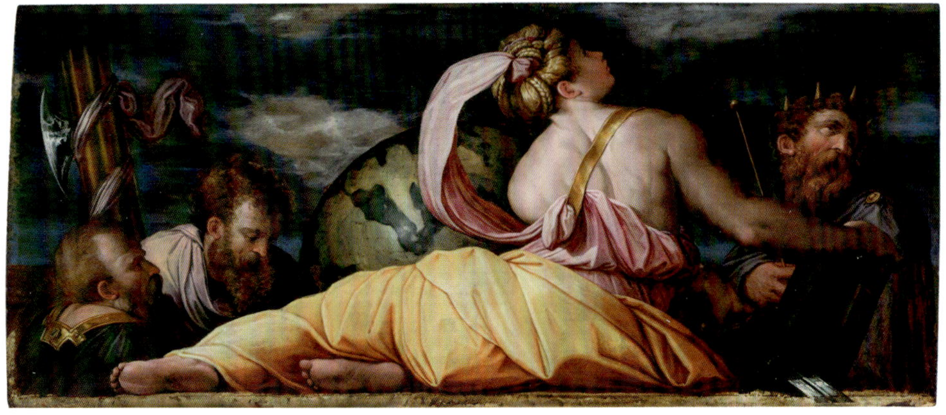

11
Giorgio Vasari, *Justice*

has been suggested that the two men to the left of *Faith* are St. Peter and St. Paul,[30] although the bearded figure with reddish hats is reminiscent of some depictions of St. Mark.[31] In any case, the two men are entirely without attributes. The uncertainty in the identification of these two figures, leaves two hypotheses concerning the example of the Virtue that was cut out. It could be Abraham, the patriarch who opens together with Noah the path of redemption after Adam's sin, an example of such unwavering faith as to sacrifice go God his own son, or, if the example of Virtue drawn from the pagan world is the one missing, one could speculate that it was Attilius Regulus. In this case, in this play of references that emerge in the reassembled ceiling, the barrel on which Noah is saved from the flood could be a pendant to the barrel that Attilius Regulus was placed in when he was put to death by the Carthaginians. In other words, an inverted meaning for a similar object, analogously to the rope leading to death Judas in *Disperation*, and to salvation in the *Faith* panel. One may add, in passing, that Attilius Regulus is one of the figures mentioned by St. Augustine's in his reflections on suicide and the ability to endure adversity (*De Civitate Dei*, Book I, ch. 15).

Completing the ensemble on the short sides of the room are two panels with the cardinal Virtues Justice and Patience, which are also flanked

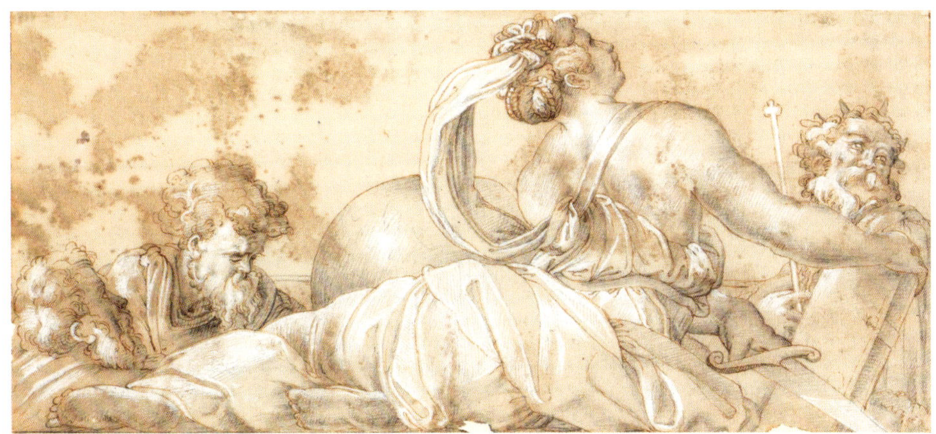

12
Excerpt from Giorgio Vasari, *Justice,*
c. 1542, drawing,
Haarlem Teylerstiching, NK94

by respective examples, Solomon for Justice and Job for Patience,[32] along with other figures that are more difficult to identify due to their total lack of attributes, for whose significance the only clues left to the viewer are their gaze and attitude.[33]

In the panel with Justice, the Virtue sits with her back turned to express impartiality, and is flanked by a globe, a book and a sword;[34] At her side, Vasari placed Solomon, the king renowned for his justice, with crown and scepter, and, on the opposite side, two men with a "bundle of rods with an axe tied together," according to the definition that Ripa used later to describe the justice that "the Judges exercise in the courts." The meaning, says Ripa, is that one should judge and punish without being hasty and "allow time for the judgment to ripen during the unbundling of the rods."[35] [fig. 11]. In the overall system of meanings in which each Virtue is confronted with the opposite concept, the opposition between divine justice and human justice is what seems to be expressed here,[36] an opposition that derives from St. Paul, who is incidentally a key figure also for the theme of the triumph of *Charity,* i.e., the main theme of the overall composition. A drawing [fig. 12] of this scene is preserved, in which the two men appear without the fasces, probably because what the composition was meant to express was first of all the opposition between the two forms of justice, with one

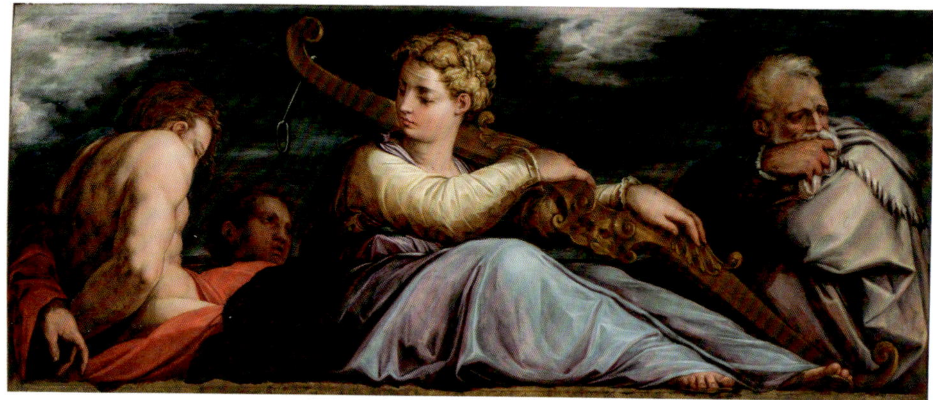

13
Giorgio Vasari, *Patience*

of the men looking up, like Justice, toward Charity—who with the pelican evokes the redemption from original sin obtained through Christ's sacrifice—while the other is looking down towards the ground. Cosimo Bartoli, Vasari's friend and frequent collaborator to the "inventions" for his paintings, had said in his *Second Reasoning* that law was necessary "to make us know sin and in despair ... had to turn to the infinity charity of God and Justice of the Faith."[37]

Solomon closes the scene by turning around, looking at what is happening in the nearby Faith panel; it is possible that it was *Infidelitas* tied to the rope that attracted his attention. After all, just as Job had to face the temptation to commit suicide, Solomon was also tempted toward idolatry by his many mistresses (*Book of Kings*, I, 11). The two examples of virtue, Job and Solomon, are thus not depicted as immune from doubt and temptation; indeed, both are depicted turning their heads away from the Virtue of which they are the traditional examples.

In the last panel that makes up the ceiling, we find a depiction of the virtue of *Patience,* expressing the theme of Christian forbearance, echoed more than once in the painting:[38] together with Job meditating on the suicide taking place before his eyes, we find a Michelangelesque "prisoner" on the opposite side of the panel, who seems bound but without ropes [fig. 13]. The appearance of being bound and the semi-nudity of this figure are traits

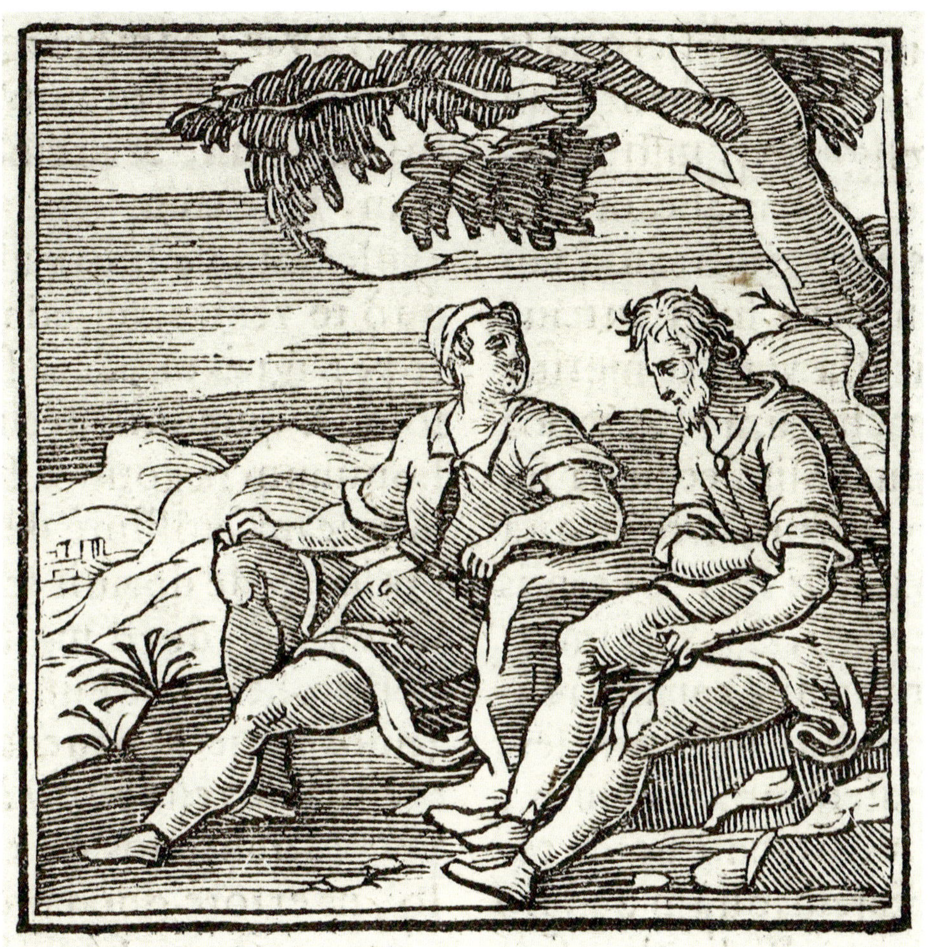

14
Emblem LXXXII, in Andreae Alciati,
Emblemata cum Commentariis
Claudii Minois I. C. Francisci Sanctii
Brocensis, et notis Laurentii Pignorii
Patavini..., Patavii, Pietro Paolo Tozzi,
1621

that belong also to the figure of Judas / Desperation, which suggest that the above figure too may be a personification of a Vice, possibly Sloth, a concept opposed to the virtuous *Patience*. The slothful man is hunched over and, like Judas, fails to respond to the light of Charity illuminating his body.[39] We may add that the image of the prisoner with his arms tied behind his back was a traditional iconographic metaphor of the human soul trapped by its own desires.[40]

In later editions of Alciati's *Emblems,* the depiction of *acedia* is represented by two men; one distraught, with his head reclining toward the ground and the other with his head turned upward, who seems to be encouraging the other. The composition echoes the attitudes of the characters in the Corner Spinelli ceiling, which might indeed have served as inspiration for the emblem [fig. 14].

The compositional design of the Corner ceiling was certainly based on the traditional theme of the triumph of Virtue over Vice, in which the personification of a Virtue could be accompanied by a figure held up as virtuous examples as well as a "prisoner," i.e. a figure personifying the opposite Vice.[41] Along with this traditional scheme, however, in Vasari's Venetian work, we also find a highly topical reflection centered on *Charity* and the sacrifice of Christ (the pelican ripping open his chest to feed the little ones), issues that at the time was at the center of the ongoing religious debate, not only among theologians and scholars, but among all the faithful.[42]

Despair, Sloth, and the missing figure that should depict Heresy or *Infidelitas* all participate in a system that echoes this debate through their connection to the image of Charity in heaven, creating a tension whose outcome is still to be decided: Judas might still be induced to open his eyes by the light and smoke of the flame, the Slothful man could be convinced to look up like the figure beside him is doing, and *Infidelitas* could be brought back to the true Faith by the rope to which he was presumably attached. The tension is reinforced by the attitude of some of the examples of Virtue, who seem to be pondering what "the prisoners of Virtue" will do: Job and the soldier, perhaps identifiable with Alexander the Great, are studying Judas; Solomon is looking towards the what might be *Infidelitas* and seems almost surprise at what he sees. From the perspective of a suspended action in progress, the fact that nothing is yet written on the plaques carried by angels in the corners of the vault[43] [fig. 1, p. 22; figs. 2–3, p. 24] might also be significant.

The only character facing the personification of Virtue in his panel is Noah, but this is probably because the interpretation of the ceiling must begin with the patriarch saved from the flood. This is suggested by the putto holding onto the foot of Charity, the only one who has no other function, given that he is carrying neither a crown nor one of the attributes of

Virtue like the others are, his purpose being only that of suggesting to the viewer where to begin reading the narrative in the ceiling.

In conclusion, the Corner scaffold could be a testimony to that hopeful historical phase inspired by a more flexible theology that still believed in the possibility of an internal and peaceful reform of the Church, keeping in mind that the work was delivered in the same months in which Bernardino Ochino, highly regarded by Pietro Aretino,[44] was allowed to preach in Venice for the Lent of 1542.

As for Vasari, he knew the people who supported an internal reform of the Church, although he avoided committing himself one way or the other.[45] As it is known, some of Contarini's Venetian friends at the beginning of the century had retired to Camaldoli,[46] a place that had also served as a refuge for Vasari after the death of Alessandro de' Medici.[47] His friend Cosimo Bartoli also sympathized with the above reformers, and in his *Second Reasoning*, had mentioned as one of his inspirators Marcantonio Flaminio, co-author with Benedetto da Mantova of the *Beneficio di Cristo*, the anonymous booklet dedicated to the centrality of Christ's sacrifice for human salvation, which circulated in manuscript since 1540 and of which Bartoli possessed a copy.[48]

We do not know who collaborated with Vasari in planning the composition of the Corner ceiling, but it seems significant that the painter chose to replicate in later works, from the Sala del Trionfo delle Virtù, in his house in Arezzo (1548) to the Hall of the Gualdrada in Palazzo Vecchio in Florence (1561–63), only the personifications of the Virtues, as if he did not find the other figures, drawn "specifically" for the other ceiling, appropriate to other contexts. Also, the way he mentions them only in passing in his *Ricordanze* might be due to a reluctance to describe them accurately now that the times had radically changed.

The Corner ceiling, given its period of execution, the spring of 1542, could also be a testimony to the ongoing debate on the principle of "double justification." Charity has her putti crown the Virtues that should guide human works and deeds and thus gives them an important function, but on the other hand, by raising the symbolic pelican, she indicates as the foundation of redemption and salvation and the central point of the work the "sacrifice of Christ. Acting virtuously is not enough and man is ever at the risk of falling, as shown also by the examples of virtue, Job and Solomon, who seem tempted by despair and idolatry. On this topic, in a 1523 letter to his friend Giustiniani in Camaldoli, Contarini had written the following words: "When man thinks he has acquired such virtues, just then he falls … we must justify ourselves by the righteousness of another, that is, of Christ."[49] Similar ideas are found in Pietro Aretino's *The Seven Psalms of Penance*, where he insisted on the importance of invoking divine grace "without which all repentance is in vain." To which he added, almost anticipating the appearance of *Charity* on a cloudy sky above the new Corner palace on rio San Polo, along with Noah saved from the flood: "Pay attention to me like you paid attention to he who your grace saved from the Flood, and clear my mind occupied by vain thoughts in the way you sometimes clear the sky encumbered by clouds."[50]

1 L. Caporossi, R. Cavigli, "Vasari at Venice. The "Suicide of Judas" at Arezzo, another addendum to the Corner ceiling," in *The Burlington Magazine*, CLVIII, 1354, 2016, pp. 10–12. I am grateful to Francesco Sorce who had the patience to examine my initial hypotheses about the iconographic program of the ceiling.

2 *Importanti dipinti, disegni, stampe e bronzi provenienti da varie proprietà*, Christie's auction (Rome, October 20, 1980), Rome 1980, vol. 71, no. 292; A. M. Maetzke, "Giuda," in *Giorgio Vasari. Principi, letterati e artisti nelle carte di Giorgio Vasari*, exhibition catalog (Arezzo, Casa Vasari and Sottochiesa di San Francesco, September 26–November 29, 1981), Florence 1981, pp. 335–36, fig. 278.

3 On Vasari's Venetian sojourn see G. Manieri Elia, "Allegoria della Fede," in *Lo Stato dell'Arte. L'Arte dello Stato. Le acquisizioni del Ministero dei beni e delle attività culturali e del turismo. Colmare le lacune - Ricucire la Storia*, exhibition catalog (Rome, Museo di Castel Sant'Angelo May 26–November 29, 2015), Rome 2015, pp. 171–72; F. Härb, *The Drawings of Giorgio Vasari (1511–1574)*, Rome 2015, pp. 191–209; G. Manieri Elia, "La Fede di Giorgio Vasari e il soffitto della 'Camera nova' in Palazzo Corner Spinelli," in *Ricche miniere*, 1, 2014, pp. 71–79; J. C. Rössler, "The 'Camera nova' by Michele Sanmicheli and Giorgio Vasari, Palazzo Corner Spinelli," in *Ricche miniere*, 1, 2014, pp. 63–69; B. Agosti, *Giorgio Vasari. Luoghi e tempi delle Vite*, Milan 2013, pp. 54–56; L. De Girolami Cheney, "Vasari's Early Decorative Cycles. The Venetian Commissions Part II," in Id., *Giorgio Vasari. Artistic and Emblematic Manifestations*, Washington 2011, pp. 51–134; A. Fenech Kroke, *Giorgio Vasari. La Fabrique de l'allégorie. Culture et fonction de la personnification au Cinquecento*, Florence 2011, pp. 326–43; M. Hochmann, *Venise et Rome 1500–1600. Deux écoles de peinture et leurs échanges*, Genève 2004, pp. 246–55; G. Romanelli, "Giorgio Vasari a Venezia," in *Pittura Veneziana dal Quattrocento al Settecento. Studi in onore di Egidio Martini*, San Giovanni Lupatoto 1999, pp. 48–53; L. Vertova, "Vasari at Venice: An Addendum," in *The Burlington Magazine*, CXLI, 1151, 1999, pp. 105–06; F. Härb, "Modes and Models in Vasari's Early Drawing Oeuvre," in *Vasari's Florence. Artists and Literati at the Medicean Court*, edited by P. Jacks, Cambridge 1998, p. 104; C. Cairns, *Pietro Aretino and the Republic of Venice. Researches on Aretino and his Circle in Venice 1527–1556*, Florence 1985, pp. 162–78; D. Mc Tavish, "Vasari e Pietro Aretino," in *Giorgio Vasari. Principi* cit., pp. 108–18; J. Kliemann, "San Michele," in *Giorgio Vasari.*

Principi cit., p. 97; R. Pallucchini, "Per la storia del Manierismo a Venezia," in *Da Tiziano a El Greco. Per la storia del Manierismo a Venezia 1540–1590*, exhibition catalog (Venice, Palazzo Ducale, September 1–December 28, 1981), Milan 1981, pp. 17–19; J. Schultz, "Vasari at Venice," in *The Burlington Magazine*, CIII, 705, 1961, pp. 500–11; J. Schultz, *Venetian Painted Ceilings of the Reinaissance*, Berkeley–Los Angeles 1968, p. 120, cat. 50; B. Nicolson, "Mannerism at the Arcade Gallery," in *The Burlington Magazine*, XCII, 562, 1950, p. 203; P. Barocchi, "Il Vasari pittore," in *Rinascimento*, VII, 2, 1955, p. 193.

4 A. M. Maetzke, "Giuda" (entry 18), in *Giorgio Vasari. Principi* cit., p. 55; L. Corti, "Giuda" (entry 25), in *Vasari. Catalogo completo*, Florence 1989, p. 44.

5 G. Romanelli, "Giorgio Vasari a Venezia" cit., p. 50.

6 In the Weidenfeld collection in London, for the events surrounding the purchase of the panel from the Galleria dell'Accademia, see G. Manieri Elia, "La Fede di Giorgio Vasari" cit., pp. 71–79; Schultz had already noted that the English panel depicting *Hope* was the most cropped of the panels J. Schultz, "Vasari at Venice" cit., p. 507, no. 33.

7 J. Schultz, "Vasari at Venice" cit., pp. 500–11; F. Härb, "Modes and Models" cit., p. 104; L. De Girolami Cheney, "Vasari's Early Decorative" cit., pp. 99–134; on the reconstruction of the ceiling see the article by R. Cavigli in the present volume.

8 Liana De Girolami Cheney had suggested a nuptial meaning: L. De Girolami Cheney, "Vasari's Early Decorative" cit., pp. 99–134; this hypothesis has already been deemed implausible by J. C. Rössler, "The 'Camera nova'" cit., p. 67.

9 The presence of Judas in the *Triumph of Hope* of the Visconti Tarot had been described by Cicognara as follows: "at the foot of Hope one sees an old man crawling on all fours with a halter around his neck and with the words *Juda traditor* written in white letters on his purple suit," L. Cicognara, *Memorie Spettanti alla Storia della Calcografia*, Prato 1831, p. 155; on the Visconti Tarot G. E. di Parravicino, "Three Packs of Italian Tarocco Cards," in *The Burlington Magazine*, III, October–December 1903, pp. 237–51; G. Moakley, *The Tarot Cards, Painted by Bonifacio Bembo for the Visconti-Sforza family. An Iconographic and Historical study*, New York 1966. Other examples of Hope with Judas are found in a stained glass window from 1519 (Musée du Cinquantenaire, Brussels) published by D. Panofsky, E. Panofsky, *Il vaso di Pandora,*

Turin 1992, fig. II, pp. 32, 36; in an illustration from Codex 1462 of the Musée Condé in Chantilly published by M. Bautz: *Virtutes. Studien zu Funktion und Ikonographie der Tugenden im Mittelater und im 16. Jahrhundert*, Berlin 1999, p. 207; Judas is found, still in opposition to Hope, in the *Allegoria di Sant'Agostino*, I. Ceretti, "L'iconografia dei vizi e delle virtù attraverso lo sguardo di un miniatore bolognese del Trecento," in *I quaderni del m.ae.s*, XIII, 1, 2010, pp. 125–46.
10 On the Venetian capital: F. Zanotto, *Il Palazzo Ducale di Venezia*, Venice 1842, vol. I, p. 312; for Marcolini's silograph: E. Parlato, "Le allegorie nel giardino delle 'Sorti'," in *Studi per le "Sorti". Gioco, immagini, poesia oracolare a Venezia nel Cinquecento*, edited by P. Procaccioli, Rome 2007, pp. 130–31 .
11 The composition for Charity was to be reused by Vasari in a a second ceiling dated around 1555 (Courtald Institute of Art, London, inv. D. 1952.RW.3504) which around the tondo with Charity reproduces, as noted by Charles Davis, a passage from Psalm 101:6–8 "similis factus sum pelican"; F. Härb, *The Drawings of Giorgio Vasari (1511–1574)*, Rome 2015, pp. 206–07, 354–55 ; as for the more usual depiction of Charity with the three putti see P. Carloni, M. Grasso, "L'eloquenza della virtù: Giorgio Vasari, Anton Francesco Doni e il linguaggio allegorico nel Cinquecento. Riflessioni attorno a una ricerca compiuta," in *Storia dell'Arte*, 92, 1994, pp. 429–30 .
12 J. Kliemann, "Philippe Thomassin (1562–1622) da Giorgio Vasari, Allegoria dell'Immacolata Concezione," in *Giorgio Vasari. Principi*, cit. pp. 106–07 ; D. Franklin, "Rosso Fiorentino, Marcillat and Vasari in Arezzo. The Reinvention of the Image of the Immaculate Conception," in *La disputa sull'Immacolata Concezione nella Toscana del Cinquecento*, proceedings of the study day (Florence, Galleria dell'Accademia, May 13, 2019), edited by C. Hollberg, Florence 2022, pp. 110–23; Vasari was to again use the image of bound and subdued figures also in the so-called *Giustizia Farnese* (1543), see S. Pierguidi, "Sulla fortuna della 'Giustizia' e della 'Pazienza' del Vasari," in *Mitteilungen des Kunsthistorische in Institutes in Florenz*, LI, 3–4, 2007, pp. 576–92.
13 J. Kliemann, "Philippe Thomassin (1562–1622)" cit. p. 106, (entry 3).
14 The position of Judas with his arm apparently bound behind his back derives from a drawing by Rosso Fiorentino, preparatory for the decoration of the Church of the Annunziata in Arezzo and which Vasari used for various figures with a negative connotation as already noted by M. Rossi, "Rosso, Pontormo, l'inferna fossa. Todes meditation vasariana," in *Pontormo e Rosso fiorentino. Divergenti vie della "Maniera,"* exhibition catalog (Florence, Palazzo Strozzi, March 8–July 20, 2014), Florence 2014, p. 331.
15 P. Rossi, "I soffitti veneziani da Pordenone a Tintoretto," in *Da Bellini a Veronese. Temi di arte veneta*. Venice 2004, p. 512.
16 L. Vertova, "Vasari at Venice" cit. pp. 105–06.
17 C. Frugoni, *La voce delle immagini. Pillole iconografiche dal Medioevo*, Turin 2010, pp. 53–54.
18 *Le ingegnose sorti composte per Francesco Marcolini da Forlì, intitolate giardino d'i pensieri. Novamente ristampate e in nove et bellissimo ordine riformate*, Venice 1550 , p. 41.
19 The episode reported by Plutarch describes Alexander the Great giving soldiers land and houses, keeping nothing for himself, because Hope is enough for him, M. Caciorgna, R. Guerrini, *La Virtù figurata. Eroi ed eroine dell'antichità nell'arte senese tra Medioevo e Rinascimento*, Siena 2003, pp. 17–27
20 At the foot of the Hope appears a young Alexander the Great, recognizable by the table with inscription, and at the bottom in a niche the statue of Noah with related inscription on the base of the statue, A. Staderini, "Allegoria delle arti liberali (inv. 64968, n. 67)," in *Dal Giglio al David. Arte civica a Firenze tra Medioevo e Rinascimento*, edited by M. M. Donato, D. Parenti, exhibition catalog (Florence, Gallerie dell'Accademia May 14–December 18, 2013), Florence 2013, p. 264 .
21 P. Querchi, *Notes on antiquarians and beards*, in *La barba nel Cinquecento. History, art, literature*, proceedings of the study seminar (Rome, Università degli Studi Roma Tre, December 16, 2022), edited by G. Crimi, Manziana 2023, p. 40
22 B. Nicolson, "Mannerism at the Arcade" cit., p. 203.
23 Reported by Mino Gabriele in A. Alciato, *Il libro degli Emblemi. Secondo le edizioni del 1531 e del 1534*, edited by M. Gabriele, Milan 2009, p. 416.
24 Vasari had not yet been in Padua, but Giovanni Corner had contacts and a house in Padua: M. Hochmann, "Tra Venezia e Roma: il cardinale Francesco Corner," in *Saggi e memorie di storia dell'arte*, 18, 1992, p. 101 .
25 C. Carlini, "Temi iconografici del '500 legati all'Hercules di Luciano, tradotto da Erasmo," in *Le Strade della Filologia* per Scevola Mariotti, Roma 2012, pp. 289–305; C. Volpi, *Le immagini degli dèi di Vincenzo Cartari*, Rome 1996, pp. 377, 380–81; E. Wind, "'Hercules' and 'Orpheus'. Two

Mock-Heroic Designs by Dürer," in *Journal of the Warburg Institute*, II, 1938–1939, pp. 206–18 .

26 A. Alciato, *Il libro degli Emblemi* cit. , p. 474.

27 A. Marranzini, "I colloqui di Ratisbona: l'azione e le idee di Gaspare Contarini," in *Gaspare Contarini e il suo tempo,* proceedings of the study conference (Venice, 1–3 March 1985), edited by F. Cavazzana Romanelli, Venice 1988, pp. 167–206.

28 A. Prosperi, *L'eresia del Libro Grande. Storia di Giorgio Siculo e della sua setta,* Milan 2011, pp. 72–78.

29 M. Firpo, F. Biferali, *Immagini ed eresie nell'Italia del Cinquecento*, Bari 2016, p. 351.

30 L. Vertova, "Vasari at Venice" cit., pp. 105–06; for the Venetian context of those years and the iconographic "spiritual" choices of some artists, see A. Gentili, *La bilancia dell'arcangelo. Vedere i dettagli nella pittura veneziana*, Rome 2009, in in particular pp. 177–80; 193–95; 217–20.

31 Close to both Mantegna's *San Marco* (1445, Städelsches Kunstinstitut, Frankfurt) and Dürer's *San Marco* (1526, Alte Pinakothek, Munich).

32 L. Vertova, "Vasari at Venice" cit., pp. 105–06; for De Girolami Cheney the figure with scepter and crown could also be Trajan, L. De Girolami Cheney, "Vasari's Early" cit., p. 107.

33 Such a way of composing the scene is reminiscent of the solution that will be adopted by Vasari for the chapel of Pope Pius V in the Vatican Palaces in 1571, where the central figure of a saint is contrasted with a father of the church and figures whose heads are only discernible and whose meaning can be deduced only from their pensive and doubtful attitudes, see G. Aurigemma, "Averroè, Ario e Sabelio, due inediti frammenti vasariani," in *Storia dell'Arte*, 136, 2013, pp. 38–45.

34 L. De Girolami Cheney, "Vasari's Early" cit, pp. 105–07; D. Mc Tavisch, "La Giustizia," in *Da Tiziano a El Greco* cit., p. 86; on the iconography of justice also A. Cecchi, "Sala del Trionfo e delle virtù," *in Giorgio Vasari. Principi* cit., p. 27.

35 C. Ripa, *Iconologia,* edited by P. Buscaroli, Milan 1992 , p. 162.

36 An interpretation already correctly suggested by L. De Girolami Cheney, "Vasari's Early" cit., p. 106.

37 C. Bartoli, *Sopra alcuni luoghi difficili di Dante*, Venice 1567 , p. 33.

38 For a survey of all Vasarian allegories: A. Fenech Kroke, *Giorgio Vasari, la fabrique* cit. p. 390 ff.

39 On acedia in the ancestor series in the Sistine Chapel, as slowness in accepting divine revelation, G. Careri, *Ebrei e cristiani nella Cappella Sistina*, Macerata 2020, pp. 171–83 .

40 E. Panofsky, *Studies in Iconology*, Turin 1975, p. 266.

41 An example are the personifications of the Virtues in the miniatures for the 11th-century Bamberg Apocalypse, A. Katzenellenbogen, *Allegories of Virtues and Vices in Medieval Art from Early Christianism to the Thirteenth Century,* New York 1964 , pp. 14–15, fig. 14.

42 M. Firpo, F. Biferali, *Immagini ed eresie* cit., pp. VIII–XXI, 351–79; on the Venetian context and the vividness of certain themes that around 1540 also began to circulate in manuscript form in the volume *Il Beneficio di Cristo*, see A. Prosperi, *L'eresia del Libro Grande* cit., pp. 38–80.

43 Perhaps in reference also to the Augustinian themes of free will and predestination, widely debated in those very years, see for example C. Ginzburg, A. Prosperi, *Giochi di pazienza, Un seminario sul* Beneficio di Cristo, Macerata 2020, especially pp. 126–30, 139–50

44 On Aretino's appreciation of Ochino's preaching see M. Firpo, *Artisti, gioiellieri, eretici. Il mondo di Lorenzo Lotto tra Riforma e Controriforma*, Bari 2011, pp. 128–31.

45 M. Firpo, "Giorgio Vasari and the Religious Crisis of the 1500s," in *Giorgio Vasari e la crisi religiosa del '500*, in *I mondi di Vasari. Accademia, lingua, religione, storia, teatro*, ed. by A. Nova and L. Zangheri, Venice 2013, pp. 43–65; M. Firpo, F. Biferali, *Immagini ed eresie* cit., especially pp. 129–49 .

46 See E. Massa, "Gasparo Contarini e gli amici tra Venezia e Camaldoli," in *Gaspare Contarini*, cit., pp. 39–41 .

47 B. Agosti, *Giorgio Vasari. Luoghi e tempi delle Vite*, Milan 2013, pp. 24–26, 45–48 ; A. M. Maetzke, "Vasari e i committenti ecclesiastici: Arezzo e Camaldoli 1537–1540," in *Giorgio Vasari. Principi* cit., pp. 50–54.

48 A. Fenech Kroke, *Giorgio Vasari. La fabrique de l'Allegorie* cit., p. 84 no. 28, 91.

49 Reported by A. Marranzini, "I colloqui di Ratisbona" cit., p. 195.

50 P. Aretino, *Prose sacre*, Lanciano 1926, p. 174.

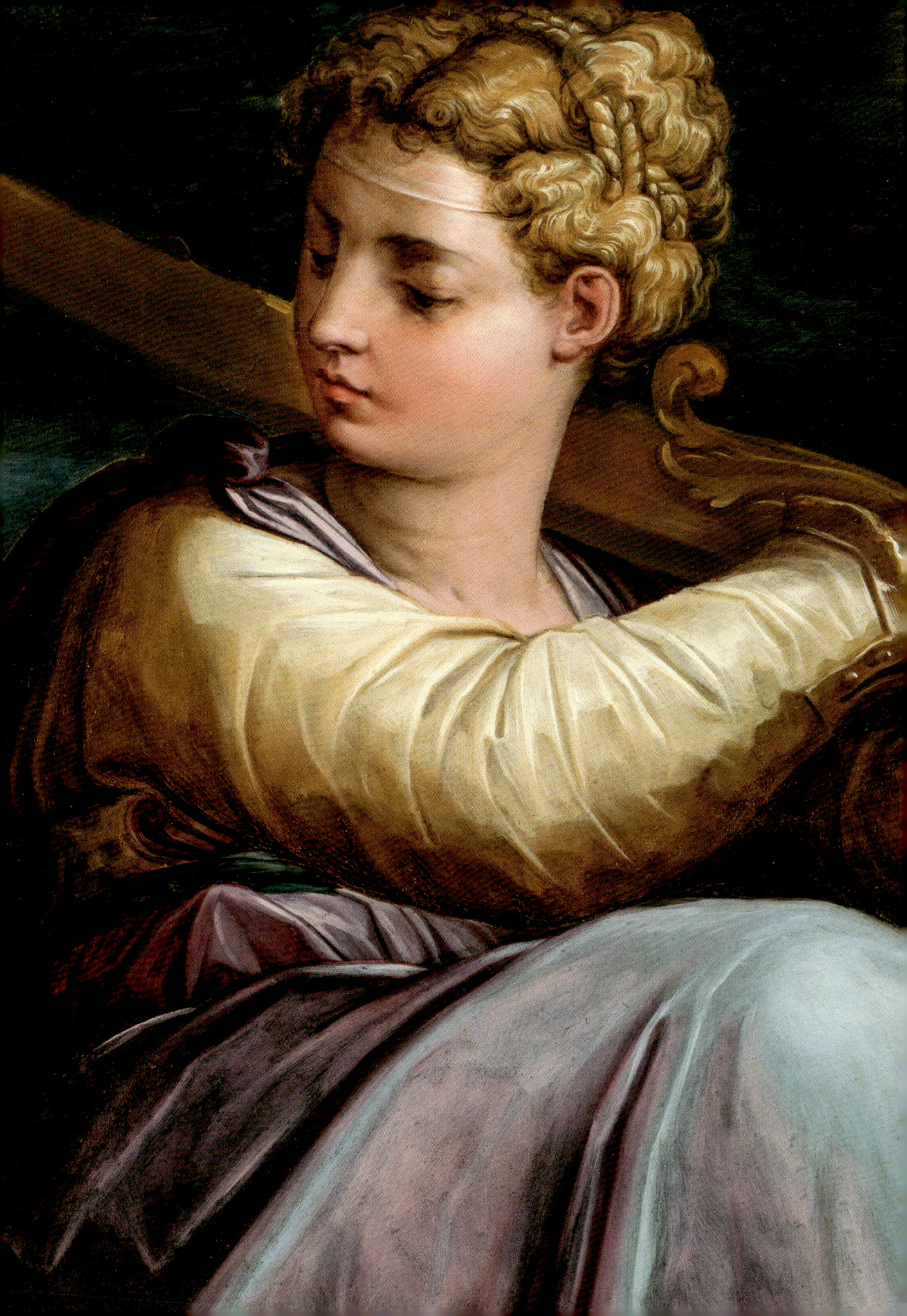

The Restoration of the Corner Ceiling: A Reading of Giorgio Vasari's "Bene Operare"

Rossella Cavigli

The restoration history

The most recent restoration interventions[1] on Giorgio Vasari's paintings for the Corner ceiling were undertaken in view of the presentation to the public of the work, never published as a whole. Over the years, the missing panels had been gradually added to the nucleus of panels already present at the Gallerie dell'Accademia in Venice. The goal of the restoration was to achieve a homogeneous level of readability for the whole, acting on the interventions carried out at different times and places, and to study the technical characteristics of the paintings in order to gather information for the reassembling of the ceiling. The greatest obstacle was the loss of the richly decorated frame that connected the panels, connecting with its gilded grid the sky found as background in all the paintings; other difficulties were the loss of one of the four corner panels depicting putti, the missing lower part in one of the remaining ones, and some missing parts from the panel with the *Faith*, which had been cut off, as became evident when the panel arrived in Venice.

The various interventions carried out on the paintings in the period after their removal from the ceiling[2] were clearly legible on the pictorial surfaces and on the wooden supports. The interventions were dictated mainly by the changed point of view of the works, which from ceiling paintings had been transformed into autonomous wall paintings. The author's rapid

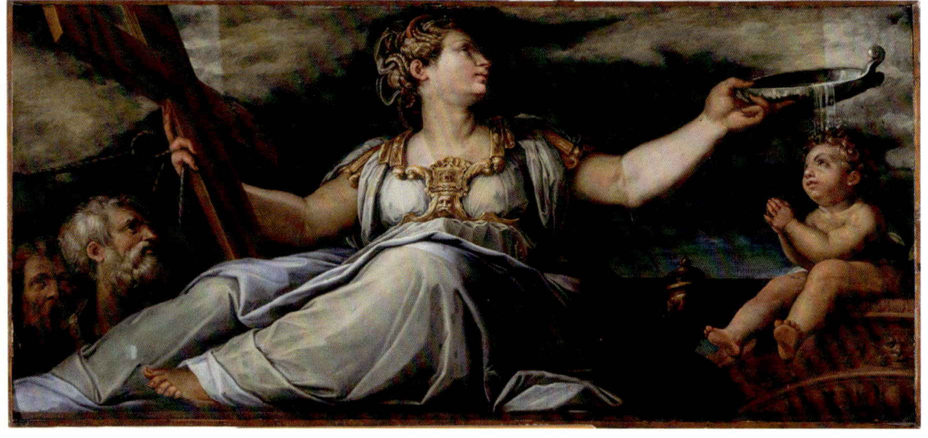

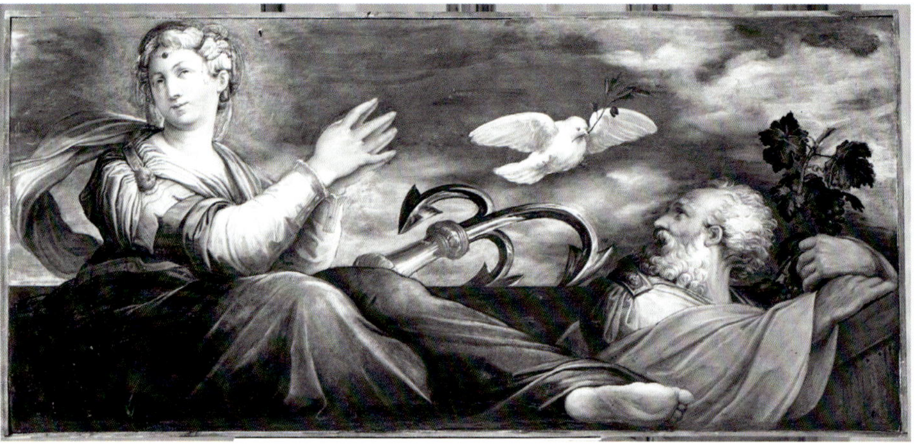

1
The *Allegory of Faith* during
restoration, with the outer laths.
Cleaning test with removal of altered
restoration varnish and, on the leg
to the left, two tests with removal of
varnish and then repainting can be
seen

2
Hope, photographed in 1952,
with the outer laths

pictorial execution, downright sketchy in some areas, appeared ill-suited to the closer point of view, now focusing on the specific parts and no longer on the whole, distorting the original impression; furthermore, the larger panels had been cut into sections, the now inappropriate cross-bars had been removed and replaced by laths nailed along the edges of the panels.[3] Those laths were still present on the panels depicting *Faith* and *Hope* [figs. 1, 2] and documented by photos of the restoration carried out in the 1980s on the panels with *Patience* and the *Suicide of Judas*. We

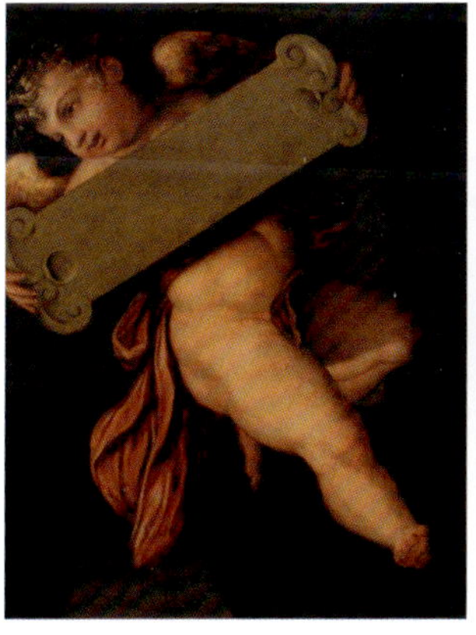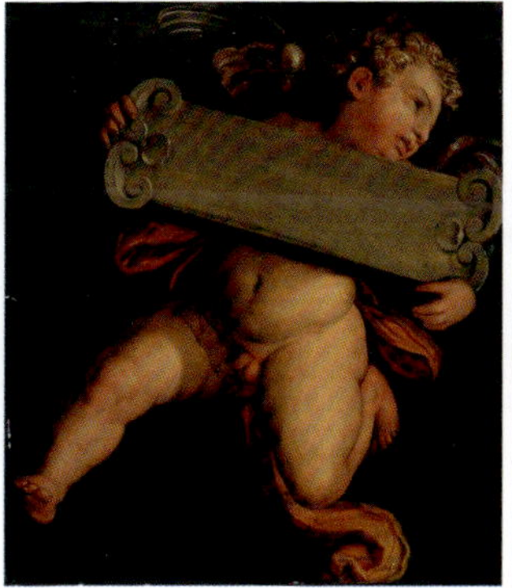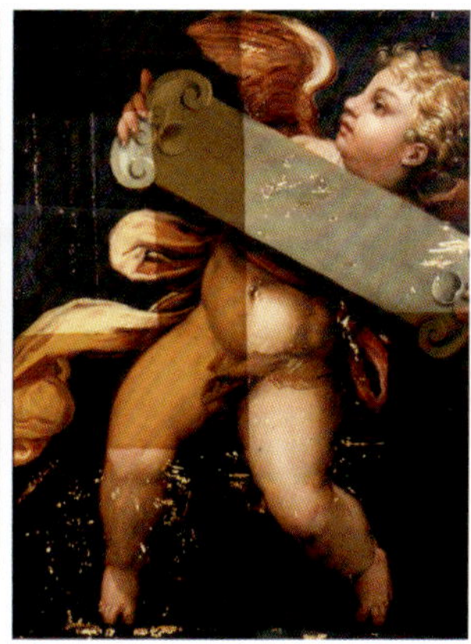

3
The three Puttos with the added
drapes in the photos of the
restoration of the 1980s

can reasonably date to the time after the dismantling of the ceiling the extensive repainting found over the balustrade, the plaques of the putti and the robes added in *Faith* [fig. 1] and *Justice* to conceal the areas where the bright underlying preparation had become visible, now that the panels were viewed up close. During that period, chastening garments were also added to the putti [fig. 3] (perhaps also to those on the center panel). These garments were removed during the aforementioned restorations along with the now yellowing varnish; this varnish was still present on the panels with *Faith* and with *Hope* when they were gathered to the whole in 2013 and 2017, respectively. The opaque appearance of *Charity*, restored in 1987,[4] was due to the presence of a wax-rich varnish that served to harmonize the countless retouches made to hide the dark punctiform deposits[5] evident especially on the brighter colors [fig. 4].

Comparison of the level of color cleaning of the last panel acquired and restored in 2003 with that of the others already in the museum led to the decision to remove from these the partially dulled varnishes, and unfortunately along with them also the retouchings and the older additions that were initially meant to be kept. The difference was evident in the tables held by the Putti: the more recently restored panel showed the quick brushstrokes functional to paintings meant to be observed from a

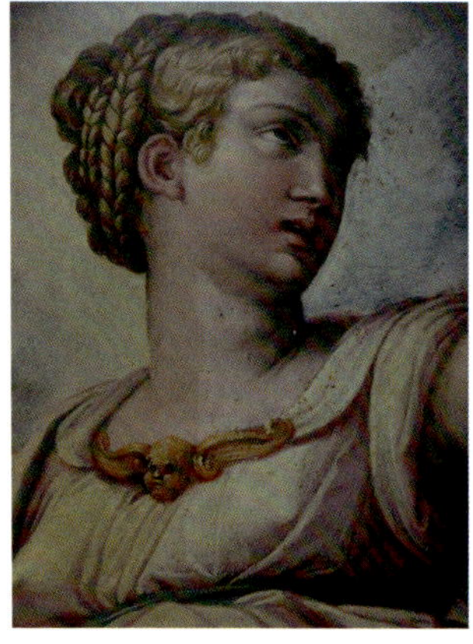
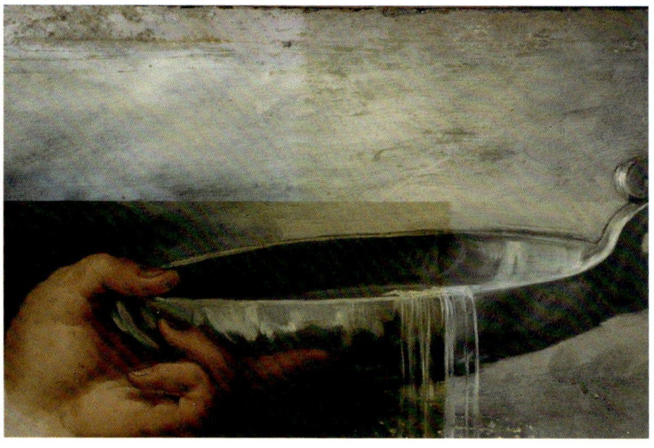

4
Detail of the *Charity* being cleaned, with the dark deposits in the area on the right, visible after removal of the altered restoration varnish, still visible on the left

5
Detail of the *Allegory of Faith* during the cleaning, with the removal of the two layers of altered varnishes: bottom left, before removal; on the right, with the more ancient varnish; top left, after the cleaning

distance, i.e. the original arrangement that would be recreated once the panels were again placed on the ceiling. The first step was the cleaning of the pictorial surfaces [figs. 1, 4–7], a more straightforward process on the paintings restored in the 1980s, where the varnishes were more recent, but more problematic in the case of the older stratifications in *Faith* and *Hope*. After the cleaning, the paintings were retouched [figs. 8–10]. On the back of the panels with *Judas* and *Faith,* it proved necessary to plaster the deep cavities caused by xylophagous insects to repair the structure of the support.[6]

The study of the ceiling composition

Giorgio Vasari's precise indications concerning the subject and the arrangement of the nine panels of the ceiling made for Giovanni Cornaro,[7] together with the iconographic studies by critics, had led most scholars to believe that all the parts of the ceiling, except for two still missing panels with Putti, once the central panel depicting *Charity,* had been found[8] [fig. 11]. The possibility, offered by the restoration, of directly comparing works

6

Detail of the *Allegory of Charity* being cleaned:
bottom right, after removal of restoration
varnish and, in the top left panel, with
retouchings highlighted by ultraviolet light

7

Detail of *Hope* with cleaning essays on different
color fields: the restoration varnishes were
removed from the portion of the sky on the right,
revealing a filler, from the neckline and ear with
the lock of hair including the figure's braid, from
portions of drapery adjoining each other, in the
center: the light blue robe, the pink stole (with a
cleaned portion also on the left), the pink sleeve,
the light blue band on the arm and an area of the
skirt between the light and shadow parts

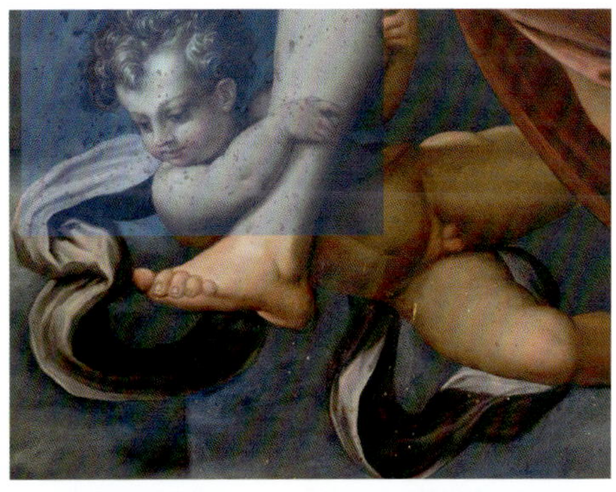

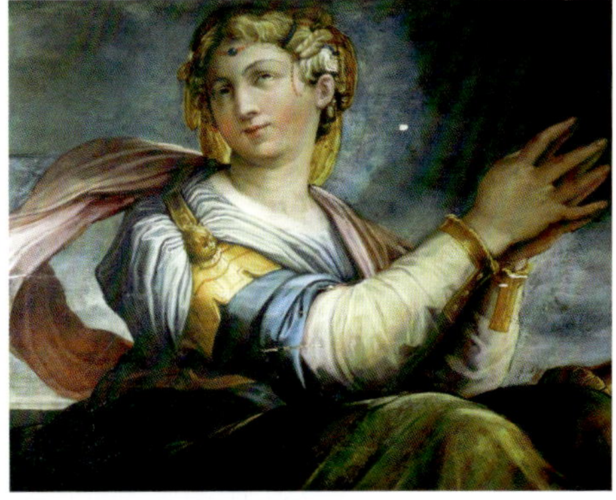

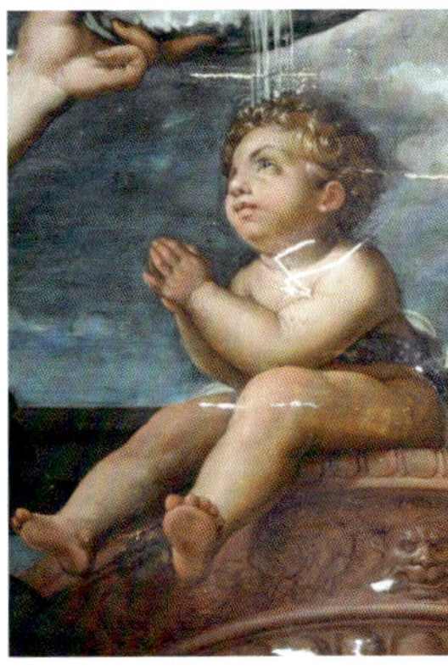

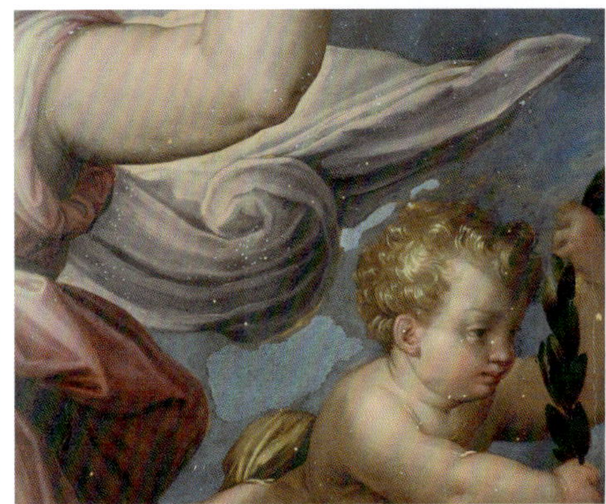

8

Detail of the *Allegory of Faith* during plastering

9

Detail of the *Allegory of Charity* being retouched,
during the application of watercolor color bases
even over the deposits of the material that
compromised the underlying color

10

Detail of the *Faith* being retouched
with watercolor based pigments

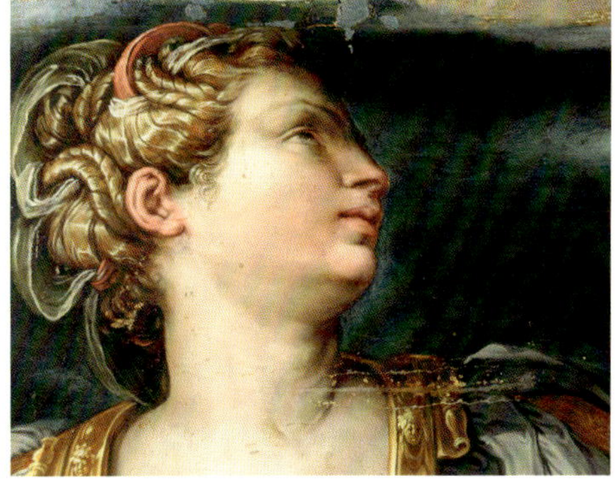

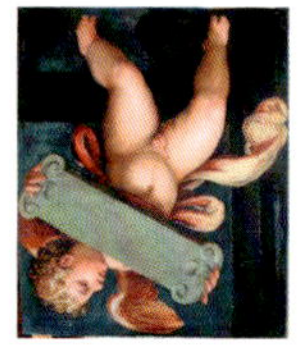
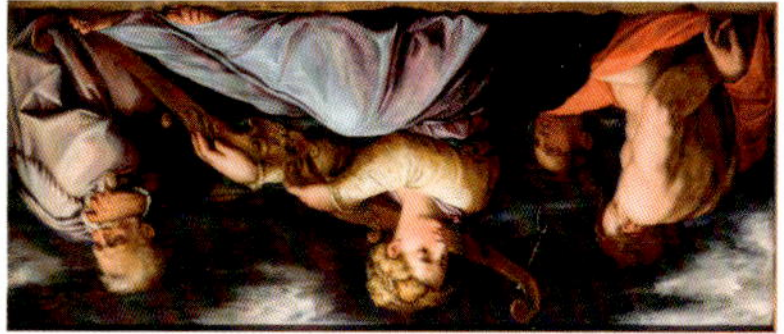

11
Hypothetical
reconstruction
of the ceiling
before the last
restoration

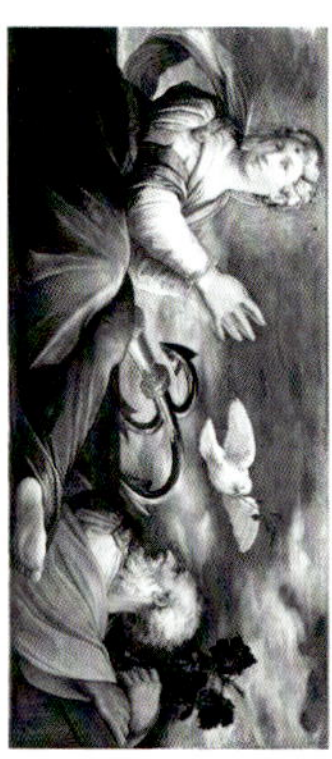
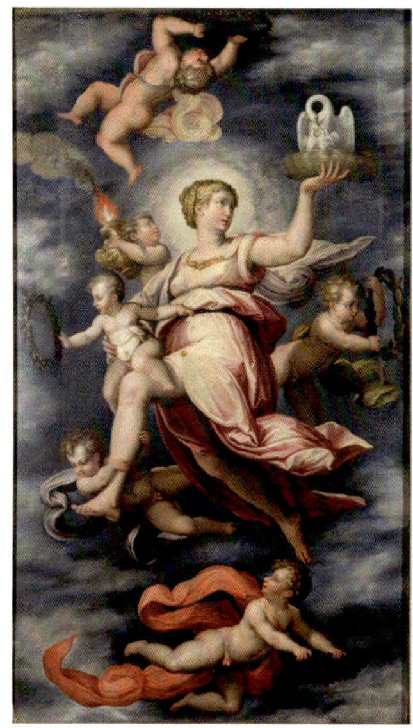
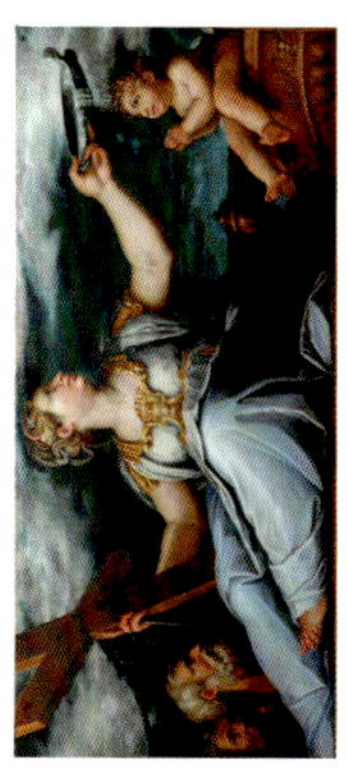

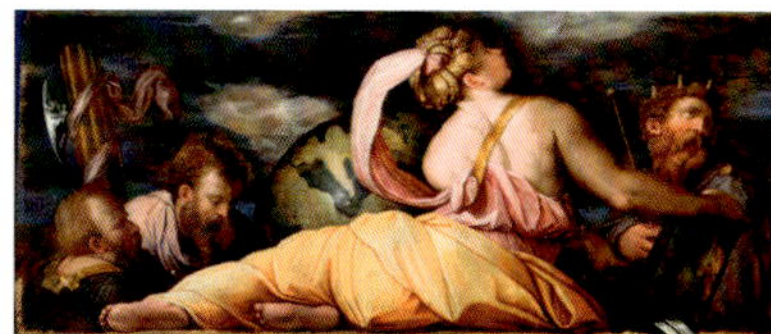
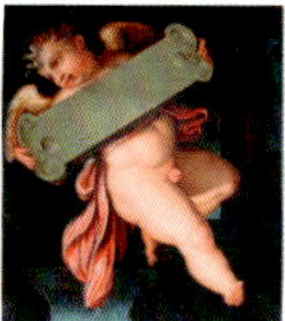

from the artist's Venetian period, including the one depicting the *Suicide of Judas in* the Museo di Casa Vasari in Arezzo, immediately revealed the similarity of the paintings, in particular with regard to the dimensions of the balustrade painted on the outer panels, clearly legible in the corner panels and in the *Judas* painting in Arezzo [fig. 12], along with the constructive similarities of the supports: the number, width and thicknesses of the slates used, the use of "butterfly joints" ("chiavi a farfalla"), the original crossbeam system. A third corner panel with a Putto had been added to the

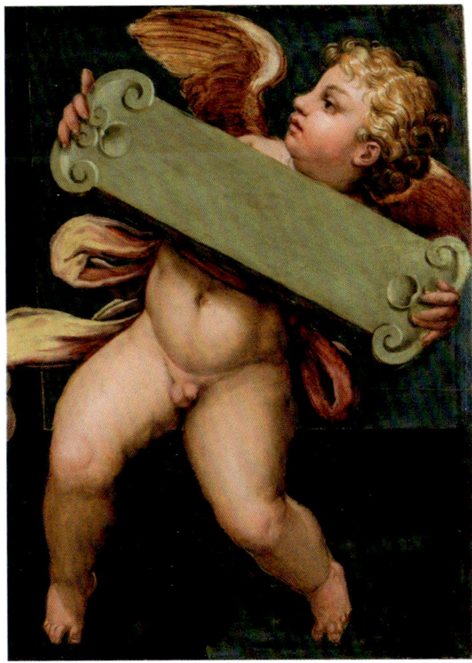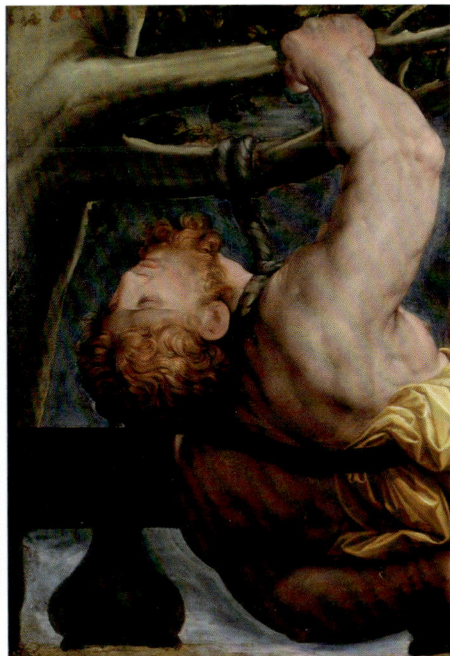

12
Comparison of the balustrade on a panel
with *Putto* and on the one with *Judas*

ensemble in the meantime, *Putto*, with *Faith* still to arrive in Venice and the *Hope* still in a private collection.

Also other elements suggested the opportunity of re-examining the figurative development of the ceiling, such as the evident curtailment of a portion of the panel in the *Allegory of Faith* that must evidently have been capable of accommodating, in addition to the cut off right foot of the main figure, a half-length figure—as in other subjects in the ensemble. Furthermore, in the remaining part of the panel one could still see traces of the robe and a rope held by *Faith*, cut off at mid-height, which must have been tied to the missing figure, like the other two ropes attached to the two men below [fig. 13]; the *Judas* panel also showed, on the right of the viewer, two interrupted figurative details-apparently a flag and a soldier's cloak.

Another clue for the reassembling of the ceiling was the empty spaces along the long sides of the central panel caused by the removal of the four Allegories, which had similar measurements [fig. 11]; these could not be filled by portions of the frame, since in a coffered ceiling the dimensions

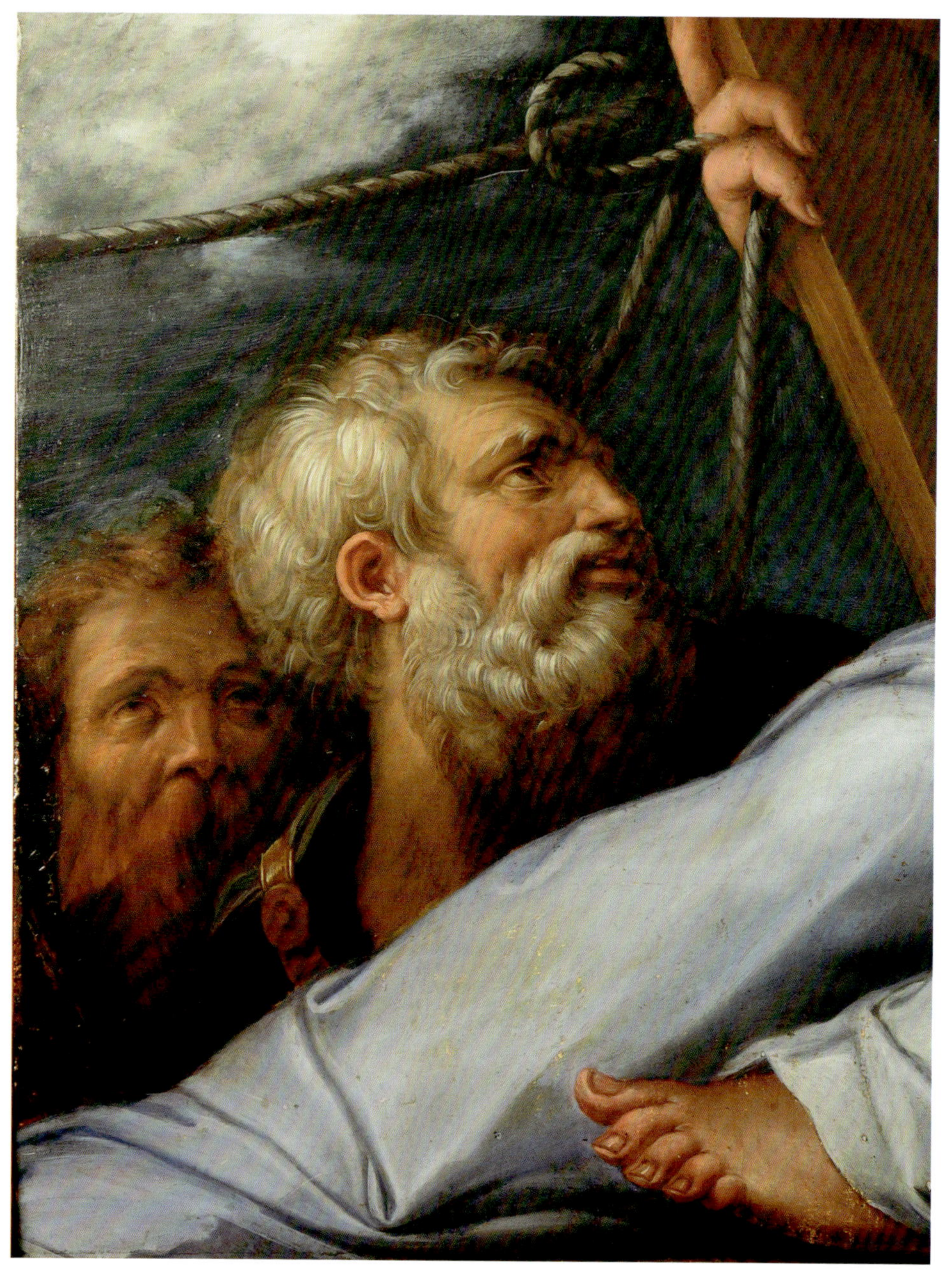

13
Detail of the *Allegory of Faith*,
after the cleaning, with what remains,
lower left, of the robe, with a shoulder
belt, of the cut character

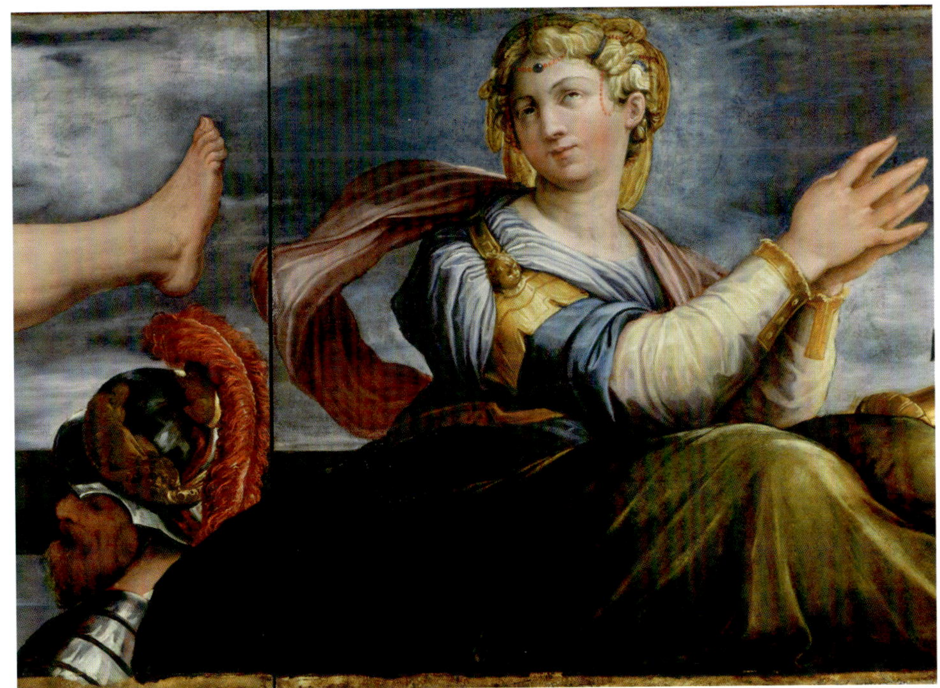

14
Detail of the two sections of the
Allegory of Hope joined together

of the frame are the same around all the painted parts, as evidenced by other ceilings of the period,[9] including those made six years after his stay in Venice by Vasari for his Arezzo residence.

The thematic connection of the character of *Judas* with the *Allegory of Hope* and the comparison with the photograph of the latter panel [fig. 2]—the only concrete document we had of the painting, which at the time still in private hands—allowed us to position the *Judas* panel to the right of *Hope*,[10] and thus correctly identifying the composition originally executed on a single panel, in agreement with Vasari's indication on the number of "pictures": the two details on the panel with *Judas* made sense when connected to the cut-off robes of Hope in the main panel [fig. 14]. The dimensions of the combined panels[11] now adequately occupied the space along the longer side of the central panel, with Virtue correctly positioned to be crowned by the putto with the olive wreath; the panels with *Justice* and *Patience*, complete

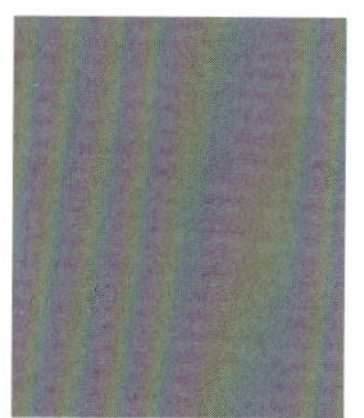
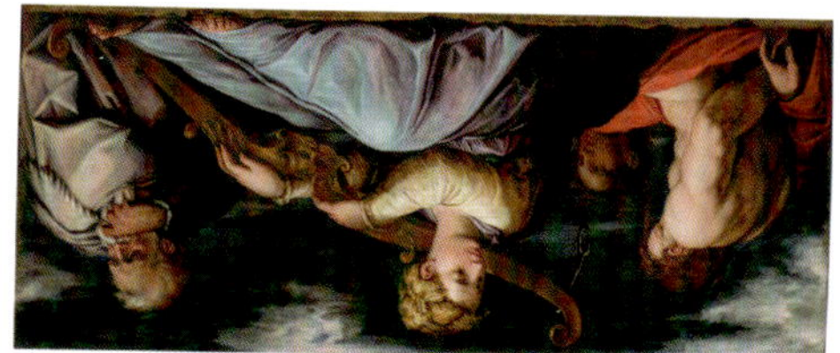
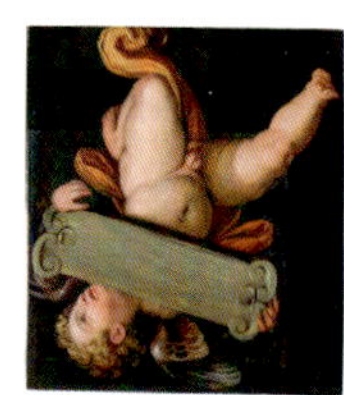
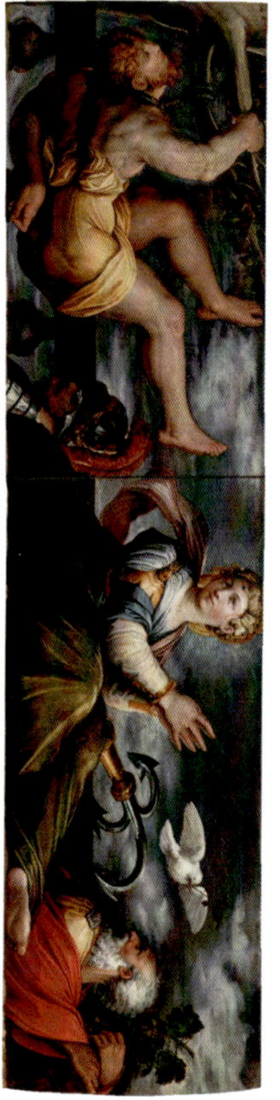
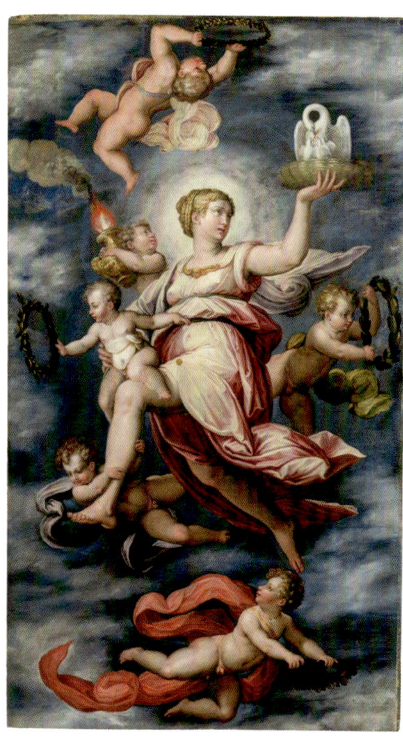
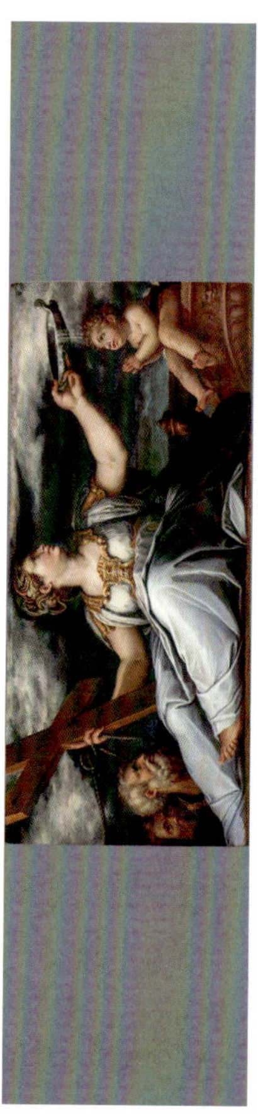
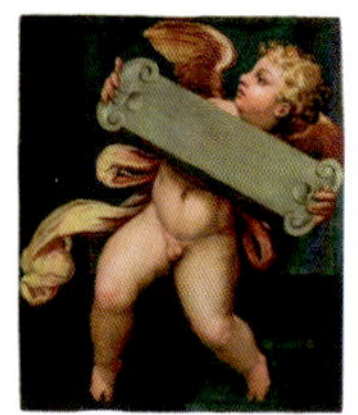
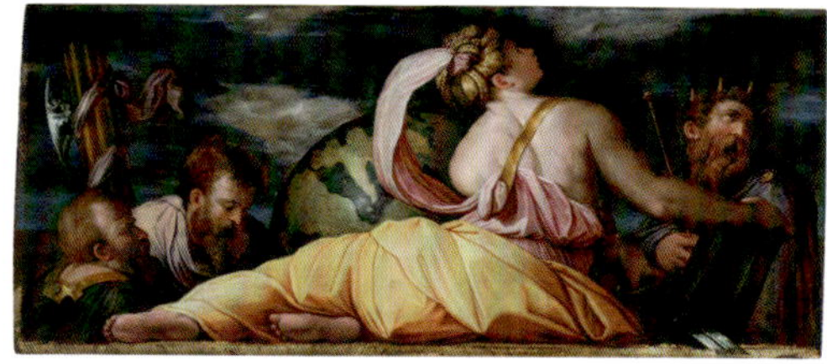
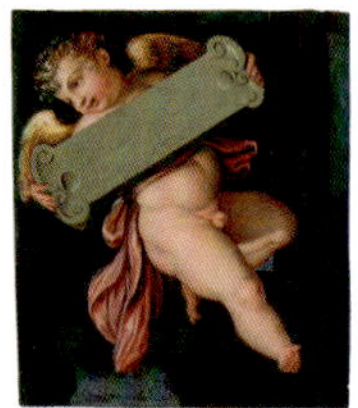

15

Hypothesis for the reassembling of the ceiling. Based on the measurements of the angles, the balustrade outlines a parallelogram that must have corresponded to the plan of the room, on the perimeter of which the panels of the ceiling were placed

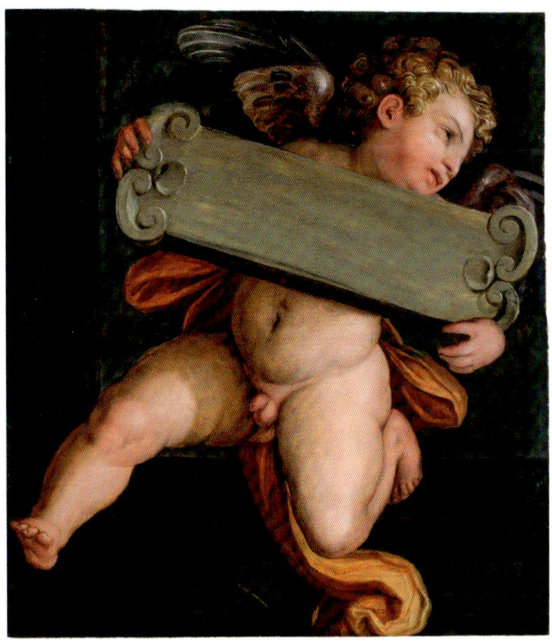

16
Putto with plaque,
69.4 × 61.8 cm, cat. 2015

with the figures on either side of the Allegories, found their place along the short sides of the ceiling, in correspondence with the garlands. In addition, the original extent of the panel with the *Allegory of Faith,* which was placed parallel to that of *Hope,* could now be identified: the position of the main figure, determined in relation to the gaze of the putto who places the wreath on her head, indicated with good approximation the extent of the reduction undergone by the panel on both sides[12] [fig. 15].

The presence on the back of the support of *Faith* of the trace of a crossbar at the exact midpoint of the whole original support, in correspondence with the one on the center panel, could be a good indication of the original placement of the panel in the ceiling (in the planking of the *Allegory of Hope* the distribution of the crossbars is different, but still symmetrical). It seems safe to assume that with the cutting of the support from this painting as well, at least a second panel with the aforementioned half-length figure was obtained, given that it was decided to sacrifice the foot of Faith to it.[13] The explanation for the slightly trimmed edges of the other panels instead could be the need to adjust them when they were inserted into the supporting structure of the ceiling; indeed, the only intact edges are the lower ones of the outer panels, as well as the left side of the *Allegory of Justice* and those of the corner panels, although with the loss of the entire lower plank in one of them [fig. 16].

The ensemble when analyzed shows many other aspects that relate the panels to one another; these include the wreaths that the Putti of the central panel are laying on the heads of the four Allegories on the adjacent panels [fig. 15] and the different plants in the garlands, each associated with a Virtue,[14] but also the gazes exchanged by the characters, typical of Vasari,[15] as in the case of the soldier thoughtfully observing the gesture of *Judas* who, with his hand hidden behind his back, is pointing to the thirty denarii received for the betrayal [fig. 17];[16] finally, there are the variations in the colors of the draperies in the figures.

A clue to the identification of the room in which the ceiling was found, still to be determined with certainty,[17] is offered by the slightly differing angles of the balustrade in the panels with the putti, which must have reflected the shape of the room;[18] the different measurements of these panels are dictated by their function of balancing the painted surface as well as the presence of four angular architectural elements—corbels or pilaster strips—that must have connected the ceiling to the walls of the room[19] [fig. 15]. Based on the angles of the balustrade, there are two possible plan combinations, but it is precisely the relationship motifs mentioned above, notwithstanding the lost parts, that help us identify the position of the Putti panels within the composition: the rotation of the panel with *Hope* according to the angle of the balustrade in the panel with which it is associated, directs the gaze of the Putto depicted there precisely towards *Noah* [fig. 15]. The sky that serves as the background of the entire composition might also be a clue to a feature of the original room: it is brighter in the central panel and in the background of the *Allegory of Hope* and the connected panel with *Putto*, darker on the other three sides, which, along with the direct effects of light and shadow on the figures, suggests the presence of a precise source of light,[20] resulting in a play of fictional and real light that is typically Mannerist and was used by Vasari also for his home in Arezzo. In joining the panels, the sky also suggests a contiguity between

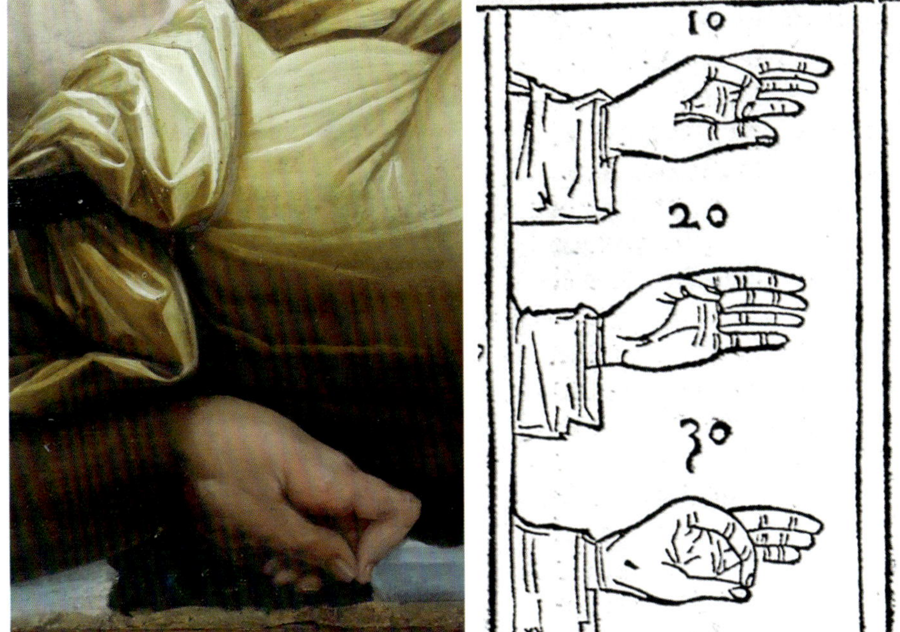

17
The hidden hand of *Judas* with the detail of
the images in Luca Pacioli's *Summa de
arithmetica geometria proportioni et
proportionalità* (Venice 1494), c. 36v,
showing the number thirty (see note 16)

the portion of blue next to Judas's head [fig. 3, p. 47], which is grayer and also materially different from the rest of the sky, and the smoke coming from the torch held by the putto in the central panel.[21] Another clue to the characteristics of the room is the position of the figures of the central panel in relation to the entrance: as a rule, their heads had to be toward the main entrance, as explicitly stated in Armenini's "precepts",[22] which Vasari followed in the ceilings of Arezzo.

The frame of a ceiling, like that of a polyptych, is a crucial connecting element between the parts, and its absence significantly influences the general perception of the work; an important indication in regards to the frame's connecting function is given by the fact that, regardless of the width that the ensemble may have had originally, the panels connected by the line of the balustrade maintain a homogeneous distance between them, corresponding to the size of the beam of the frame, and that this

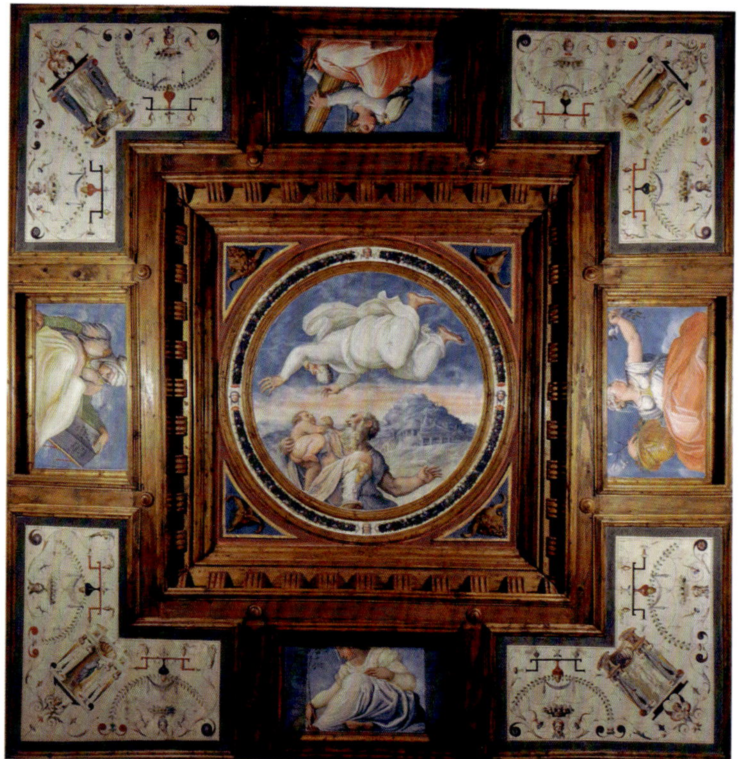

18
The ceiling of the Chamber of
Abraham of Casa Vasari in Arezzo,
showing the three horizontal levels at
which the panels can be positioned

measure doubles around the central panel: this datum is compatible with
the solution usually adopted for the central panel, whose height is nor-
mally offset in relation to the surrounding ones. This difference in height is
also found in the ceilings of the Chamber of Abraham and the Hall of the
Triumph of Virtue in Arezzo [figg. 18, 19], in the latter case with the variant
of the central panel being placed on the lowered plane, due to the little
space available under the upper floor. In the case of the Corner ceiling we
are probably dealing with the same model used shortly thereafter in Paolo
Veronese's ceilings in San Sebastiano in Venice, in which the main paintings are recessed [fig. 20], given the sophisticated break-through effect of
the sky whose color lightens in the central panel, and in which the size of
the putti is reduced compared to those in the corner panels. Vasari was

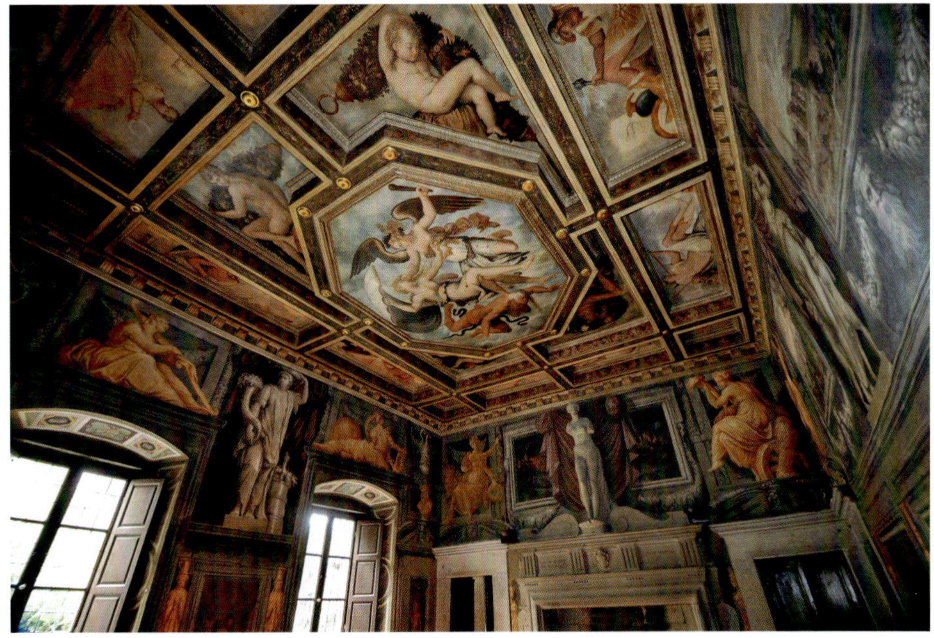

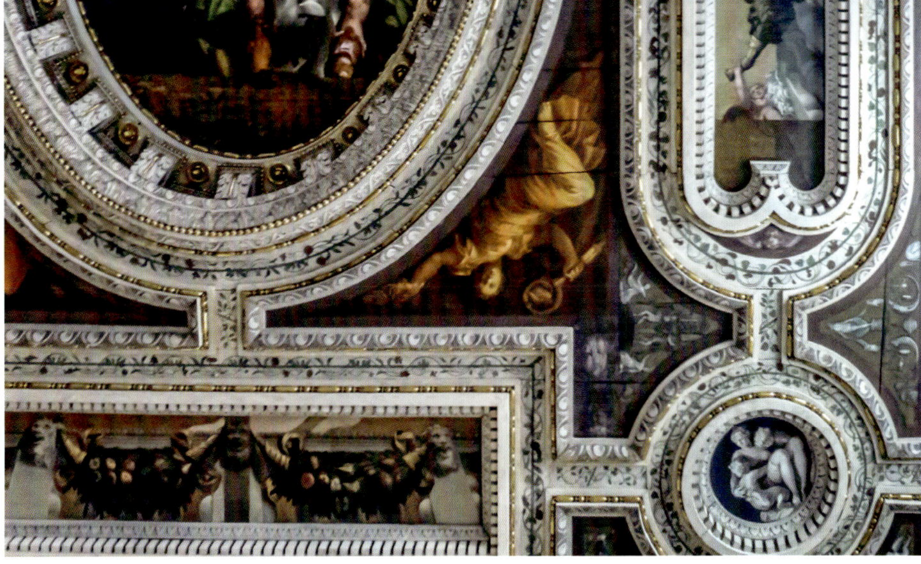

19
View of the Hall of the Triumph of Virtue
in Casa Vasari in Arezzo with the ceiling,
the central panel is in a lower position
compared to the rest of the panels

20
Detail of Paolo Veronese's ceiling
in the church of San Sebastiano
in Venice, showing the different
horizontal levels at which the panels
can be located

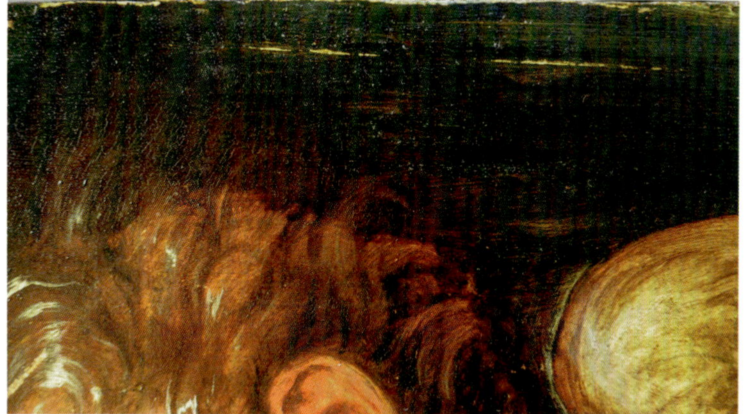

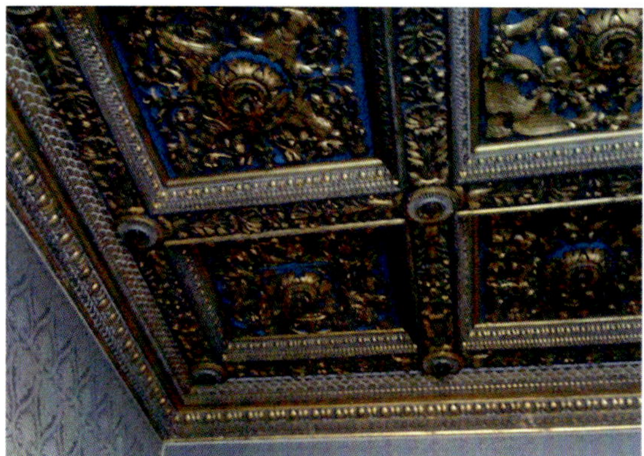

21
Detail of the *Putto*, cat. 1372,
with remnants of the gold in the
frame, not parallel to the upper edge
of the panel

22
Detail of the ceiling in Palazzo Corner
Spinelli in Venice

to use light contrasts also in the Hall of the Triumph of Virtue, but there he placed the brighter panels, the ones depicting the deities of the signs of the Zodiac, on the perimeter of the ceiling and recessed compared to the central one, and varying the luminosity by using two different painting techniques, tempera for the perimetric paintings mentioned above and oil for the central panels, i.e. those related to the earthly sphere, depicting the stages in man's life, and the panel containing the allegory of *Virtue*.[23]

A useful indication concerning the decoration of the ceiling frame is found in the payment document, which describes it as gilded and carved with leaves, "fusarole," and moldings as well as Vasari's note in the *Life* of Michele Sanmicheli:[24] indeed, traces of gold leaf remain on the panels, which do not run parallel to their edges, but to the balustrade [fig. 21], attesting to the frame's function as a link between the illusionistic space marked by this architectural element and the room itself. By comparing

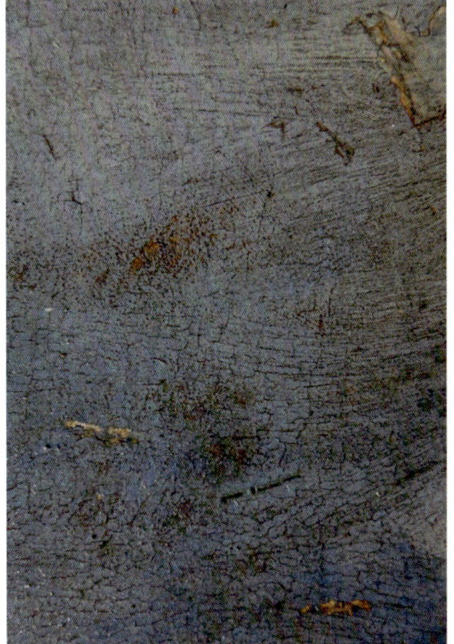

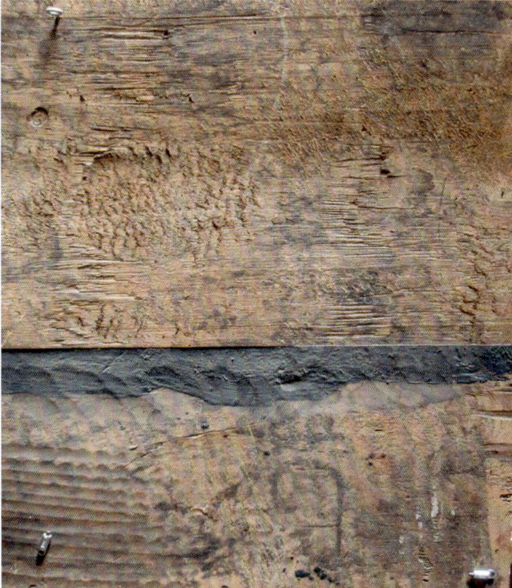

23
Detail of the panel with the *Allegory of Charity* with the canvas visible underneath the painting material

24
Back of the *Putto* panel, cat. 1373

what is described in the document and the frames of ceilings similar in size and period to the Corner ceiling, it is possible to get an idea of the decorative pattern applied. Elements derived from the classical repertoire recur in another ceiling present in the Corner Spinelli palace, alsocoffered, but with carved and gilded rosettes on a blue background, possibly the one based on a design by Sanmicheli,[25] and made just after the Vasari ceiling [fig. 22]; the same modules though only painted can be seen also on the frame of the Hall of the Triumph of Virtue, a difference in line with the different function of the room; similarly, gilded "fusarole" appear in the aforementioned ceilings of the sacristy and the church of San Sebastiano, accompanied by painted plant motifs.

The execution technique of the ceiling

The study of the techniques used in the Corner ceiling, besides material testing, also included the examination of archival sources and the technical indications provided by Vasari himself in his writings.[26]

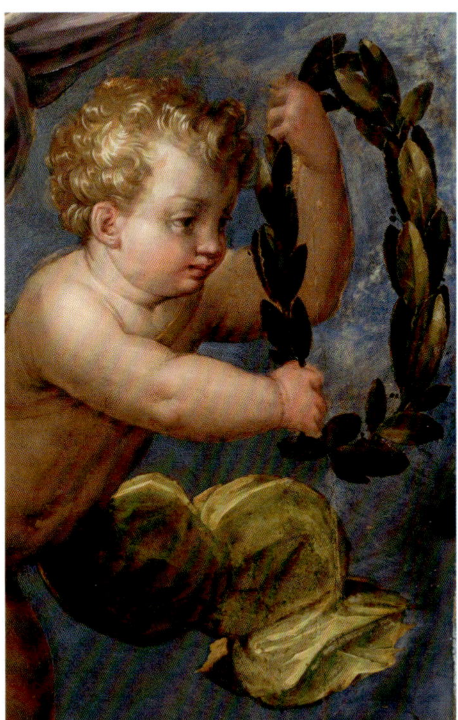

Detail of the *Allegory of Charity* with the robe of the putto with the warm tone of the "imprimitura" exposed

In attempting to trace the stages of the work's realization, one may start with Vasari's *Ricordanze* with regard to the amount to be paid by the patron for the planking, one of the main expenses; the choice of wood as a support was typical of the Tuscan production of the period, whereas in the Veneto area, the use of cheaper and more manageable canvas supports was already widespread, in advance compared to other areas of Italy. After the supports were assembled,[27] strips of canvas were applied to reinforce the points most subject to movement in the wood: in the x-ray taken on the *Faith* panel,[28] in the areas where the planks are joined and on a slit in the planking, it is possible to detect continuous lines of filler, also visible from the back, with canvas strips on top; these are visible also in the panels with *Charity* [fig. 23] and *Judas*; on the latter panel a filler with carbon black was also used, perhaps only locally, with the function of insulating the wood from moisture.[29] Black filler is also present on the joints of the corner panels with *Putti* [fig. 24]. Canvas strips were used by Vasari also for the *Immaculate Conception* in the church of the Santi Apostoli in Florence, painted two years earlier.[30] In the chapter on the construction of panels in

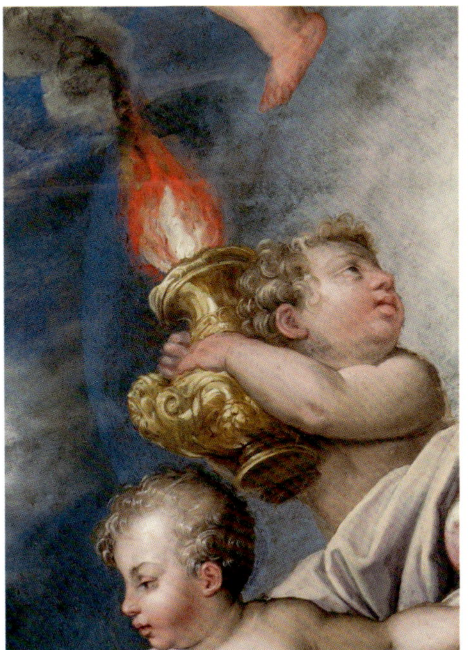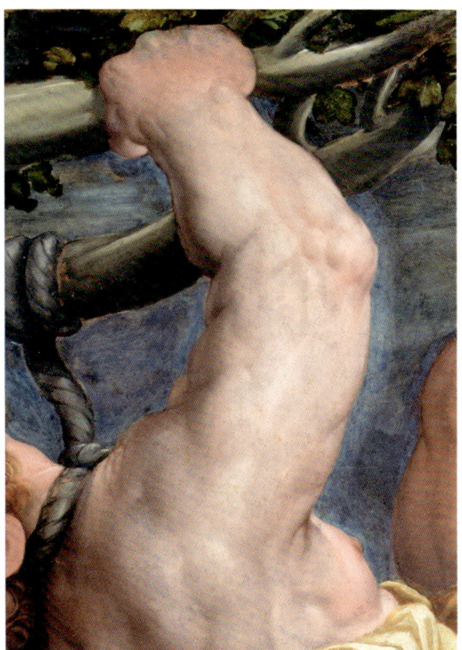

26
Details with the lighter color effects on the panel
with the *Allegory of Charity* and around the arm
of *Judas*

the introductory part of the *Vite*, Vasari merely describes the old, already obsolete, method of covering the entire planking before the preparation was laid. In general, Vasari is not interested in describing the technical aspects in detail, unlike Armenini and Borghini, the ones to which we owe the description of the techniques actually used by the artists of the period, including Vasari and his collaborators.[31]

After the panels were assembled, a thin layer of plaster and glue was added, so thin as to leave the trace of the wood grain of the support, visible with raking light. In Vasari's biography of his collaborator, Cristofano Gherardi nicknamed Doceno, Vasari highlights the division of labor in the preparatory stages to painting, in which his assistants were in charge of the application of the oil priming ("mestica" or "imprimitura") before the drawing.[32]

Underneath the layers of oil painting, it is possibile to detect primings with varying hues,[33] used by savings [fig. 25]; this technique, reserved for paintings to be viewed from a distance, recalls the indications Vasari gave

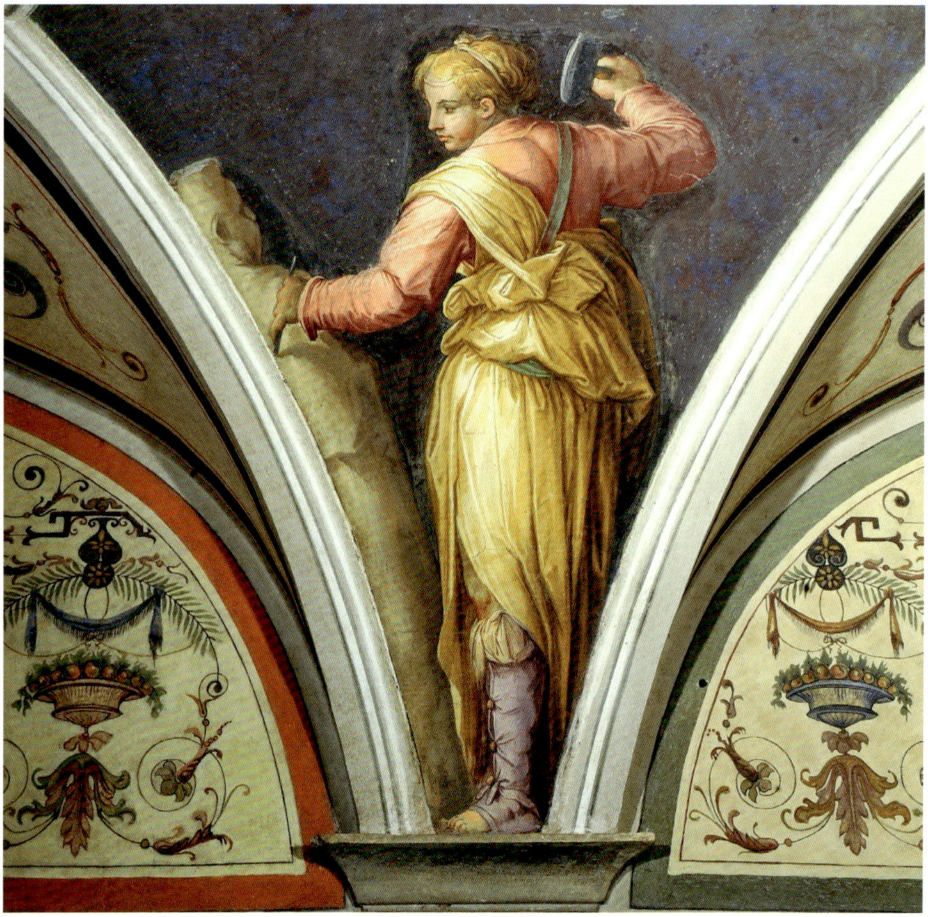

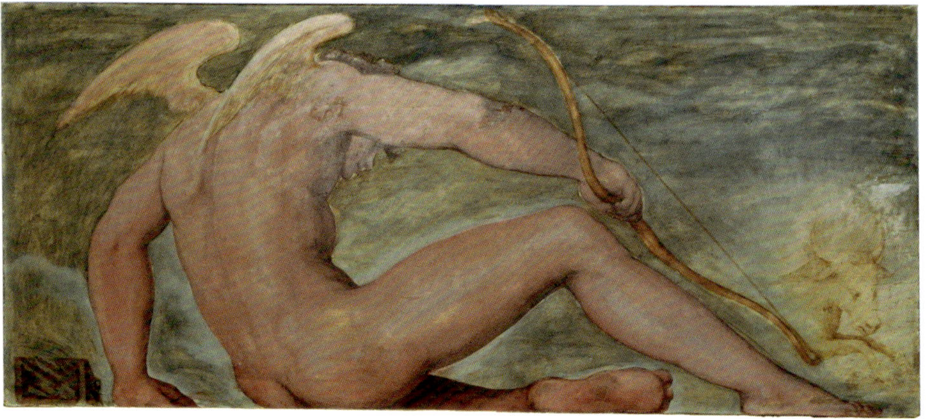

27
Details of the decorations in Casa Vasari in Arezzo, of the vault of the Hall of Fame and the Arts with the light color effects around the yellow robe of the *Allegory of Sculpture* and of the panel with *Mercury*, in the ceiling of the Hall of the Triumph of Virtue, with the lighter color along the outline of the figure

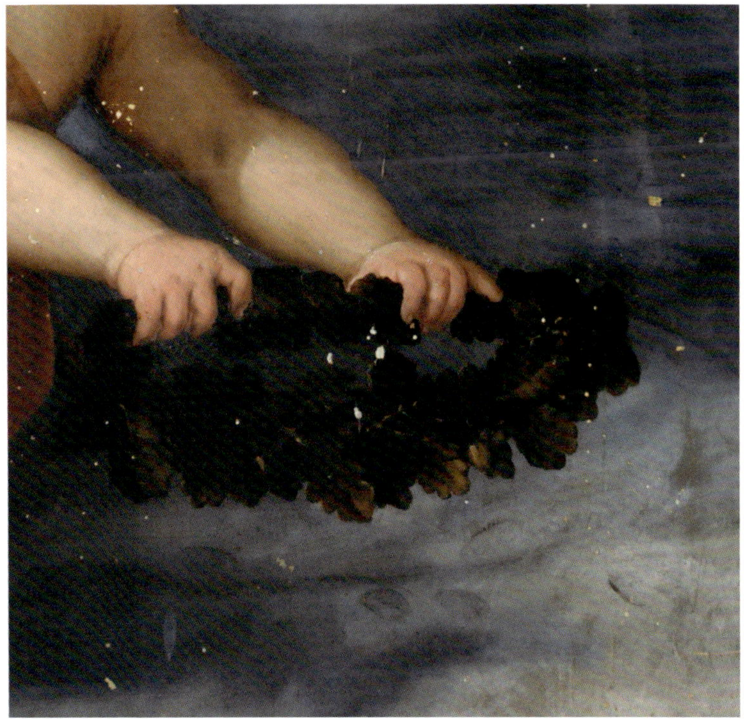

28
Detail of the *Allegory of Charity* with
the "pentimento" in the garland of
oak leaves: note below another type
of leaf, evidently judged not suitable
to the *Allegory*

for frescoes, namely the need for the wall to "show clarity."[34] Indeed, the light-colored highlight used in the sky to make the figure of *Judas* and the torch stand out from the background [fig. 26], can also be found on the wall paintings Vasari executed as soon as he returned from Venice on the vault of the Hall of Fame and the Arts in Arezzo[35] and on the panels with the gods on the ceiling of the Hall of the Triumph of Virtue, painted later, in tempera [fig. 27]. On the central panel there are repaintings with evident "pentimenti" on the leg of *Charity,* on the putto above her head and on the crown of leaves, now of oak [fig. 28], with areas left unfinished [fig. 29]. In describing the process of pictorial execution, Vasari makes frequent references in his biographies of artists, including that of his collaborator Doceno, to a first "rough drafting" with colors.[36] The various phases of painting are described in the introduction to his *Lives* in the chapter "On

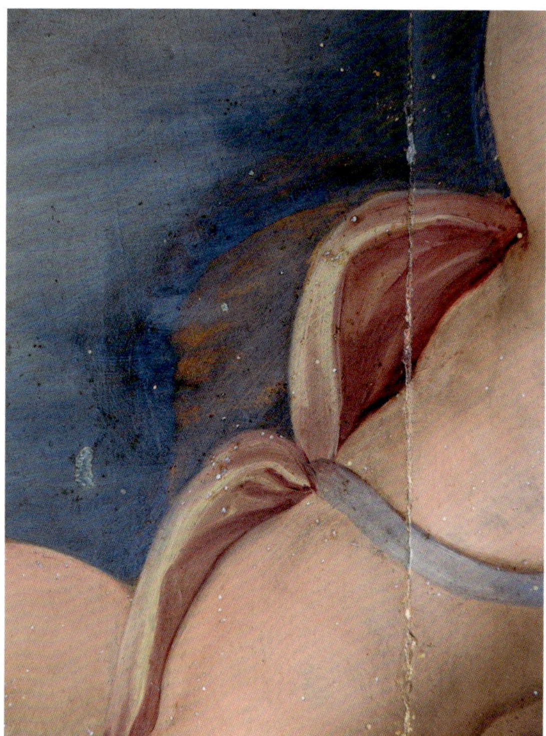

Detail of the *Allegory of Charity* with the "pentimento" in the robe of the Putto at the top, left uncovered

painting with oil on wood and canvas...": the oil technique brightens and softens the colors, allowing for blurring and blending when working with fresh paint; after this first intervention, the artist will resume the work later to finish it off. The main goal is the "union" of colors, an achievement of the Vasari's period made possible by this new technique. Vasari defines painting as a balance between light, dark and half-light tones, combined to achieve relief and perspective[37] and devotes a chapter on "How colors should be united in oil, fresco or tempera..."[38] so that they are not put together too brightly, as this produces discordance; the only exception being the rendering of "sbattimenti," that is, the shadows produced by one figure on another, because they are illuminated by the same light source, which also must be painted "with gentleness and unitarily." These light effects are well exemplified in the ceiling, along with the principle, evident in the depiction of the Allegories, that the main figures should have light and

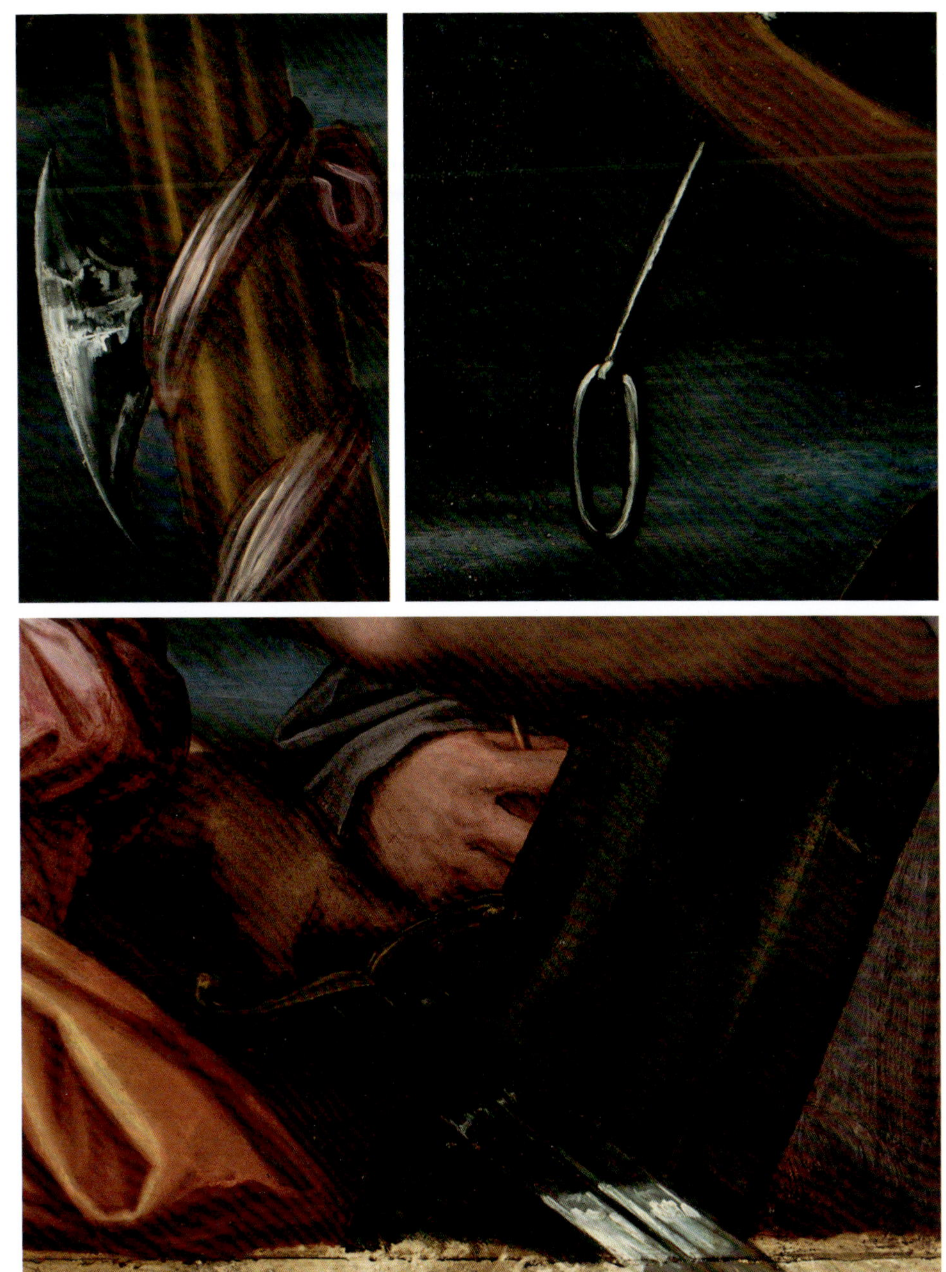

30
Details of the metal objects
in the ceiling

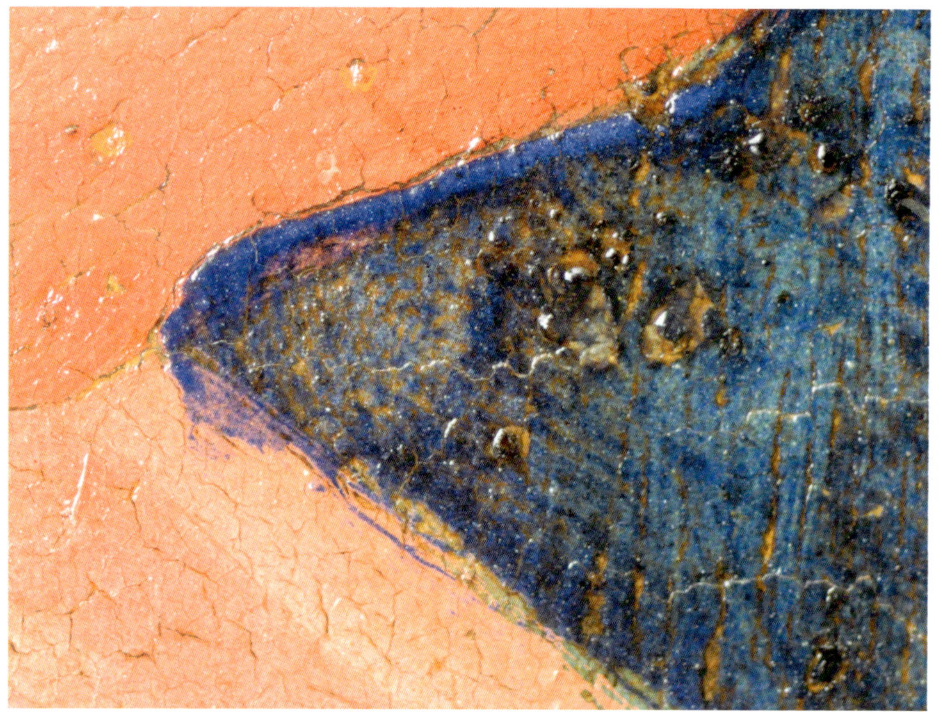

31
Detail from the central panel of the
ceiling with a blue layering probably
of lapis lazuli

pleasing colors, whereas the background should have darker ones in order to highlight them.[39]

The ceiling also testifies to Vasari's particular attention to the rendering of "lustri" or bright spots on metal objects [figs. 15, 30], an effect he praises in various passages of the *Lives*;[40] these can be found in many prominent details in the side panels: the helmet, breastplate and anchor in the *Allegory of Hope*, the ring of the yoke in that of *Patience*, the axe blade and sword in *Justice*, and the cup held by *Faith.* As for the specific use of the precious blue lapis lazuli pigment, of which two variants are specifically mentioned in the documents due to their significant cost, it will be ascertained by further investigations [fig. 31]. [41]

Of great interest is the study of the lower margins of the panels, those intended to be hidden by the frames, because they show evidence of the

32
Detail of the robe of *Patience* with the black glazing, reinforced on the shadows, and its deposit along the edge under the foot of the Allegory, flush with the frame present at the time of its application

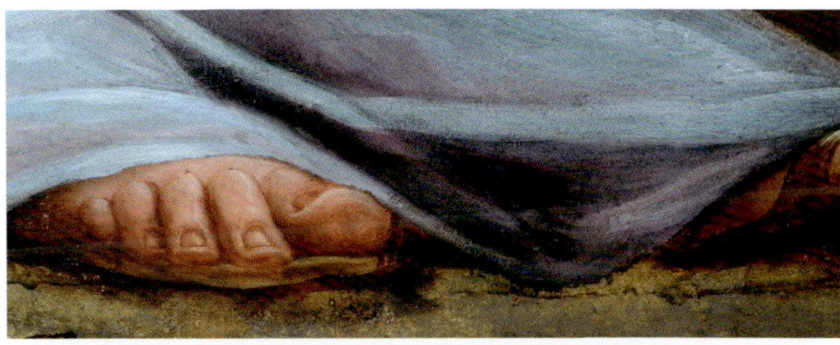

33
Detail of the dark glaze deposit on the lower edge of the *Allegory of Justice*

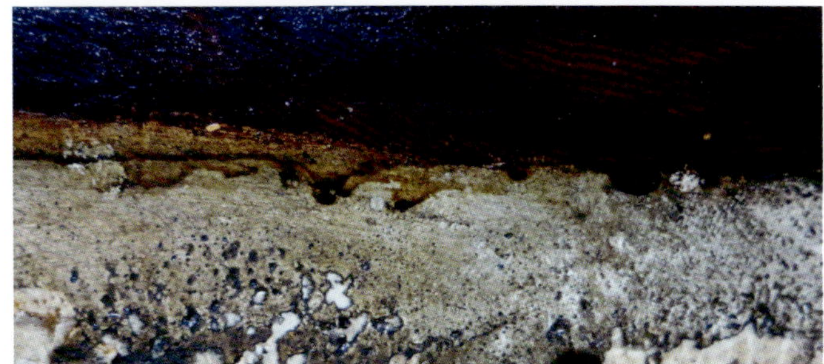

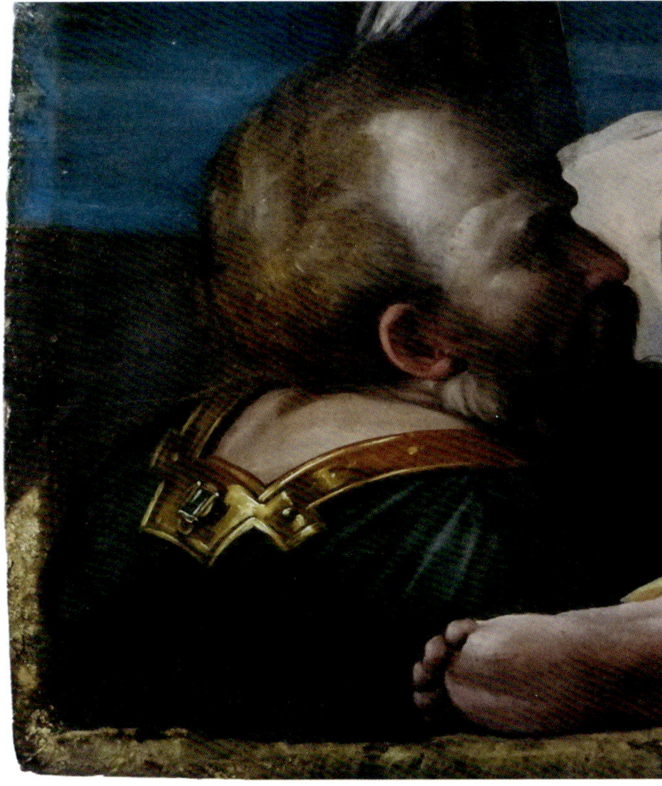

34
The vertical side of the panel with the *Allegory of Justice* spared from the application of the black glaze due to the presence of a frame at the time of its application

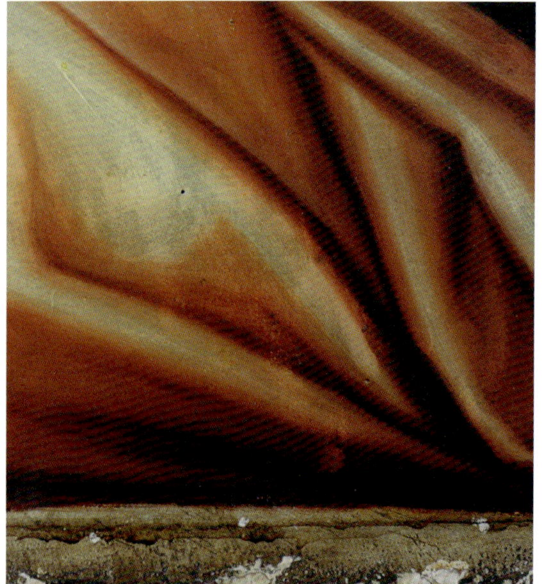

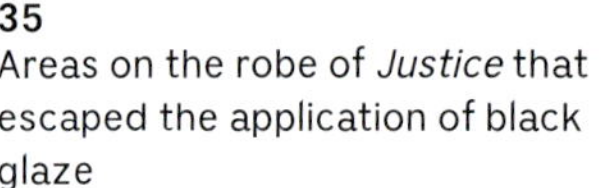

35
Areas on the robe of *Justice* that
escaped the application of black
glaze

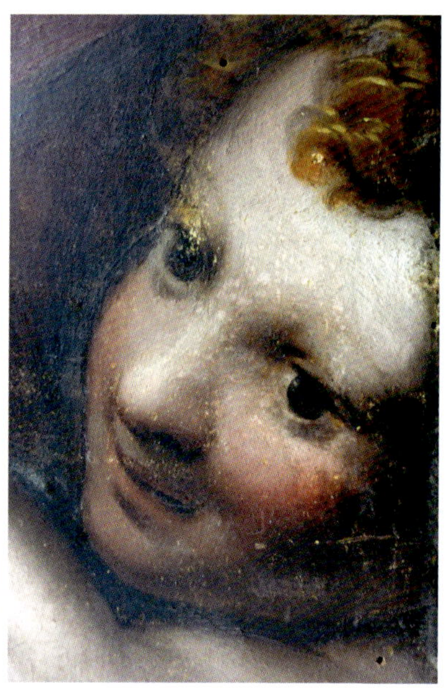

36
Character in Francesco Morandini's
Martyrdom of St. Lawrence from the
Badia di San Fedele in Poppi (Arezzo)
with the damaged areas stripped of
their dark finish

various stages in the execution. For the most part, only the ground is present. In some parts, however, the final part of some figurative details is
drafted, minus the last pictorial layers [fig. 30, the sword]; among these
final layers a dark-colored glaze stands out, due to the thicker deposits it
has left flush with the frames that were present at the time of its application over the entire painted surface [figs. 32–34]: as the deposits dried,
they sometimes tore the gold leaf from the frame, which remained thus
attached to the paint [fig. 21]. The color of this transparent layer is shiny
black and it seems to have been applied almost everywhere, albeit in different amounts, with only some areas spared, due to oversight, such as the
yellow-orange robe of *Justice* [fig. 35].

A relevant reference can be found in the document attesting the payment of the ceiling to Vasari, which specifies a sum destined " to Battista,
his assistant, for his 'dousing' [*beveraggio*] of the ceiling,"[42] possibly referring to the painter Giovan Battista Cungi, who in Venice worked on the

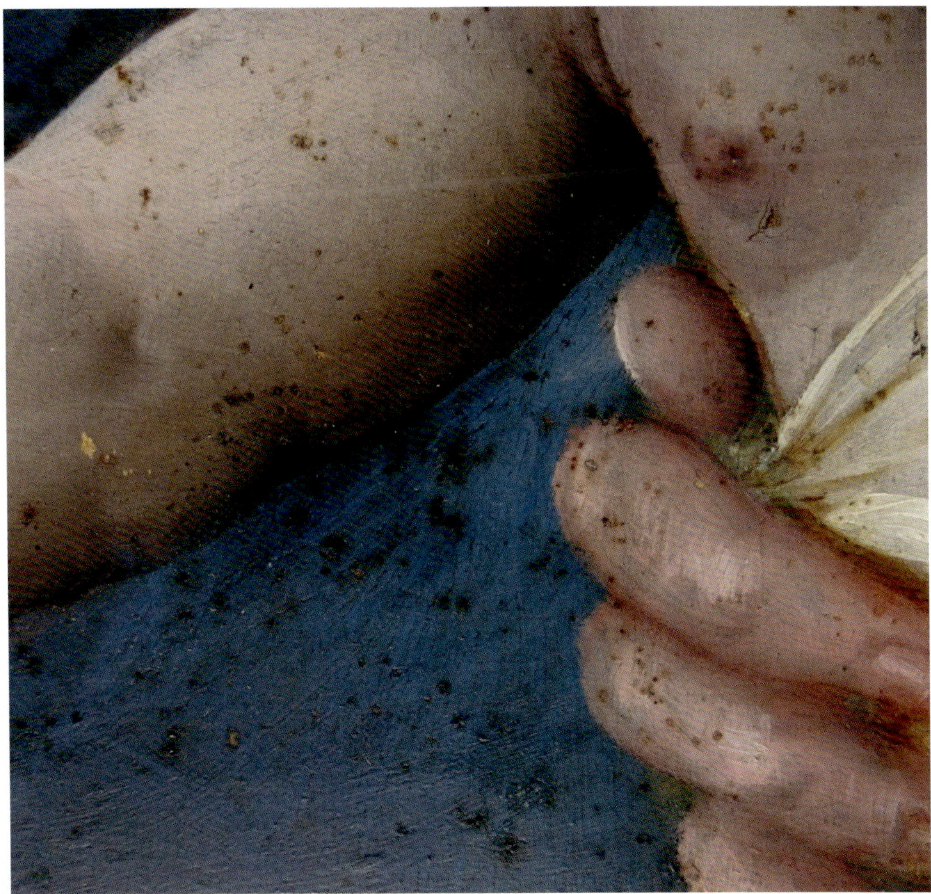

37
Detail of the *Allegory of Charity*
with dark deposits distributed over
the sky and on the embodiments of
a Putto and the Allegory's hand

scenes for Pietro Aretino's *Talanta*.[43] A preliminary survey shows that this peculiar technique was used in by Vasari and other artists in his circle, such as Stradano[44] and Morandini, in whose *Martyrdom of St. Lawrence* from the Badia di San Fedele in Poppi (Arezzo) it is clearly evident [fig. 36]. When drying, this glazing left on the surface a peculiar marbling with an opaque-glossy effect barely perceptible on the darker backgrounds of the skies, such as those of the *Faith*; the small blackened lumps, spread somewhat over all the panels, would appear to be deposits originating from this material [fig. 37].[45]

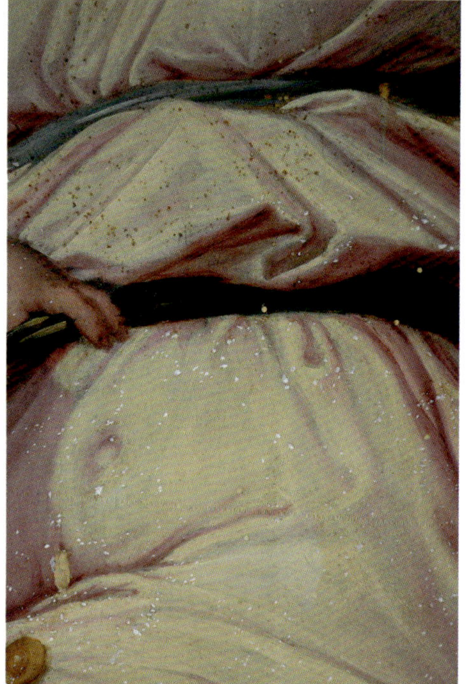 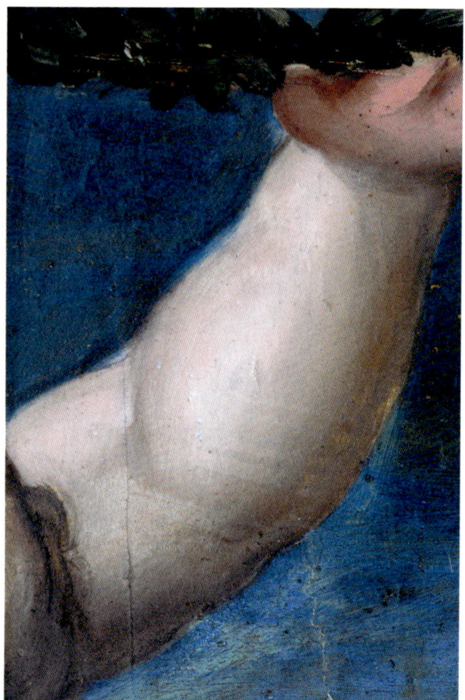

38
Detail of the drapery of the *Charity in the* process of applying watercolor bases over dark deposits: at the bottom, on the curve of the thigh, a lighter area spared by a finishing varnish is evident

39
Detail of the *Allegory of Charity with the* arm of the putto at the top, showing the uneven spreading of the finishing varnish

When Vasari describes the last finishing stage in painting, he does not provide specific technical indications, for which we once again have to turn to Armenini, who speak explicitly of "velare" (glaze) and to Borghini.[46] However, the study of the visual characteristics and application technique of the black glaze, a pigmented but transparent substance, cannot fail to recall Pliny's passage[47] on Apelles' mythical "atramentum," a passage well known to Vasari, who will mention it, with Giovan Battista Adriani's letter, in the second edition of the *Lives*.[48] The passage, which circulated widely, referred to the invention, attributed by Pliny to Apelles, of a process capable of softening bright hues and enhancing their depth. As for the origin of this glaze, Vitruvius wrote it came from the burning of a resin, of wood, of pine bark, or wine lees.[49] In sixteenth-century sources, among the many black and brown pigments we find listed "Greek pitch smoke,"[50] a glaze obtained with pitch cooked in walnut oil, whose presence has been detected in Raphael's paintings in the National Gallery in London.[51] On the central panel of the ceiling, which has a brighter tone than the rest of the composition, the presence of a transparent layer can be observed, thanks to the contrast offered by some points left bare [figs. 38–39], with the same modality of the areas in which the dark glaze is absent.

1 The restoration, financed by Venetian Heritage, was the result of a collaboration of the Ministry's relevant offices at the Gallerie dell'Accademia in Venice and the State Museum of Casa Vasari in Arezzo, custodian of the ceilings in the house painted by Vasari and the panel from his Venetian period with the *Suicide of Judas*. The direction was entrusted to Giulio Manieri Elia and the work was non-continuously carried out, at the laboratory of the Misericordia, on the painted surfaces by the writer and on the wooden supports by Roberto Saccuman, under the coordination of Maria Chiara Maida, from April 2013 to June 2018 (the work on the supports, already begun in 2004, was completed in 2020).

2 For historical events see Giulio Manieri Elia's essay in the present volume and G. Manieri Elia, "La Fede di Giorgio Vasari e il soffitto della "Camera Nova" in palazzo Corner Spinelli," in *Ricche Minere*, I, 1, 2014, pp. 71–79.

3 See the article by Roberto Saccuman in the present volume, p. 106.

4 Intervention of Bernardo Cardi, see A. Giovannetti, Giorgio Vasari, "Il Trionfo della Carità," entry 15, in *Pinacoteca di Brera. Scuole dell'Italia centrale e meridionale*, Milan 1992, p. 39. The 1987–1990 restorations in Venice were carried out by Gloria Tranquilli and Rosa Bagarotto, with Gigi Savio working on the supports; the 1982 restoration of *Suicide of Judas* was by Carlo Guido, while the one in 2003 was carried out by Barbara Ferriani, along with Ciro Castelli on the support.

5 The hypothesis is that the material is original, rather than dejections left by insects: see the conclusion of the present article. Under the deposit, the color appears degraded, probably due to the acidity of the material. FTIR analysis, performed, like the XRF, by Enrico Fiorin at the Scientific Laboratory of the Gallerie dell'Accademia in Venice at Misericordia, showed the presence of oxalates, the result of interaction between the materials.

6 Selective methods and preparations suitable to the specific materials to be removed were used in the cleaning; after filling in the color losses, the retouching was carried out using handcraft varnish paint with watercolor bases. The filling of the back was done with pigmented putty based on cellulose pulp. See the restoration report at the Misericordia Archives. For the treatment on the supports see the article by Roberto Saccuman in the present volume.

7 Vasari describes his work on the ceiling in the *Ricordanze* and in several passages of the *Vite*. See G. Vasari, *Il Libro delle Ricordanze di Giorgio Vasari*, edited by A. del Vita, Arezzo 1927, pp. 39–40: "I remember how on the eight of April 1542, the Magnificent Sir Giovanni Cornaro, a Venetian nobleman, commissioned me via order of Sir Michele da San Michele, from Verona, Architect of St. Mark, a wooden ceiling or soffit to be painted in oil with nine large paintings, one in the middle with Charity with her putti around her crowning in four paintings Faith, Hope and Justice and Patience, which are all accompanied by various figures according to a design made specifically and also four paintings

with inside four putti in the corners; which work I promised to deliver complete the next first of August and he had to give me all the panels of his own and four ounces of ultramarine azure and as price and payment of the said work give me the sum of one-hundred twenty scudi at 7 grossi per scudo, as we stated, so in total 120 scudi." G. Vasari, *Le Vite de' più eccellenti pittori, scultori et architettori* (Florence 1550 and 1568), edited by R. Bettarini and P. Barocchi, Florence 1966–1987, https://www.memofonte.it/home/files/pdf/vasari_vite_giuntina.pdf 3/2006: p. 895 [Il. 464: *Vita di Cristofano Gherardi detto Doceno*] "Vasari and Cristofano stayed in Venice a few months, painting for the magnificent sir Giovanni Cornaro the ceiling or true soffit of a room, in which went nine large oil paintings"; pp. 933–34 [Il. 520: *Vita di Michele Sanmicheli*] "And in Venice.... he worked at another building, also of the Cornara famIly, which is San Benedetto a l'Albore for sir Giovanni Cornari, of whom Michele was a close friend of; and was the reason that in this [building] Vasari made nine oil paintings for the ceiling of a magnificent room, all adorned with carved wood and rich gold leaf"; p. 1111 [Il. 812: *Vita di Tiziano*] "The year 1541 . . . The same year, Vasari having been in Venice thirteen months to make, as said, a coffered ceiling for sir Giovanni Cornaro"; p. 1233 [Il. 991: *Autobiografia*] "the nine paintings in the palace of sir Giovanni Cornaro, that is, in the ceiling of a room of his palace, which is in San Benedetto."

8 See F. Härb, "Modes and Models in Vasari's Early Drawing Oeuvre," in *Vasari's Florence. Artists and Literati at the Medicean Court*, edited by P. J. Jacks, Cambridge 1998, pp. 83–110, 104; the third Putto was identified in 1999: L. Vertova, "Vasari at Venice: An Addendum," in *The Burlington Magazine*, CXLI, 1151, 1999, pp. 105–06. See note 2.

9 J. Schultz, *Venetian Painted Ceilings of the Renaissance*, Berkley–Los Angeles 1968, pp. 15–16, 120.

10 L. Caporossi, R. Cavigli, "Vasari at Venice. The Suicide of Judas at Arezzo, Another Addendum to the Corner Ceiling," in *The Burlington Magazine*, CLVIII, 1354, 2016, pp. 10–12. See Luisa Caporossi's article in the present volume. The photographic plate, preserved in the then Gabinetto Fotografico of the Sovrintendenza delle Gallerie of Naples and documented in August 1952, dated back to the exhibition *Fontainebleau e la maniera italiana*, in Naples, where *Hope* was exhibited along with *Justice* and *Patience*. Since then, the painting, privately owned till October 2017, was known in publications via a trimmed b/w image. The clean image showed the painting with edges fitted with laths similar to those on the other panels. A number of authors associated the Judas panel to the ceiling, but without providing evidence.

11 For the dimensions of *Hope* we referred to entry no. 16876 in the Zeri Foundation Archives: https://catalogo.fondazionezeri.unibo.it/scheda/opera/18133/Vasari%20Giorgio%2C%20Allegoria%20della%20Speranza.

12 The reason why the longer panels were cut was probably re-use requirements; examination of the state of preservation of the support in the *Faith* and the general presence of gores on the backs of all the ceiling panels also makes one wonder on conservation conditions that may have caused the degradation of parts of it, such as, possibly, the loss of the bottom plank of the third *Putto*.

13 For the foot, compare with Giovanni Stradano's version of the allegory in the Hall of the Gualdrada in Palazzo Vecchio in Florence; See C. Orsi, *Vasari in Venice*, Milan 2002, pp. 16–17. See the article by Luisa Caporossi in the present volume, p. 54.

14 Olive for *Hope*, laurel for *Faith*, oak for *Justice*, and probably myrtle for *Patience*, a plant associated with Venus and thus with the feminine universe with which the virtue is associated. Vasari describes one of his painting in which Justice crowns Truth with oak leaves, see G. Vasari, *Vite* cit., p. 1234 [Il. 991].

15 Vasari in the introduction to the *Vite*, the so-called *Teoriche*, says: "This invention requires for itself an appropriateness created by concordance and obedience, so that, if one figure moves to greet the other, do not make the other looking back in order to reply; and with this similitude all the rest." Ibid., p. 261 [l. 45].

16 The character's right hand, hidden behind his back, points to the number thirty, as suggested by the image in Luca Pacioli's *Summa de aritmetica geometria proporzioni et proporzionalità*, Venice 1494, c. 36v: see *Luca Pacioli tra Piero della Francesca e Leonardo*, exhibition catalog (Sansepolcro, Museo Civico, June 9–September 24, 2017), edited by S. Zuffi, Venice 2017, p. 28. The gesture of the character, whose particular role within the entire composition has been noted, could allude to the author himself: in Matthew, the thirty denari are said to have been used to buy "the field of the potter" intended for the burial of foreigners [Mv, 27,7]: it was well known that the last name of Vasari, a foreigner in Venice, came from his ancestors who worked as *vasai* or potters.

17 J. C. Rossler, "The "Camera Nova" by Michele Sanmicheli and Giorgio Vasari, Palazzo Corner Spinelli," in *Ricche Minere*, I, 1, 2014, pp. 63–69.
18 The angles measure 87, 93, 89 degrees, so the missing *Putto* panel had to have an angle of 91 degrees to reach a total of 360 degrees.
19 The relationship between the panels and the ceiling beams is made more difficult to establish by the loss of the crossbars of the supports that could have included elements serving to anchor them to the beams, as in Vasari's ceiling for the Hall of the Five Hundred in Palazzo Vecchio in Florence. Seepage from the ceiling produced the gores on the back of the panels. The coffered ceilings in Casa Vasari in Arezzo were part of the restructuring project of the building following its purchase in 1541: the special arrangement of the beams on the Chamber of Abraham leaves room for the central panel and those on the sides are positioned in the structure of the ceiling on the medium level of the tree on which the panels can be positioned.
20 See G. Manieri Elia, "La Fede" cit., p. 77 and note 24 in the present article, for the reference to two balconies.
21 See Luisa Caporossi's article in the present volume, p. 46.
22 G. B. Armenini, *De' veri precetti della pittura* (Ravenna 1586), edited by M. Gorreri, Turin 1988, p. 181: book III, ch. IV, "therefore a general recommendation common to any vault that be half-barrel in shape, will be the following, that the heads of the figures, in the narratives in the middle, be directed towards the main entrance of that place."
23 The contrast, now accentuated by the alteration of greens to browns, probably serves to emphasize the distance between the celestial and earthly spheres, which is subject to the influences of the former, see *Restauri nella Casa del Vasari. La Sala del Camino*, edited by A. M. Maetzke, Arezzo 1977, p. 12, almost an apotropaic representation of Achilles' famous shield, for the benefit of the master of the house.
24 G. Romanelli, "Giorgio Vasari a Venezia," in *Pittura veneziana dal Quattrocento al Settecento*, edited by G. M. Pilo, San Giovanni Lupatoto 1999, pp. 48–53: *Venezia, 1542. Pagamenti a Vasari e aiuti per il soffitto di Ca' Corner in corte dell'Albero* (Palazzo Mocenigo in San Stae, Corner-Mocenigo Archives, b. 96), pp. 50, 53. Iseppo Battiloro keeps store in San Lio for the supply of a large quantity of "pezze d'oro battuto," to gild "fusaroli," leaves and "soazze," i.e., frames; a few months later gold was supplied by goldsmith Francesco Bragadin, to gild the *fusaroli* of the carvings of the chests

of two balconies in the room, in all 182 pieces minus 13 left over = 169. See note 7.
25 Ibid., p. 51. It is reasonable to think, then, that Sanmicheli—as the architect of the project for the "Camera Nova"—must have been responsible for the design of the frame, perhaps called by Vasari himself.
26 In addition to the recollections mentioned in footnote 7, there are also descriptions of artistic techniques in Vasari's *Vite*.
27 See the article by Roberto Saccuman in the present volume.
28 Thanks are due to the National Gallery in London, which provided the X-ray for study purposes.
29 Charcoal had been in use for a long time due to its resistance to moisture and its aid to stabilize wood; see R. Cavigli, "Osservazioni sulla tecnica pittorica del Polittico della Misericordia," in *Ripensando Piero della Francesca. Il Polittico della Misericordia di Sansepolcro*, edited by M. Betti, C. Frosinini, P. Refice, Florence 2011, pp. 203–18: pp. 204–05.
30 C. Giovannini, M. Sailer, G. Seroni, in *Capolavori & Restauri*, exhibition catalog (Florence, Palazzo Vecchio, December 14, 1986–April 26, 1987), Florence 1986, p. 451 "thin strip of canvas"; see also M. Ciatti, "Immacolata Concezione," in *OPD restauro*, 13, 2001, pp. 213–16: p. 213. The presence of canvas is apparent using raking light in the *Altar-piece of St. Roch* in the Museo nazionale d'arte medievale e moderna of Arezzo, painted by Vasari between 1536 and 1537.
31 G. Vasari, *Le Vite* cit., p. 266 [I. 51]. G. B. Armenini, *De' veri precetti* cit., p. 139: "they used the ancient precepts … on the joints one sees that everywhere certain strips of linen cloth were placed with good glue"; strips of canvas have also been detected in the *St. George and the Dragon* by Stradano, a painter of the Vasari circle, of the abbey of Sante Flora e Lucilla at Arezzo. R. Borghini, *Il Riposo* (Florence 1584), edited by M. Rosci, Milan 1967, pp. 172–73, describes the system of applying hemp fibers on the joints, as, for example, in Vasari's *Martyrdom of St. Stephan* in the church of Santo Stefano dei Cavalieri in Pisa (as observed by restorer Nadia Presenti) and on Francesco Morandini's *Pentecost* in the church of San Marco in Poppi (Arezzo).
32 In the *Vita di Cristofano Gherardi detto il Doceno*, in G. Vasari, *Le Vite* cit., p. 893 [II. 461]: "they all began [with Cungi] to plaster the three panels [for San Michele in Bosco in Bologna] and to lay the priming, until Giorgio would arrive [to draw]." In *Teoriche*, p. 267 [I. 52]. For the study

of the preparatory drawing see the article by Serena Bidorini, Ornella Salvadori and Silvia Salvini in the present volume.

33 Vasari himself in the *Ricordo* and in the biographies of Doceno and Sammicheli reports that he painted the ceiling in oil, see note 7 in the present article. A thin paint film and fast execution is also found in the *Convito per le nozze di Ester e Assuero*; see S. Casciu, "Il Convito per le nozze di Ester e Assuero. Ricerche e indagini diagnostiche," in *Kermes. Arte e tecnica del restauro*, VI, 17, 1993, pp. 3–12: p. 10.

34 G. Vasari, *Le Vite* cit., p. 265 [I. 50].

35 G. Vasari, *Il libro delle ricordanze* cit., p. 40; G. Vasari, *Vite* cit., p. 1233 [II. 991]: "...the year 1542, and I returned to Tuscany; where, before I wished to begin working on anything else, I painted in the vault of a room, which of my own order had been made in the aforesaid house, all the Arts that are used in drawing, or which depend on it."

36 Ibid., p. 893 [II. 462]: Doceno and Cungi drafted the panels for San Michele in Bosco, and Doceno did the scenes of the comedy *Talanta*; he also painted the "oil draft" of the Night chariot, see p. 895 [II. 464]; p. 725 [II. 205]: for Rosso Fiorentino's draft; p. 981 [II. 592]: for the "drafts" left by Tintoretto; p. 984 [II. 596], referring Andrea Schiavone and, p. 1114 [II. 817], referring to Titian; in the autobiography see pp. 1228, 1232, 1237 [II. 983, 989, 995–96].

37 On the combining of colors see G. Vasari, *Le Vite* cit., pp. 261, 262, 264 [I. 44, 45, 49]. In the chapter on sketches, cartoons and perspective he writes, p. 262 [I. 46]: "Having measured them [the drawings] with the compass or by eye, they are enlarged from the small dimension to the larger ones, according to the work that is to be done ... it is enough that the perspectives are as beautiful insofar as they appear correct when viewed and by escaping move away from the eye... The painter then has to take care that they gradually fade with the gentleness of colors," p. 263 [I. 47].

38 Ibid., p. 264 [I. 48, 49].

39 Ibid.: "the most charming, most pleasant and most beautiful colors in the main figures ... because these are always the ones most taken into consideration and more looked at than the others, which serve almost as a background for the coloring of these."

40 In his autobiography, Vasari describes the armor of the portrait of Alessandro de' Medici: "making the burnished of that armor white, shiny and proper," ibid., p. 1228 [II. 984]; he admires the "lustri" or bright spots on the armors in by Piero della Francesca and Sodoma, p. 488 [I. 356], p. 941 [II. 531], and those of Signorelli p. 591 [I. 526].

41 Indirectly, via X-ray fluorescence examination that ruled out the presence of other blues of the time. See note 7 for the *Ricordo*, then the documents in the Corner-Mocenigo Archive b. 96 (Palazzo Mocenigo di San Stae): "On the day 20 of June ... six ducati, 16 soldi, for one ounce and 4 saggi of ultramarine azure, at four ducati per ounce; and four ducati, 8 soldi, for two ounces and one saggio of lower ultramarine azure, at two ducati per ounce, bought to be used in the paintings for the ceiling of the new chamber painted by sir Zorzi, Florentine"; "On day 26 given three ducati 12 soldi to sir Francesco Giallo, miniaturist, who brough them to master Zorzi, painter, they are for the amount of ounces, one of fine ultramarine azure for four small paintings in the ceiling val. L. 21." In G. Romanelli, "Giorgio Vasari a Venezia" cit., p. 50.

42 Ibid.: "On day 17 of August, one hundred and twenty-three ducati, 21 soldi, for which master Zorzi, Florentine painter serves as creditor ... they are one hundred ducati for a total of five paintings, which he made for the ceiling of the new chamber, and twenty ducati obtained for four little putti in four painting he made, that are placed in the four corners of the said ceiling and three ducati and 21 soldi counted to Battista, his assistant, for his dousing of the ceiling." "Beveraggio, beverage, beverone, questo altro intruglio," in M. Cortellazzo, P. Zolli, *Dizionario etimologico della lingua italiana*, 5 vols., Bologna 1997, vol. 1, p. 135; "beverone" was a term used in the past to indicate a transparent but pigmented substance applied to homogenize certain chromatic imbalances in the painted surface, perhaps in reference to its undesirable effects of aggressive cleaning. Oxalates and oil were detected via FTIR. The varnish seems to have been also sprayed.

43 Like Doceno, a native of Sansepolcro; G. Vasari *Le Vite* cit., p. 894 [II. 463]. A number of panels in the Museo Civico of Sansepolcro have been attributed to him that have a transparent gray finish, as reported by restorer Daniela De Ritis.

44 The chance of comparing the paintings of the artists offered by the exhibition *Il Cinquecento a Firenze* (Florence, Palazzo Strozzi, September 21, 2017–January 21, 2018) made possible these observations on the subject. See also A. Conti, *Michelangelo e la pittura a fresco. Tecnica e conservazione della Volta Sistina*, Florence 1986, p. 29.

45 Like the widespread deposits on the central

panel: see note 5 in the present article. A large number of similar deposits are also observed on the central panel of the *Sala del Trionfo della Virtù*.

46 G. B. Armenini, *De' veri precetti* cit.; R. Borghini, *Il Riposo* cit., p. 220, suggests making the background with little oil and letting it dry well, and then correcting and giving "the last film of very fine colors, and tempered with little oil, which in such a way will always be charming and vivid."

47 G. Pliny Secundus, *Naturalis Historia* [*Natural History*], ed. by G. B. Conte with the collaboration of A. Barchiesi and G. Ranucci, "The Millennia," Turin 1982–1988, 5 vols., Book XXXV, p. 337: "In Athens, painters obtained the atramentum from marc, and called it tryginon. Apelles had the idea of making from burnt ivory that color which is called elephantine"; p. 341: "of the blacks the atramentum"; pp. 395, 397: "when the work was completed he would pass a coat of atramentum so lightly that, forming a reflective layer, it produced a white color due to the brightness and at the same time defended the painting from dust and dirt; this could be seen only up close, but nevertheless then, with extreme caution, he dosed the light to prevent the brightness of the colors from striking the eye as through a mirror plate, while for those looking from a distance this procedure made, without being noticed, the colors that were too bright more diluted."

48 G. Vasari, *Le Vite* cit., p. 288 [II. XIII]: *Lettera di Messer Giovambatista di Messer Marcello Adriani a Messer Giorgio Vasari . . .*: "Never was anyone found after him who knew how to use it, and this was a brown color, or varnish if you wish, which he subtly spread over the works when finished; which by its reverberation aroused the clarity in some of the colors and defended them from dust, and was not visibile except to those who regarded from up close; and this he did with exquisite ability, so that the clarity of some of the bright colors might less offend the sight of those who from a distance, as through a glass, looked at them, tempering with more and less, as he judged to be fitting." On the "atramentum" see also L. Dolce, "Dialogo della pittura intitolato l'aretino (Venice 1557)," in *Trattati d'arte del Cinquecento tra manierismo e controriforma*, edited by P. Barocchi, Bari 1960–1962, 3 vols., vol. I, pp. 141–206, pp. 183–84. See A. Conti, *Michelangelo e la pittura* cit., p. 25, on the sixteenth-century tradition and, in the notes, for some Venetian editions of Pliny's passage: p. 38, note 4: Antonio Brucioli (Venice 1548) and Ludovico Domenichi (Venice 1561). Attention to this subject continued, as in G.B. Armenini, *De veri precetti* cit., p. 141: "some say that Apelles used in finishing his works a liquor as varnish, with which he revived all the colors, covering them with more and with less, according to which he saw needed it." For a summary on the subject see A. Cerasuolo, *Prestezza e Diligenza. La tecnica nella pittura e nella letteratura artistica del Cinquecento*, Florence 2014, pp. 78–80.

49 Vitruvius mentions its use for walls, describing its application. See A. Conti, *Michelangelo e la pittura* cit., pp. 35, 173.

50 G. B. Armenini, *De' veri precetti* cit., p. 142.

51 A. Roy, M. Spring, C. Plazzotta, "Raphael's Early Work in the National Gallery: Paintings before Rome," in *National Gallery Technical Bulletin*, 25, 2004, pp. 4–35: p. 11: Raphael occasionally employs a translucent brown lacquer made of burnt conifer resin, pitch (p. 35, note 42, on the Ansidei Madonna); p. 24 he employs a brown lacquer of conifer pitch cooked in walnut oil.

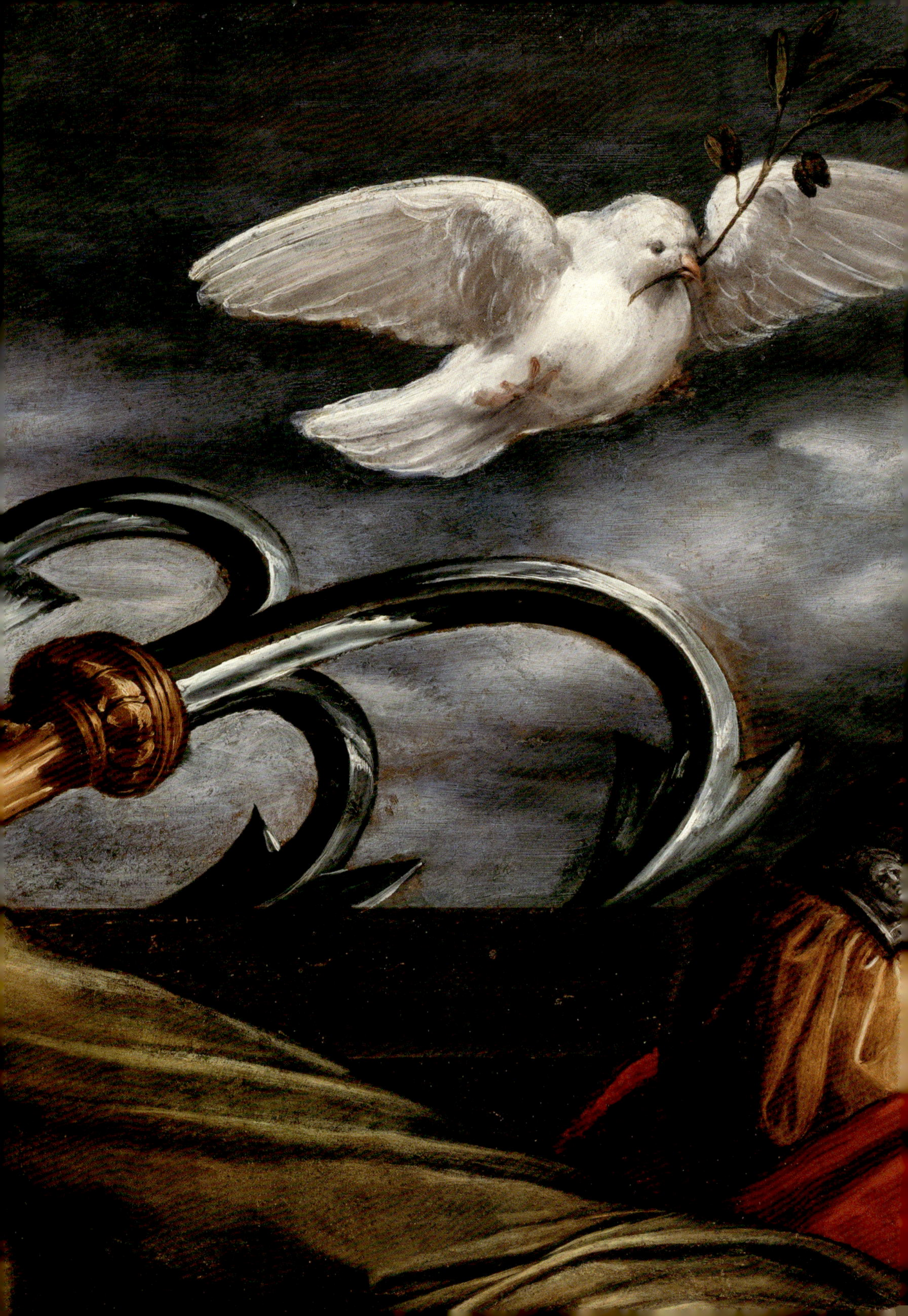

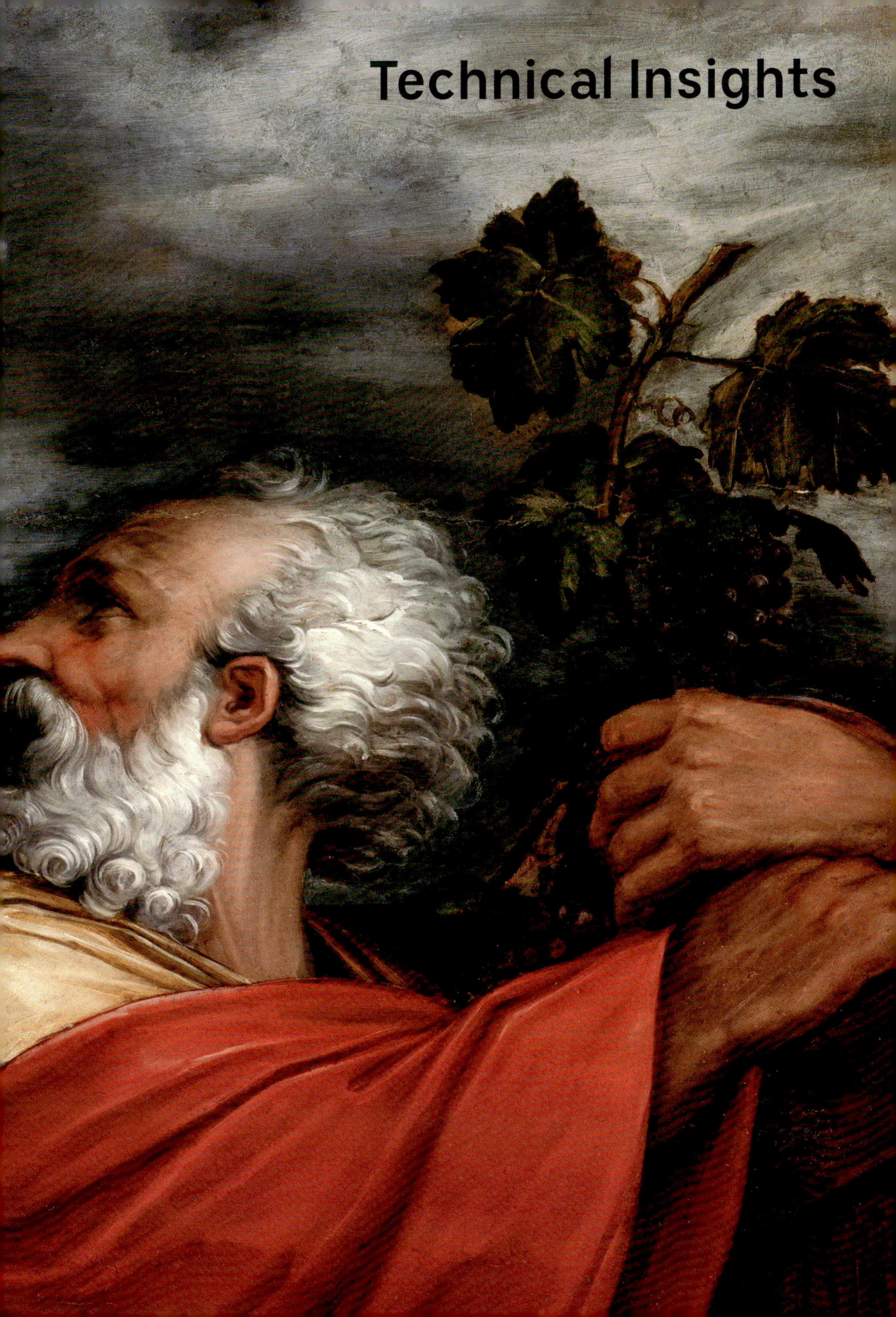
Technical Insights

The Restoration of the Corner Ceiling Panel Supports

Roberto Saccuman

Work on the ensemble of panels that make up the ceiling of Ca' Corner, now displayed in a room at the Gallerie dell'Accademia in Venice, began in the spring of 2004, was continued at different times and concluded with one last intervention in 2020, with the timing of the work being dictated by the museum's gradual acquisition of the panels.[1]

The first painting to be restored and studied was the central panel where *Charity* is depicted, a panel composed of six planks of poplar wood,[2] with sharp edges, attached with wooden pegs on the joint lines, with "butterfly joints" added to reinforce the gluing. At the time of assembly, the size of the panels was certainly greater at least lengthwise as clearly evidenced by the fact that the butterfly joints at one end are cut in half, thus limiting the effectiveness of the joints, evidently because of the need to fit the panel in its compartment [fig. 1]. The presence of wooden inserts under the pictorial film [fig. 1] filling pre-existing holes, suggests that the panel had been already prepared before it was delivered to Giorgio Vasari.[3] The back of the panel, therefore the side intended to be the extrados of the coffered ceiling, shows numerous traces of the work done to thin and even out the planking using a curved iron tool. The result is especially homogeneous in the sections that were to adhere to elements of the structure, probably the ceiling beams or the three crossbars applied according to a construction

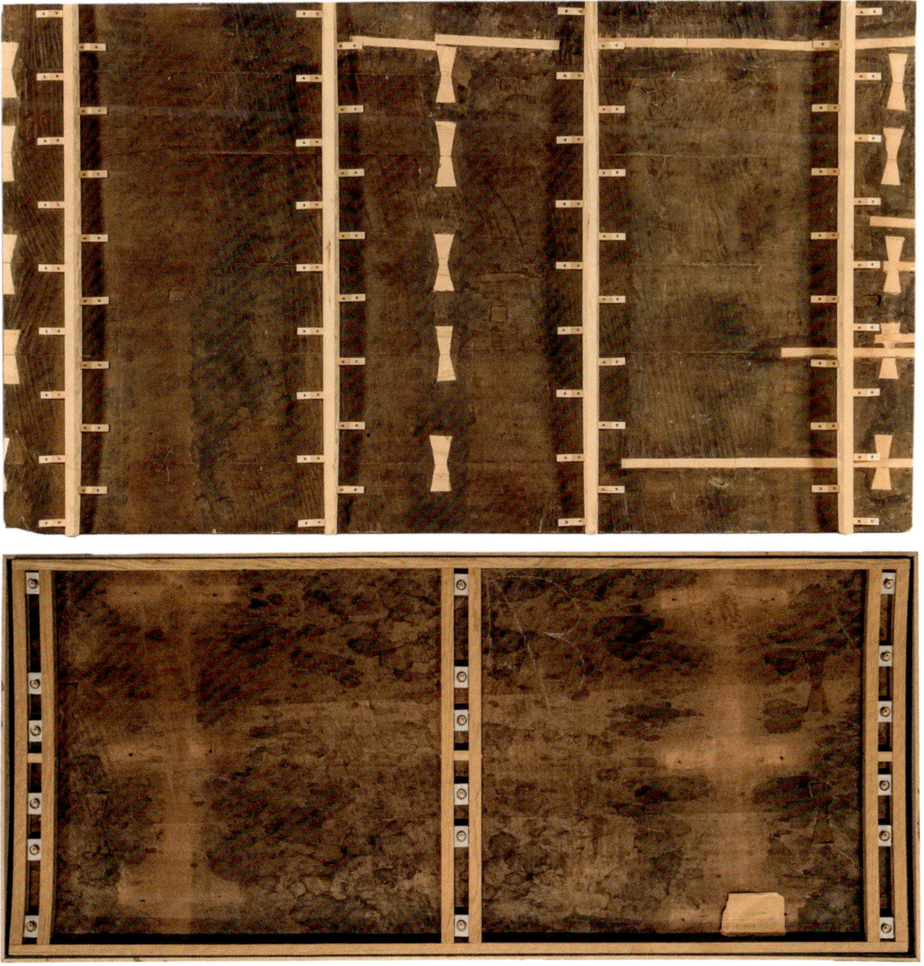

1
Photo of the back of the panel with
the *Allegory of Charity* where traces
of work on the wood, of restoration
dowels inserted prior to the pictorial
layers, and the signs of the resizing
of the support are evident. The
panel is at it appeared when arrived
in the workshops of the Gallerie
dell'Accademia at the Misericordia,
with the trapezoidal crosspieces,
before the 2004 intervention. A
similar system was present before
the intervention on the panel with
Putto, restored in 2003

2
The back of the panel with the
Allegory of Justice where the traces
left by the crosspieces and brackets
that originally supported them are
clearly visible. The same image shows
the elastic restraint system applied to
the panels and the perimeter frame in
which they are inserted

3
Detail of the technique for uniting
Hope and the *Suicide of Judas,* and of
the elastic anti-deformation restraint
system applied on all the panels on
which work was done. The lighter-
colored panel is *Hope,* thinned, while
the darker one is *Judas,* showing
traces of work on the wood and
of fillings, light-colored in this case,
applied in the cavities caused by
xylophagous insects, in order to
protect the wood

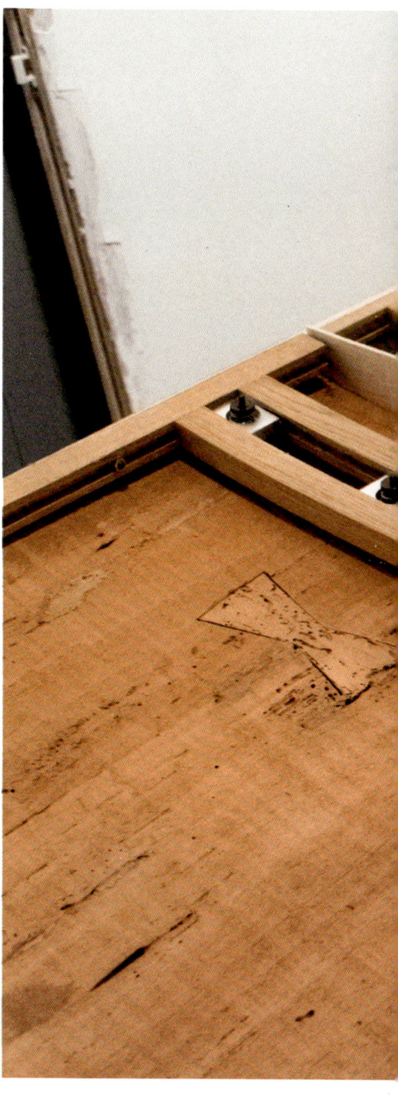

methodology widely in use in Venice in those years, as evident in the other ceiling panels [fig. 2].[4]

At the time of the intervention, four trapezoidal crossbars were present with the sides adapted so as to correspond to the deformation already present on the panel and fixed by a series of opposite brackets, all made from basswood, as are the inserts wedged into the cracks present in the grain of the wood. The inadequacy of this system and the presence of new cracks prompted us to replace it with a more modern one meant to elasti- cally contain the movements of the wood; the same system was later ap-

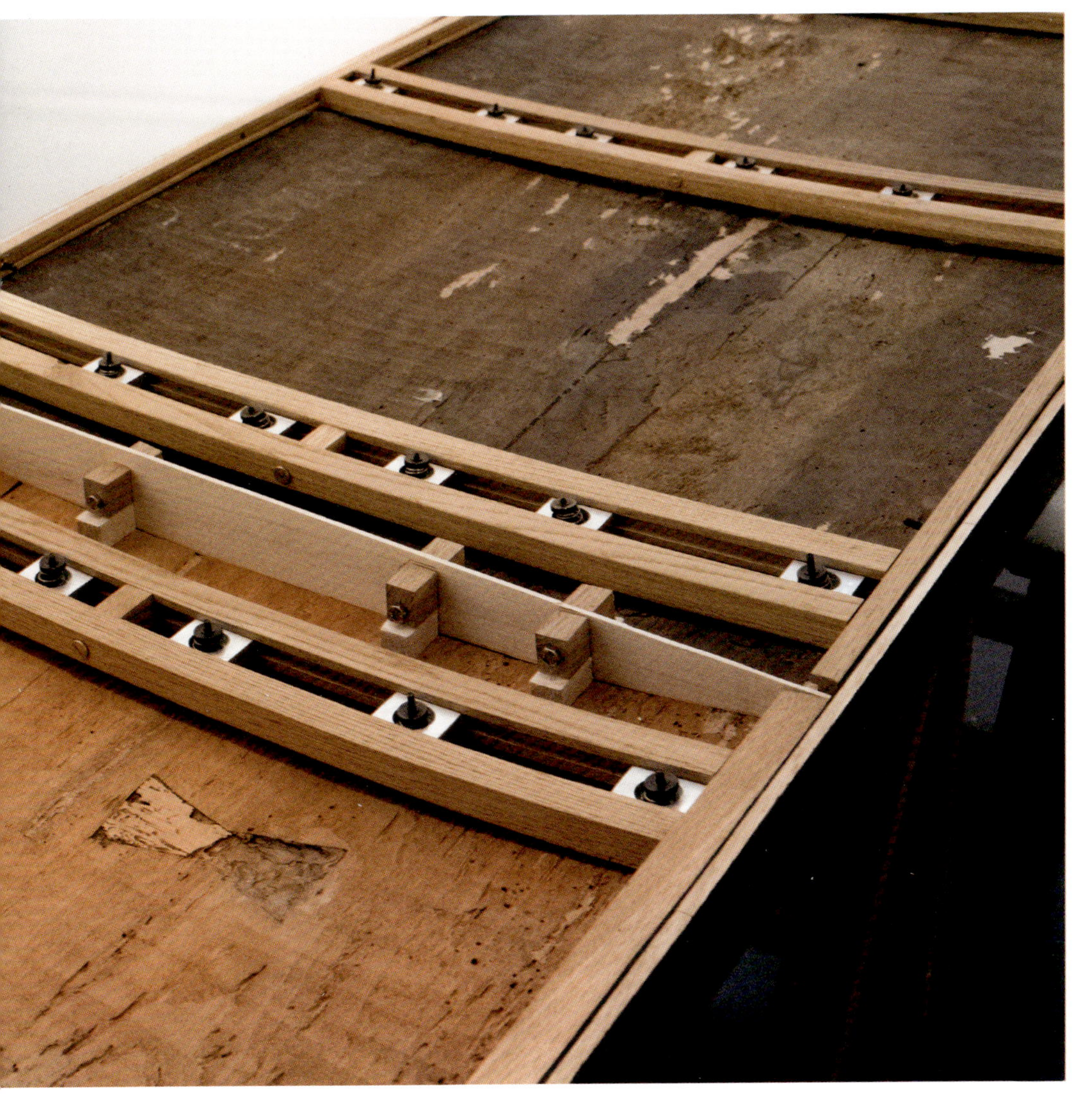

plied to the other panels [fig. 2]. Two different types of frames had been used for two of the corner panels, a metal frame dating back to the 1980s, and a frame of laminated wood, with springs, applied during the restoration of the painting carried out in 2003.[5]

After the dismantling of the ceiling, they followed different paths and their conservation history was consequently affected in different ways. A common element, however, appears to be the removal of the original crossbars and, in order to protect the edges, the application of laths along the perimeter, fixed with numerous nails allowing them to be mounted in frames and to improperly replace the crossbars. These additions however became an obstacle to the natural movements of the wood, especially at the extremities of the planks, giving rise to cracks and partial detachment of the joints. For this reason, it was decided to remove them. From traces present on the backs of the perimeter panels, it appears the original retaining structure consisted of crossbars, probably with inverted T shapes, as in other works from the Veneto region, fixed with brackets that were glued and nailed, the traces of which are still clearly visible and proved useful to identify the positioning of the panels when the ceiling was re-assembled.[6]

Of special interest were the panels with *Hope* and the *Suicide of Judas*.[7] The two panels were originally part of a single panel, cut after the ceiling was dismantled, after which the two parts went their separate ways. *Judas* arrived only in 1981 in Arezzo, at the Giorgio Vasari's House Museum, while the *Hope* panel was in England for a long time before returning to Italy, during which period it underwent a restoration that greatly reduced its thickness to remedy the warping of the wooden support, a deformation found also in the other panels. Once the two panels were both available, in order to rejoin them the wooden supports were analyzed. The study of rings in the wood showed from the outset that they were compatible, evidencing the continuity and correspondence between two sides, in full agreement with the reunited pictorial surfaces. There was concern that the thinning could have led to further warping due to the cutting of the wood from which the panel had been made, but in practice the result of the joining of the two panels proved acceptable, and the panels were fitted with two elastic retaining frames, corresponding to the dimensions of the individual panels, and then inserted into a single perimetric frame [fig. 3].

The reassembling of the entire ceiling as it originally appeared in Palazzo Corner required a technical solution capable of guaranteeing the proper conservation of the works while making them accessible to and enjoyable by the public. The main problem was the warping of the panels, which made it necessary to build a supporting frame along the perimeter, which, combined with a the frame behind the panels, would allow for the original horizontal positioning of the panels. These frames were made of oak wood[8] and the perimeter edge on which the individual panels were to rest was appropriately shaped according to the deformation of the sides, ensuring the horizontal support would evenly support the weight of the panels and adapt itself to the existing deformations, keeping tension to a minimum.

The missing elements, namely a panel with one of the corner putti and parts of the panel depicting the *Allegory of Faith* were replaced with carbon fiber panels, shaped according to the curve in the panel to which they were to be associated to offer a better legibility of the entire ensemble.

1 See the text by Giulio Manieri Elia in this volume.

2 18.3 cm to 30 cm wide. The good quality of the wood indicates very careful selection and processing of the material, respecting the type of lumber in use in Venice at that time.

3 See footnote 7 in Rossella Cavigli's text in this volume.

4 The ceiling perimeter panels have three planks placed horizontally measuring about 22 cm wide and 2.5/1.6 cm thick, with "butterfly joints" inserted in half-wood measuring 22 × 7 cm.

5 The restoration performed by Ciro Castelli was not modified.

6 From the traces it appears that the crossbars were 5 cm wide and the kittens 20 cm; there were three of them on the major and longest panels, two on the others. See Rossella Cavigli's text in this volume.

7 The work on this panel was carried out at the restoration laboratory of the National Museum of Medieval and Modern Art in Arezzo, in collaboration with Rossella Cavigli. Francesca Bartolomei and Giovanni Gualdani also collaborated to the interventions on the supports.

8 The frames were made from composite laths according to the glulam technique then shaped as needed; this ensures greater stability of the wood over time therefore less interaction with the work.

Beyond the Visibile: The Preparatory Drawing

Serena Bidorini, Ornella Salvadori, Silvia Salvini

Reflectographic studies[1] carried out on the ceiling panels provided significant information that can help better understand the work of the artists who collaborated with Vasari on the Corner ceiling.[2]

IR imaging investigations showed the preparatory design and some "pentimenti," although in several areas the underlying drawing was already visible to the naked eye. In addition, reflectograms performed on the panels with *Judas* and *Hope* showed the absolute homogeneity of the two parts confirming that they belong to a single whole [fig. 1].

On the *Faith* and the three *Putti*, the charcoal stroke appears sharp, free and rapid [figs. 2, 3], in line with the drawing detected in Vasari's paintings on wood *Convito per le nozze di Ester e Assuero* in the National Museum of Medieval and Modern Art in Arezzo and *Ultima Cena* in the Cenacle of Santa Croce in Florence;[3] like the paintings in Venice, these too are characterized by the occasional use of a double sign [fig. 4]. On the other panels of the Corner ceiling the drawing is generally less apparent[4] [figs. 5–7]. Numerous "pentimenti" are found on all the panels except those with the putti [figs. 6–7].

Several engraved straight lines outlining the geometric elements were observed with the naked eye: on the lictor beam of *Justice*, on the cross held by *Faith*, and on the balustrade [fig. 8], the only architectural element of the whole; in the latter case, the lines stop in the vicinity of the figures,

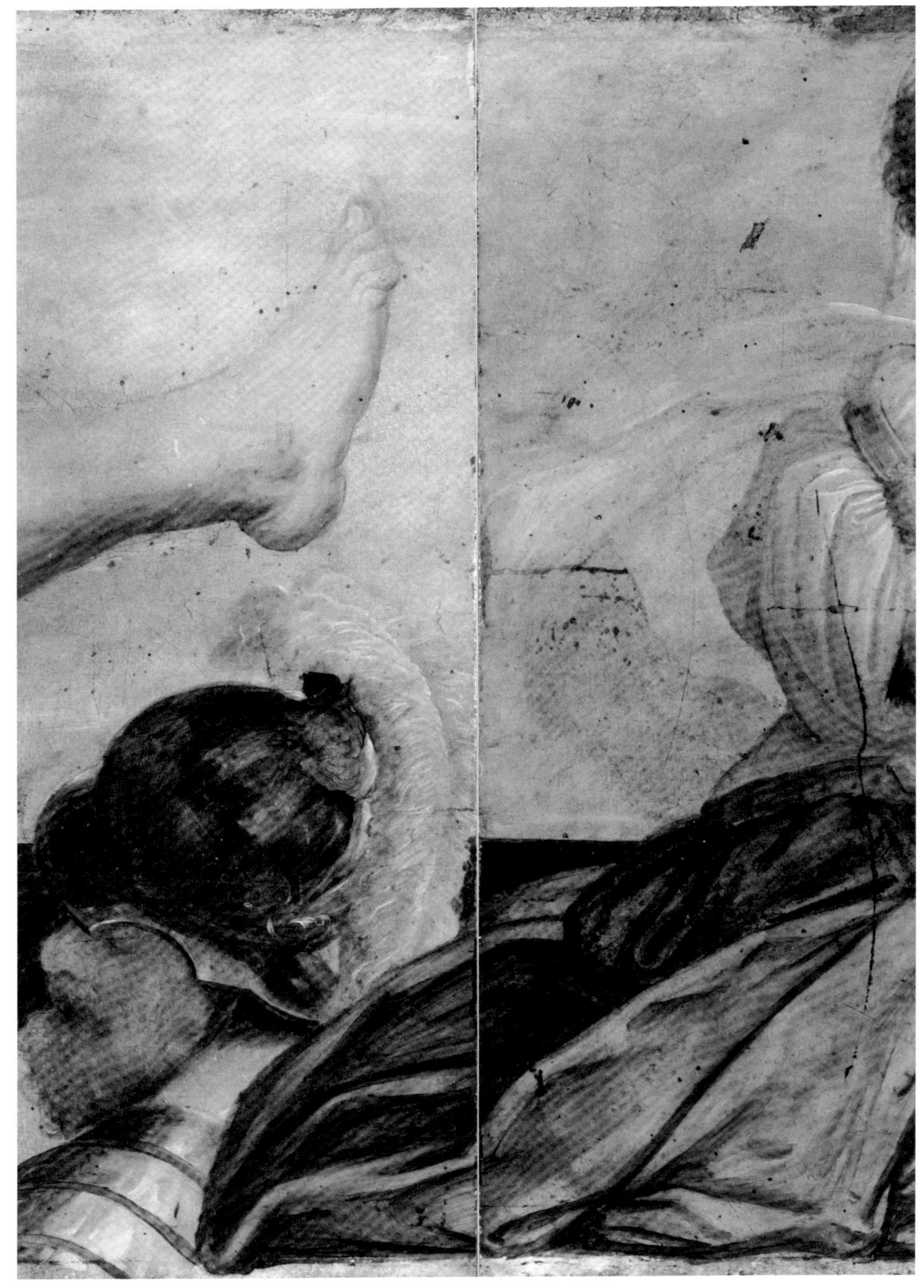

1

Comparison of the reflectograms of the two panels with *Hope* and *Judas,* with elements of homogeneity evident in the area of union; in the lower area of the robe of the Allegory, the continuation in the hatching pattern of the shadows, divided by the cut, is evident, as are the different brushstrokes in the area of darker color, the homogeneity of which is barely perceptible to the naked eye

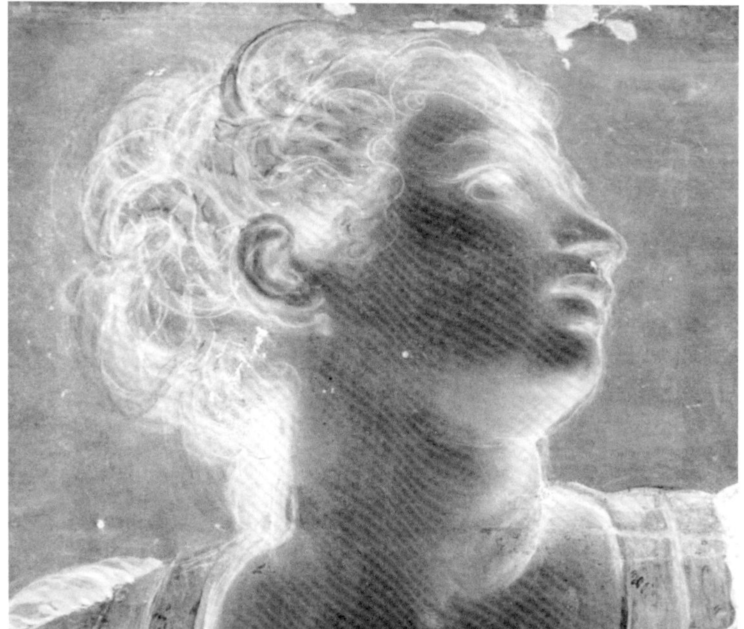

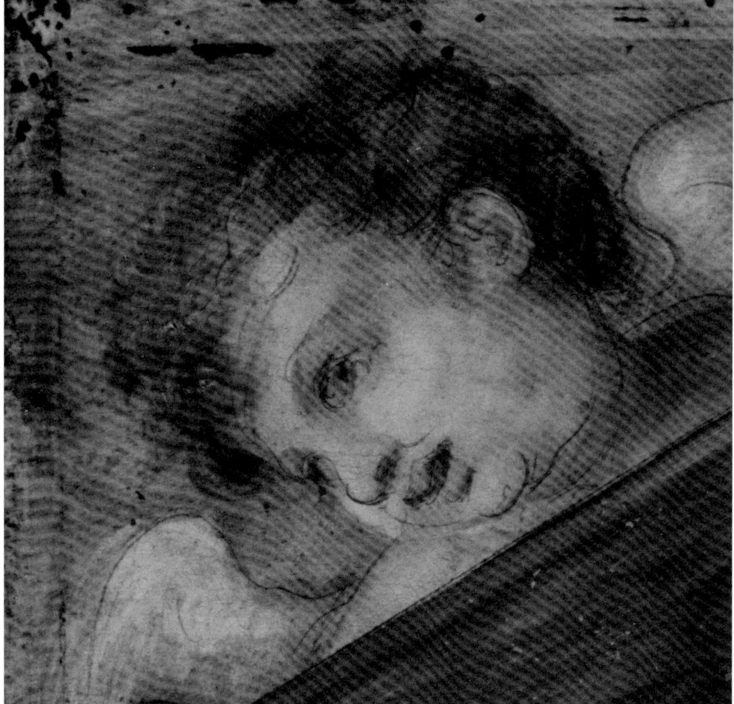

2
The *Faith*, IR reflectography. Detail in which the preparatory drawing of the head is evident with sharp, sometimes doubled stroke

3
Putto, cat. 1373, IR reflectography. Detail of head drawing with sharp, doubled stroke

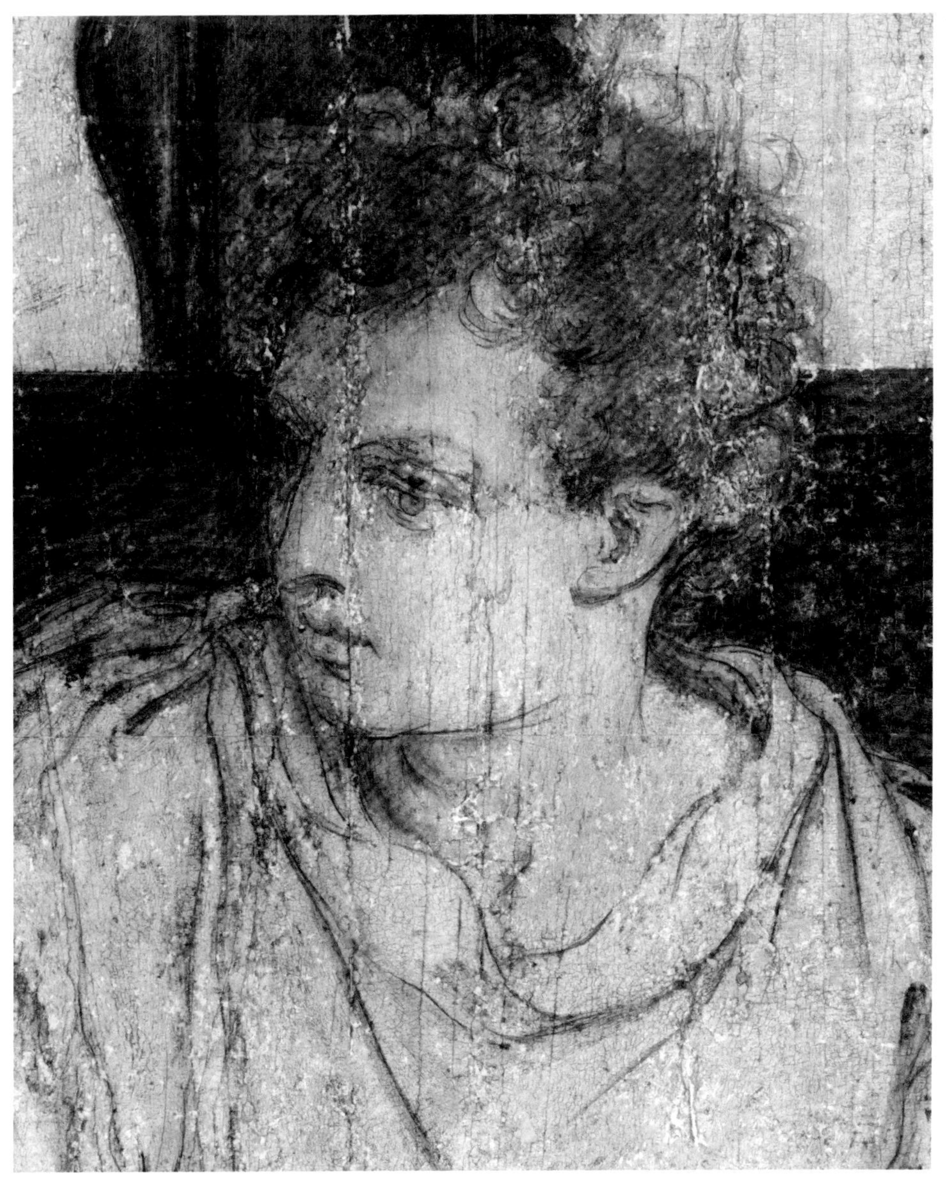

4
Giorgio Vasari, Last *Supper*, Cenacolo
di Santa Croce in Florence. Detail of
IR survey; also evident here is the
sometimes doubled stroke found in
some of Vasari's figures

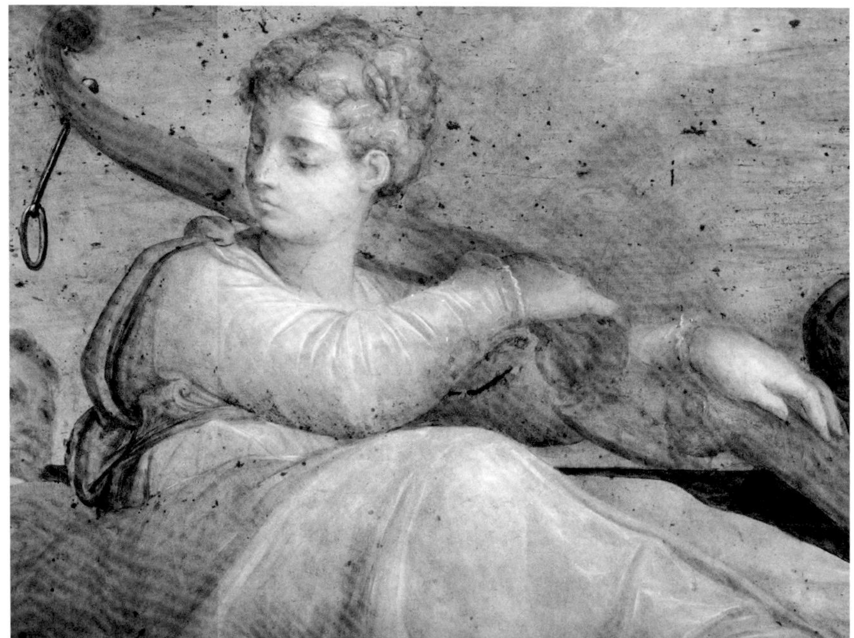

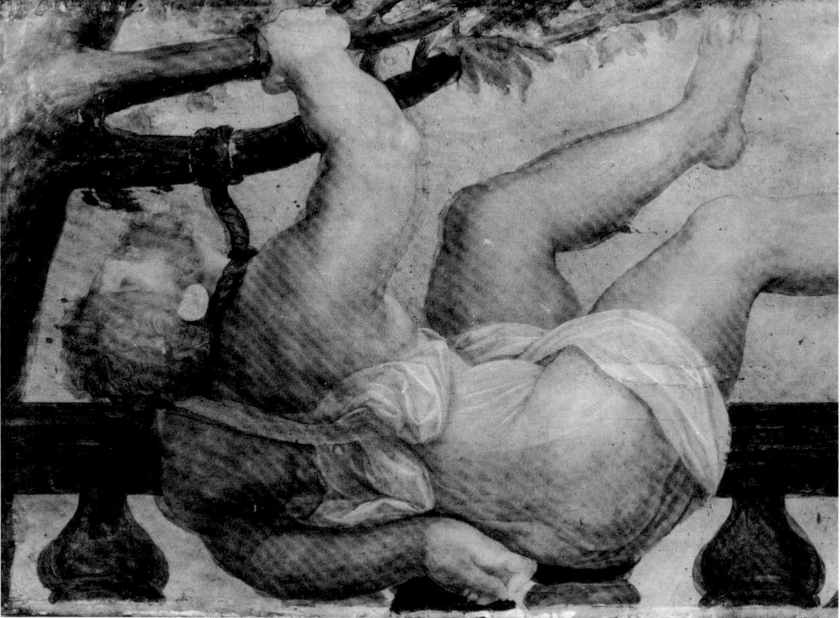

6
Judas, IR reflectography. Numerous "pentimenti" are evident on the entire figure. Clearly visible in this image is the deviation of the legs, especially the left, both arms, the back, the rope, and even two elements of the balustrade

5
Allegory of Patience, IR reflectography. Detail. The drawing is less obvious but you can still see markings, probably made with a brush around the main figure

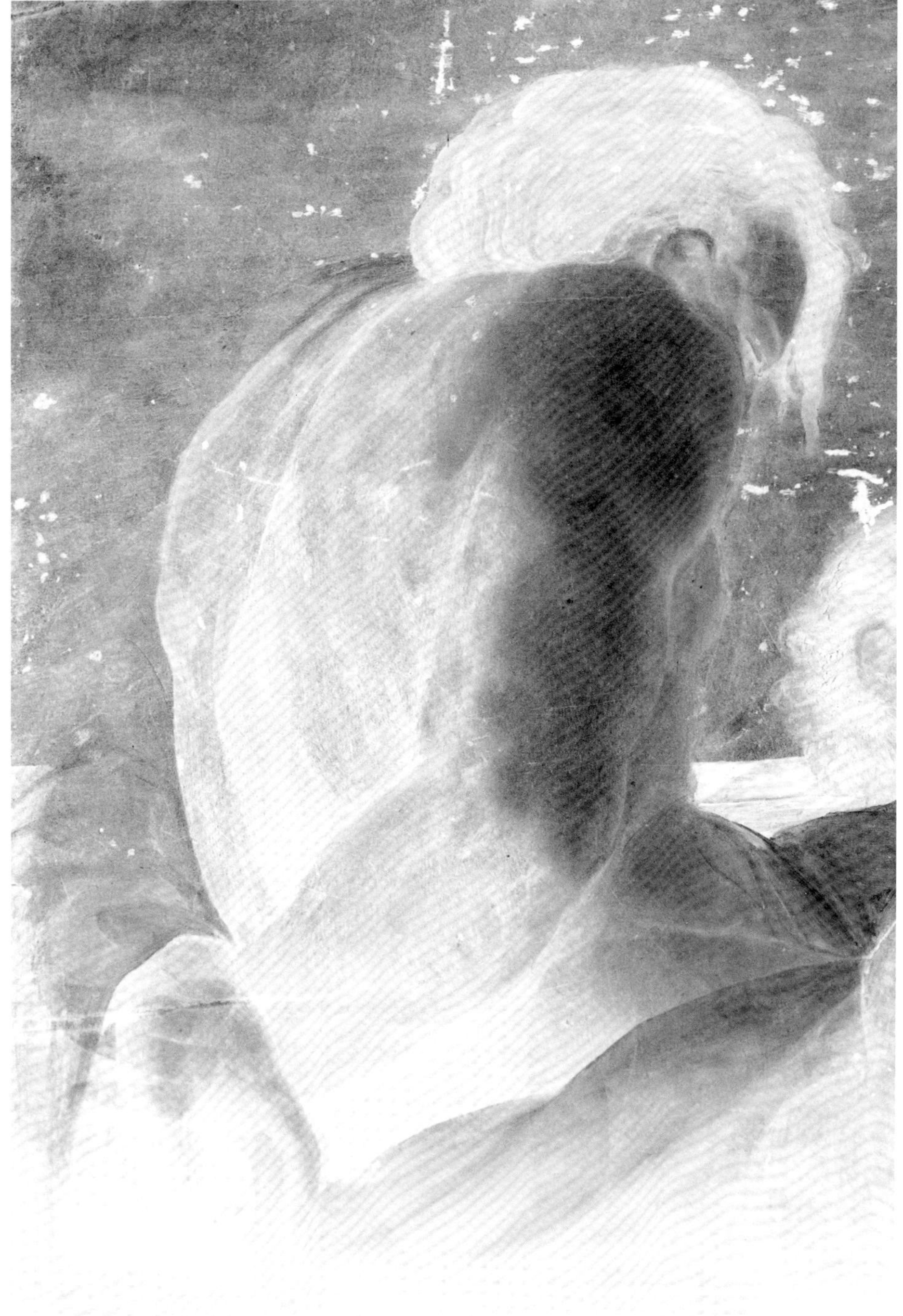

7
The *Allegory of Patience*,
IR reflectography. "Pentimento"
in the hand of the figure on the left

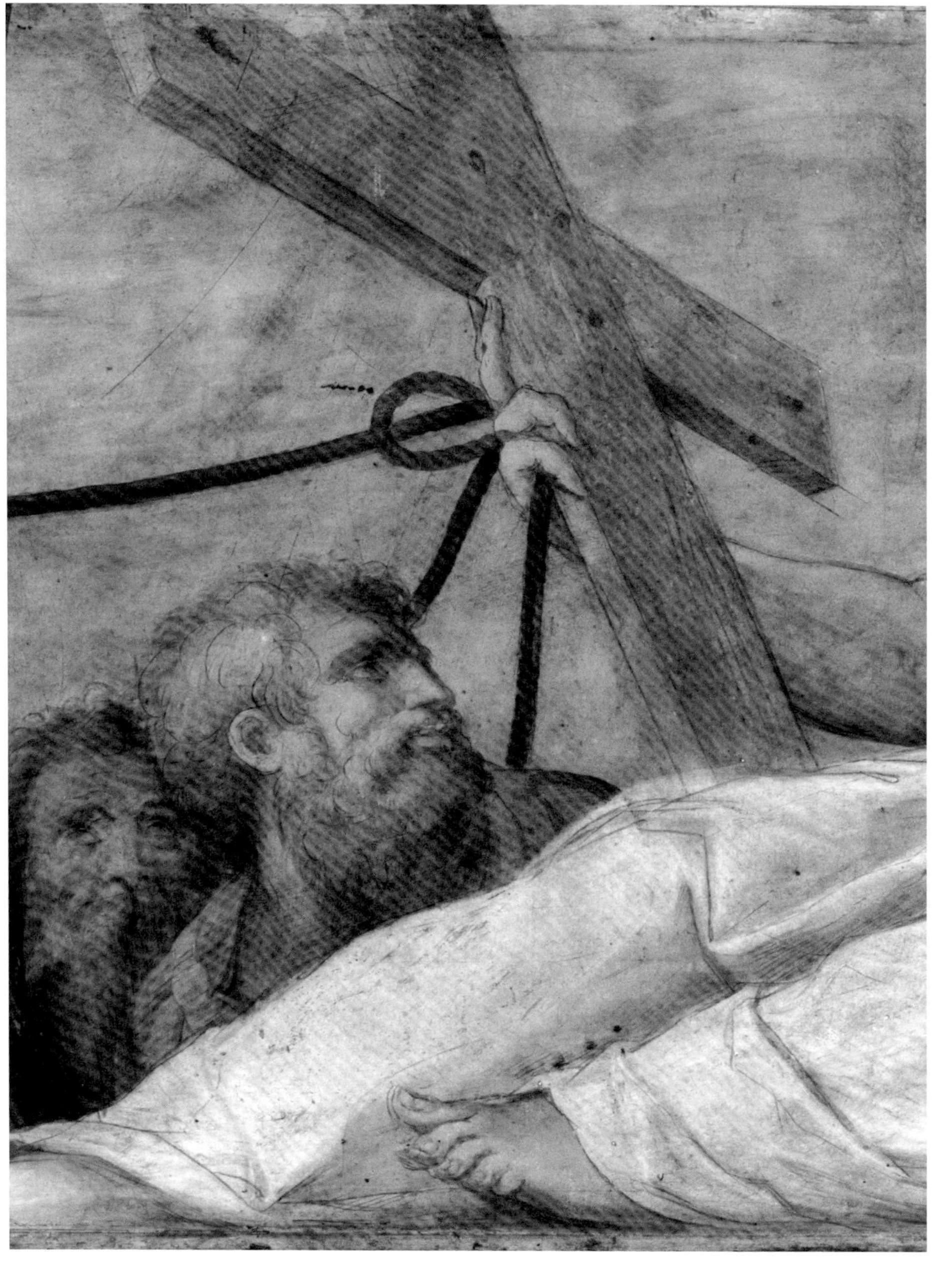

8

Allegory of Faith, IR reflectography. Detail of the many
lines outlining the cross of *Faith*, with "pentimenti," the
outermost lines of which are incisions also visible in X-ray.
Note the hatching shadow area on Peter's shoulders and
on Paul's beard, related to the shadow of the figure that
was cut out from the panel

which were evidently already planned, similarly to the engraved lines of the architectural elements of the *Last Supper*, while in the *Convite* the drawing of the figures goes over the lines.[5]

Vasari was to partly replicate the Virtues of the Corner ceiling in the Palazzo della Cancelleria, in Rome, and in his house in Arezzo, on the walls of the room with the *Triumph of the Virtue*, specifically *Justice* and *Patience*,[6] with echoes also on the ceiling of the Chamber of Abraham. In Florence, Giovanni Stradano was to paint in the Hall of the Gualdrada in the *Eleonora of Toledo apartment* in Palazzo Vecchio the four allegories with a similar horizontal format.

1 Infrared reflectography is a noninvasive imaging technique used to investigate the layers underneath the color, namely the preparatory drawing and the pentimenti. Reflectographies on the allegories of *Justice* and *Patience were* performed in 2004 with a INOA scanner equipped with InGaAs sensor, the remaining panels were analyzed between 2017 and 2018 using an OSIRIS camera (Opus Instruments) with 1–1.7 µm spectral range and InGaAs sensor.
2 See notes 7 and 42 in Rossella Cavigli's text in the present volume.
3 See S. Casciu, "Il Convito per le nozze di Ester e Assuero. Ricerche e indagini diagnostiche," in *Kermes. Arte e tecnica del restauro*, VI, 17, 1993, pp. 3–12, reflectographs performed by Theobaldo Pasquali (Panart) using a camera with a Hamamatsu sensor ranging up to 1700 nm; *Dall'alluvione alla rinascita: il restauro dell'Ultima Cena di Giorgio Vasari. Santa Croce cinquant'anni dopo* (1966–2016), edited by R. Bellucci, M. Ciatti, C. Frosinini, Florence 2016, p. 143, figs. 1, 2, pp. 178–79, pls. VI. VII. Works from the years 1546–49.
4 We cannot rule out that the information on the preparatory drawing provided by the IR may have been distorted by the presence of a colored "mestica" over the preparation and that the drawing was actually made using some other technique. Another work of the artist in which the drawing has not clearly identified is the Pala Albergotti in Arezzo; see T. Radelet, "Potenzialità delle analisi multispettrali nell'utilizzo preliminare al restauro della Pala Albergotti," in *L'ingegno e la mano. Restaurare il mai restaurato. Il restauro della Pala Albergotti di Giorgio Vasari nella Badia delle Sante Flora e Lucilla di Arezzo*, ed. by I. Droandi, Florence 2009, pp. 33–43, p. 39.
5 The engravings can also be detected with X-rays; see note 28 in Rossella Cavigli's article in the present volume. E. Bianco, A. Casaccia, I. Corsini, C. Mignani, D. Minotti, "L'Ultima Cena del Vasari: un restauro al limite del possibile," in *Dall'alluvione alla rinascita* cit., pp. 142–143, S. Casciu, "Il convito per le nozze" cit., p. 7.
6 The studies carried out for the restoration and related studies showed that the graphic reliefs of the two allegories painted on the wall do not correspond to the same figures painted on the ceiling panels, ruling out the hypothetical reuse of a cartoon.

Bibliography

Le ingegnose Sorti composte per Francesco Marcolini da Forlì, Intitolate Giardino di Pensieri. Novamente ristampate e in Nove et Bellissimo Ordine Riformate, Venice 1550

C. Bartoli, *Sopra alcuni luoghi difficili di Dante*, Venice 1567

L. Cicognara, *Memorie Spettanti la Storia della Calcografia*, Prato 1831

F. Zanotto, *Il Palazzo Ducale di Venezia*, Venice 1842

G. Vasari, *Le Vite de' più eccellenti pittori, scultori ed architetti*, ed. by G. Milanesi, Florence 1871

G. E. di Parravicino, "Three Packs of Italian Tarocco Cards," in *The Burlington Magazine*, III, 9, October-December 1903, pp. 237–51

P. Aretino, *Prose sacre*, Lanciano 1926

Il Libro della Ricordanze di Giorgio Vasari, ed. by A. Del Vita, Arezzo 1927–1929

Antiquitäten Tapisserien Gemälde alter und neuer Meister, auction catalog, Internationales Kunst, Berlin 1930, lot 455

A. Venturi, *Storia dell'arte italiana. La pittura del Cinquecento*, vol. IX, t. 4, Milan 1936

A. Von Schneider, *Aus der Sammlung Robert Scholz – Forni*, Hamburg 1937

Lo Zibaldone di Giorgio Vasari, ed. by A. Del Vita, Rome 1938

E. Wind, "'Hercules' and 'Orpheus'. Two Mock-Heroic Designs by Dürer," in *Journal of the Warburg Institute*, II, 1938–1939, pp. 206–18

M. Goering, P. Gazzola, *Giorgio Vasari*, in U. Thieme, F. Becker, *Allgemeines Lexikon der Künstler*, XXXIV, 1940, pp. 119–28

B. Nicolson, "Mannerism at the Arcade Gallery," in *The Burlington Magazine*, XCII, 562, 1950, pp. 203–05

R. Causa, *Fontainebleau e la Maniera italiana*, exhibition catalog (Naples, Mostra d'oltremare e del lavoro italiano nel mondo, July-October 1952), Florence 1952

P. Barocchi, "Il Vasari pittore," in *Rinascimento*, VII, 2, 1955, pp. 193

L. Dolce, "Dialogo della pittura intitolato l'aretino (Venice 1557)," in *Trattati d'arte del Cinquecento tra manierismo e controriforma*, ed. by P. Barocchi, Bari 1960–1962, 3 vols.

J. Schultz, "Vasari at Venice," in *The Burlington Magazine*, CIII, 705, 1961, pp. 500–11

A. Katzenellenbogen, *Allegories of Virtues and Vices in Medieval Art from Early Christianism to the Thirteenth Century*, New York 1964

G. Moakley, *The Tarot Cards, Painted by Bonifacio Bembo for the Visconti-Sforza Family. An Iconographic and Historical study*, New York 1966

G. Vasari, *Le Vite de' più eccellenti pittori, scultori et architettori* (Florence 1550 e 1568), ed. by R. Bettarini and P. Barocchi, Florence 1966–1987

R. Borghini, *Il Riposo* (Florence 1584), ed. by M. Rosci, Milan 1967

J. Schultz, *Venetian Painted Ceiling of the Renaissance*, Berkeley–Los Angeles 1968

E. Panofsky, *Studi di iconologia*, Turin 1975

L. Olivato, L. Puppi, *Mauro Codussi*, Milan 1977

Restauri nella Casa del Vasari. La Sala del Camino, ed. by A. M. Maetzke, Arezzo 1977

Importanti dipinti, disegni, stampe e bronzi; provenienti da varie proprietà, vol. 71, Christie's auction, Rome, 20 October 1980, Rome 1980, no. 292

Giorgio Vasari. Principi, letterati e artisti nelle carte di Giorgio Vasari a Casa Vasari, exhibition catalog (Arezzo, Casa Vasari, Sottochiesa di San Francesco, 26 September—29 November 1981), ed. by L. Conti, M. Daly Davis, A. M. Maetzke, Florence 1981

A. Cecchi, "Sala del Trionfo e delle virtù," in *Giorgio Vasari. Principi* cit., pp. 26–29

J. Kliemann, "San Michele," in *Giorgio Vasari. Principi* cit., p. 97

J. Kliemann, "Philippe Thomassin (1562-1622) da Giorgio Vasari, Allegoria dell'Immacolata Concezione," in *Giorgio Vasari. Principi* cit., pp. 106–07

A. M. Maetzke, "Vasari e i committenti ecclesiastici: Arezzo e Camaldoli 1537–1540," in *Giorgio Vasari. Principi* cit., pp. 50–54

A. M. Maetzke, "Giuda," in *Giorgio Vasari. Principi* cit., pp. 335–36, fig. 278

D. Mc Tavish, "Vasari e Pietro Aretino," in *Giorgio Vasari. Principi* cit., pp. 108–18

R. Pallucchini, "Per la storia del Manierismo a Venezia," in *Da Tiziano a El Greco. Per la storia del Manierismo a Venezia 1540–1590*, exhibition catalog (Venice, Palazzo Ducale, 1 September–28 December 1981), Milan 1981

G. Plinio Secondo, *Naturalis Historia* [Natural History], directed by G.B. Conte in collaboration with A. Barchiesi and G. Ranucci, «I millenni», Turin 1982–1988, 5 vols.

C. Cairns, *Pietro Aretino and the Republic of Venice. Researches on Aretino and His Circle in Venice 1527-1556*, Florence 1985

Capolavori & Restauri, exhibition catalog (Florence, Palazzo Vecchio, 14 December 1986–26 aprile 1987), Florence 1986

A. Conti, *Michelangelo e la pittura a fresco. Tecnica e conservazione della Volta Sistina*, Florence 1986

G. B. Armenini, *De' veri precetti della pittura* (Ravenna 1586), ed. by M. Gorreri, Turin 1988

A. Marranzini, *I colloqui di Ratisbona: l'azione e le idee di Gaspare Contarini*, in *Gaspare Contarini e il suo tempo*, proceedings of the conference, (Venice, 1–3 March 1985), ed. by F. Cavazzana Romanelli, Venice 1988, pp. 167–206

E. Massa, "Gasparo Contarini e gli amici tra Venezia e Camaldoli," in *Gaspare Contarini e il suo tempo* cit., pp. 39-91

L. Corti, "Giuda" (entry 25), in *Vasari. Catalogo completo*, Florence 1989, p. 44

A. Giovannetti, "Giorgio Vasari, Il trionfo della Carità," entry no. 15, in *Pinacoteca di Brera. Scuole dell'Italia centrale e meridionale*, Milan 1992, p. 39

M. Hochman, "Tra Venezia e Roma: il cardinale Francesco Corner," in *Saggi e memorie di Storia dell'arte*, 18, 1992, pp. 97–110, 203–06

D. Panofsky, E. Panofsky, *Il vaso di Pandora*, Turin 1992

C. Ripa, *Iconologia*, ed. by P. Buscaoli, Milan 1992

S. Casciu, "Il Convito per le nozze di Ester e Assuero. Ricerche e indagini diagnostiche," in *Kermes. Arte e tecnica del restauro*, VI, 17, 1993, pp. 3–12

P. Carloni, M. Grasso, "L'eloquenza della virtù. Giorgio Vasari, Anton Francesco Doni e il linguaggio allegorico nel Cinquecento. Riflessioni attorno a una ricerca compiuta," in *Storia dell'Arte*, 92, 1994, pp. 426–43

C. Volpi, *Le immagini degli dèi di Vincenzo Cartari*, Rome 1996

M. Cortellazzo, P. Zolli, *Dizionario etimologico della lingua italiana*, 5 vols., Bologna 1997

F. Härb, "Modes and Models in Vasari's Early Drawing Oeuvre," in *Vasari's Florence. Artists and Literati at the Medicean Court*, ed. by P. Jacks, Cambridge 1998, p. 104

M. Bautz, *Virtutes. Studien zu Funktion und Ikonographie der Tugenden im Mittelater und im 16 Jahrhundert*, Berlin 1999

G. Romanelli, "Giorgio Vasari a Venezia,"
in *Pittura Veneziana dal Quattrocento al
Settecento. Studi in onore di Egidio Martini*,
ed. by G. M. Pilo, San Giovanni Lupatoto 1999,
pp. 48–53

L. Vertova, "Vasari at Venice: an addendum,"
in *The Burlington Magazine*, CXLI, 1151, 1999,
pp. 105–06

M. Ciatti, "Immacolata Concezione," in *OPD
restauro*, 13, 2001, pp. 213–16

F. Härbs, "Prospero Fontana alias Giorgio Vasari:
Collaboration and the Limits of Autorship,"
in *Francesco Salviati e la Bella Maniera*,
conference proceedings ed. by P. Costamagna,
M. Hochmann, Paris 2001, pp. 578–79

C. Orsi, *Vasari a Venezia*, Milan 2002

M. Caciorgna, R. Guerrini, *La Virtù figurata. Eroi
ed eroine dell'antichità nell'arte senese tra
Medioevo e Rinascimento*, Siena 2003

M. Hochmann, *Venise et Rome 1500-1600: deux
écoles de peinture et leurs échanges*, Genève
2004

P. Rossi, "I soffitti veneziani da Pordenone a
Tintoretto," *in Da Bellini a Veronese. Temi di arte
veneta*, Venice 2004, pp. 509–35

A. Roy, M. Spring, C. Plazzotta, "Raphael's Early
Work in the National Gallery: Paintings before
Rome," in *National Gallery Technical Bulletin*, 25,
2004, pp. 4–35

E. Parlato, "Le allegorie nel giardino delle 'Sorti'",
in *Studi per le "Sorti". Gioco, immagini, poesia
oracolare a Venezia nel Cinquecento*, ed. by
P. Procaccioli, Viella 2007, pp. 113–37

S. Pierguidi, "Sulla fortuna della "Giustizia" e
della "Pazienza" del Vasari," in *Mitteilungen des
Kunsthistorische in Institutes in Florenz*, 51, 3–4,
2007, pp. 576–92

A. Alciato, *Il libro degli Emblemi, secondo
le edizioni 1531–1534*, ed. by M. Gabriele,
Milan 2009

A. Gentili, *La bilancia dell'arcangelo. Vedere i
dettagli nella pittura veneziana*, Rome 2009

T. Radelet, "Potenzialità delle Analisi
Multispettrali nell'utilizzo preliminare al restauro
della Pala Albergotti," in *L'ingegno e la mano.
Restaurare il mai restaurato. Il restauro della
Pala Albergotti di Giorgio Vasari nella Badia
delle Sante Flora e Lucilla di Arezzo*, ed. by
I. Droandi, Florence 2009, pp. 33–43

I. Ceretti, "L'iconografia dei vizi e delle virtù
attraverso lo sguardo di un miniatore bolognese
del Trecento," in *I quaderni del m.ae.s*, XIII, 1,
2009–2010, pp. 125–46

C. Frugoni, *La voce delle immagini. Pillole
iconografiche dal Medioevo*, Turin 2010

R. Cavigli, "Osservazioni sulla tecnica pittorica
del Polittico della Misericordia," in *Ripensando
Piero della Francesca. Il Polittico della
Misericordia di Sansepolcro*, ed. by M. Betti,
C. Frosinini, P. Refice, Florence 2011, pp. 203–18

L. De Girolami Cheney, *Giorgio Vasari: Artistic and
Emblematic Manifestations*, Washington 2011

L. De Girolami Cheney, "Vasari's Early Decorative
Cycles. The Venetian Commissions," part. II,
In Id., *Giorgio Vasari, Artist and Emblematic
Manifestations,* Washington 2011

A. Fenech Kroke, *Giorgio Vasari. La Fabrique
de l'allégorie. Culture et fonction de la
personnification au Cinquecento*, Florence 2011

M. Firpo, *Artisti, gioiellieri, eretici. Il mondo di
Lorenzo Lotto tra Riforma e Controriforma*,
Bari 2011

A. Prosperi, *L'eresia del Libro Grande. Storia di
Giorgio siculo e della sua setta*, Milan 2011

C. Carlini, "Temi iconografici del '500 legati
all'Hercules di Luciano, tradotto da Erasmo,"
in *Le Strade della Filologia*, ed. by S. Mariotti,
Rome 2012, pp. 289–305

B. Agosti, *Giorgio Vasari. Luoghi e tempi delle
Vite*, Milan 2013

G. Aurigemma, "Averroè, Ario e Sabelio, due
inediti frammenti vasariani," in *Storia dell'Arte*,
136, 36, 2013, pp. 38–45

M. Firpo, "Giorgio Vasari e la crisi religiosa del
'500," in *I mondi di Vasari. Accademia, lingua,
religione, storia, teatro*, ed. by A. Nova and
L. Zangheri, Venice 2013, pp. 43–65

G. Manieri Elia, "Allegoria della Pazienza," in
Giorgio Vasari e l'Allegoria della Pazienza, ed. by
A. Bisceglia, exhibition catalog (Florence, Palazzo
Pitti-Galleria Palatina, 26 November 2013–5
January 2014), Leghorn 2013, pp. 54–57

A. Staderini, "Allegoria delle arti liberali (inv.
64968 – n. 67)," in *Dal Giglio al David. Arte civica
a Firenze tra Medioevo e Rinascimento*, ed. by
M. M. Donato and D. Parenti, exhibition catalog
(Florence, Gallerie dell'Accademia, 14 May–
18 December 2013), Florence 2013, p. 264

A. Cerasuolo, *Prestezza e Diligenza. La tecnica nella pittura e nella letteratura artistica del Cinquecento*, Florence 2014

G. Manieri Elia, "La Fede di Giorgio Vasari e il soffitto della "Camera nova" in palazzo Corner Spinelli," in *Ricche miniere*, 1, 2014, pp. 71–79

M. Rossi, "Rosso, Pontormo, l'inferna fossa. Todesmeditation vasariana," in *Pontormo e Rosso fiorentino. Divergenti vie della "Maniera"*, exhibition catalog (Florence, Palazzo Strozzi, 8 March–20 July 2014), Florence 2014, pp. 329–37

J. C. Rössler, "The 'Camera nova' by Michele Sanmicheli and Giorgio Vasari, Palazzo Corner Spinelli," in *Ricche miniere*, 1, 2014, pp. 63–69

F. Härb, *The Drawings of Giorgio Vasari (1511–1574)*, Rome 2015

G. Manieri Elia, "Allegoria della Fede," in *Lo Stato dell'Arte – L'Arte dello Stato. Le acquisizioni del Ministero dei beni e delle attività culturali e del turismo. Colmare le lacune – Ricucire la Storia*, exhibition catalog (Rome, Museo di Castel Sant'Angelo, 26 May–29 November 2015), Rome 2015, pp. 171–72

E. Bianco, A. Casaccia, I. Corsini, C. Mignani, D. Minotti, "L'Ultima Cena del Vasari: un restauro al limite del possibile," in *Dall'alluvione alla rinascita: il restauro dell'Ultima Cena di Giorgio Vasari. Santa Croce cinquant'anni dopo (1966–2016)*, ed. by R. Bellucci, M. Ciatti, C. Frosinini, Florence 2016, pp. 141–71

L. Caporossi, R. Cavigli, "Vasari at Venice. The "Suicide of Judas" at Arezzo, another addendum to the Corner ceiling," in *The Burlington Magazine*, CLVIII, 1354, 2016, pp. 10–12

Dall'alluvione alla rinascita: il restauro dell'Ultima Cena di Giorgio Vasari. Santa Croce cinquant'anni dopo (1966–2016), ed. by R. Bellucci, M. Ciatti, C. Frosinini, Florence 2016

M. Firpo, F. Biferali, *Immagini ed eresie nell'Italia del Cinquecento*, Bari 2016

Luca Pacioli tra Piero della Francesca e Leonardo, exhibition catalog (Sansepolcro, Museo Civico, 9 June–24 September 2017), ed. by S. Zuffi, Venice 2017

G. Manieri Elia, in *Il giovane Tintoretto*, ed. by R. Battaglia, P. Marini and V. Romani, exhibition catalog (Venice, Gallerie dell'Accademia, 7 September 2018–6 January 2019), Venice-Milan 2018

M. Favilla, R. Rugolo, "Gli apparati decorativi di Palazzo Corner dal Seicento all'Ottocento," in B. Buratti, M. Favilla, G. Guidarelli, R. Rugolo, *Palazzo Corner Mocenigo a Venezia, sede della Guardia di Finanza*, Rome–Venice 2019

G. Careri, *Ebrei e cristiani nella Cappella Sistina*, Macerata 2020

C. Ginzburg, A. Prosperi, *Giochi di Pazienza: un seminario sul* Beneficio di Cristo, Turin, Macerata 2020

D. Franklin, "Rosso Fiorentino, Marcillat and Vasari in Arezzo. The Reinvention of the Image of the Immaculate Conception," in *La disputa sull'Immacolata Concezione nella Toscana del Cinquecento*, proceedings of the Study Day (Florence, Galleria dell'Accademia, 13 May 2019), ed. by C. Hollberg, Florence 2022, pp. 110–23

P. Querchi, "Appunti sugli antiquari e le barbe," in *La barba nel Cinquecento. Storia, arte, letteratura*, proceedings of the study group (Rome, Università degli Studi Roma Tre, 16 December 2022), ed. by G. Crimi, Manziana 2023

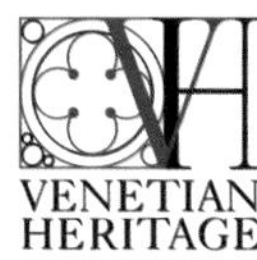

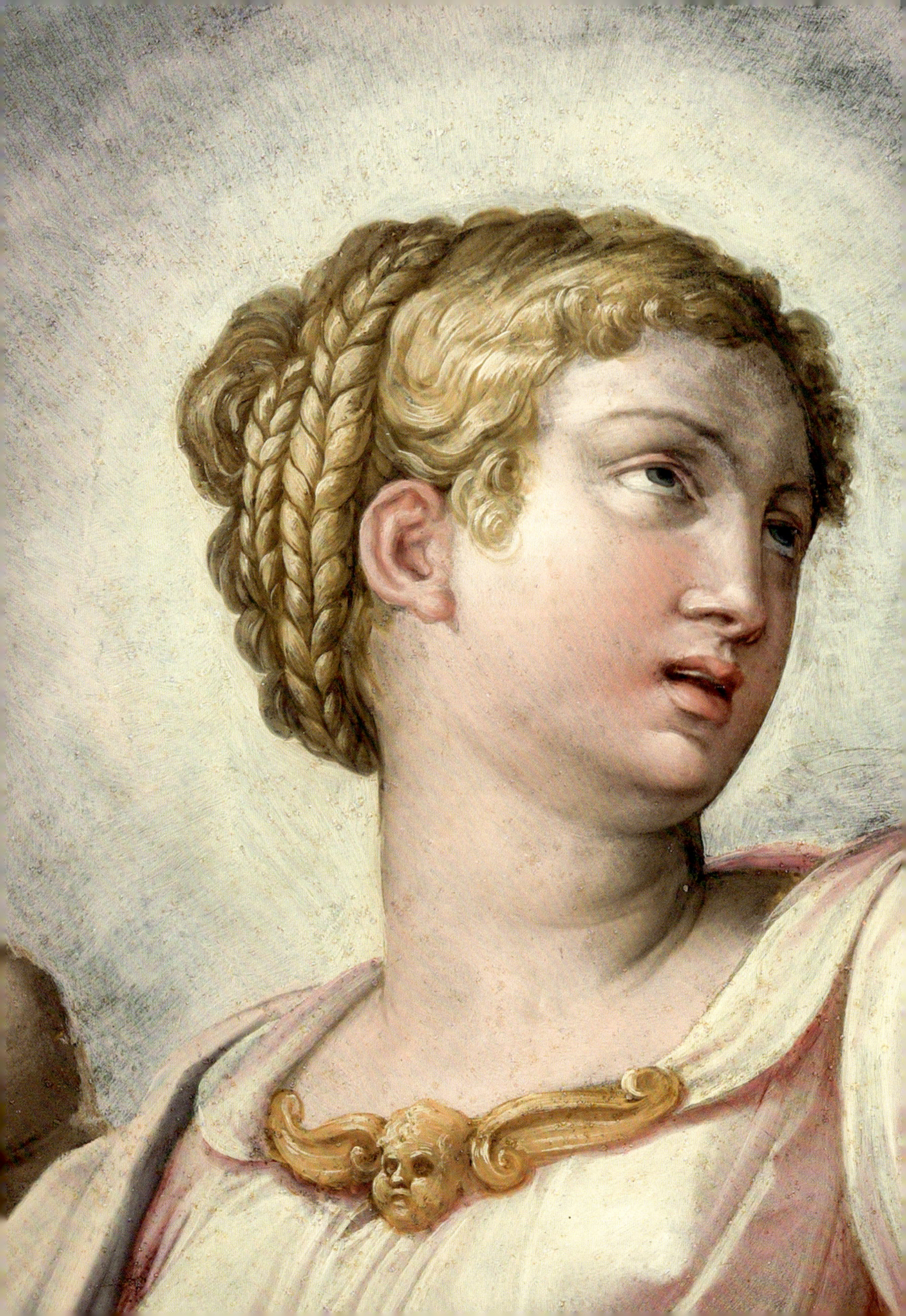

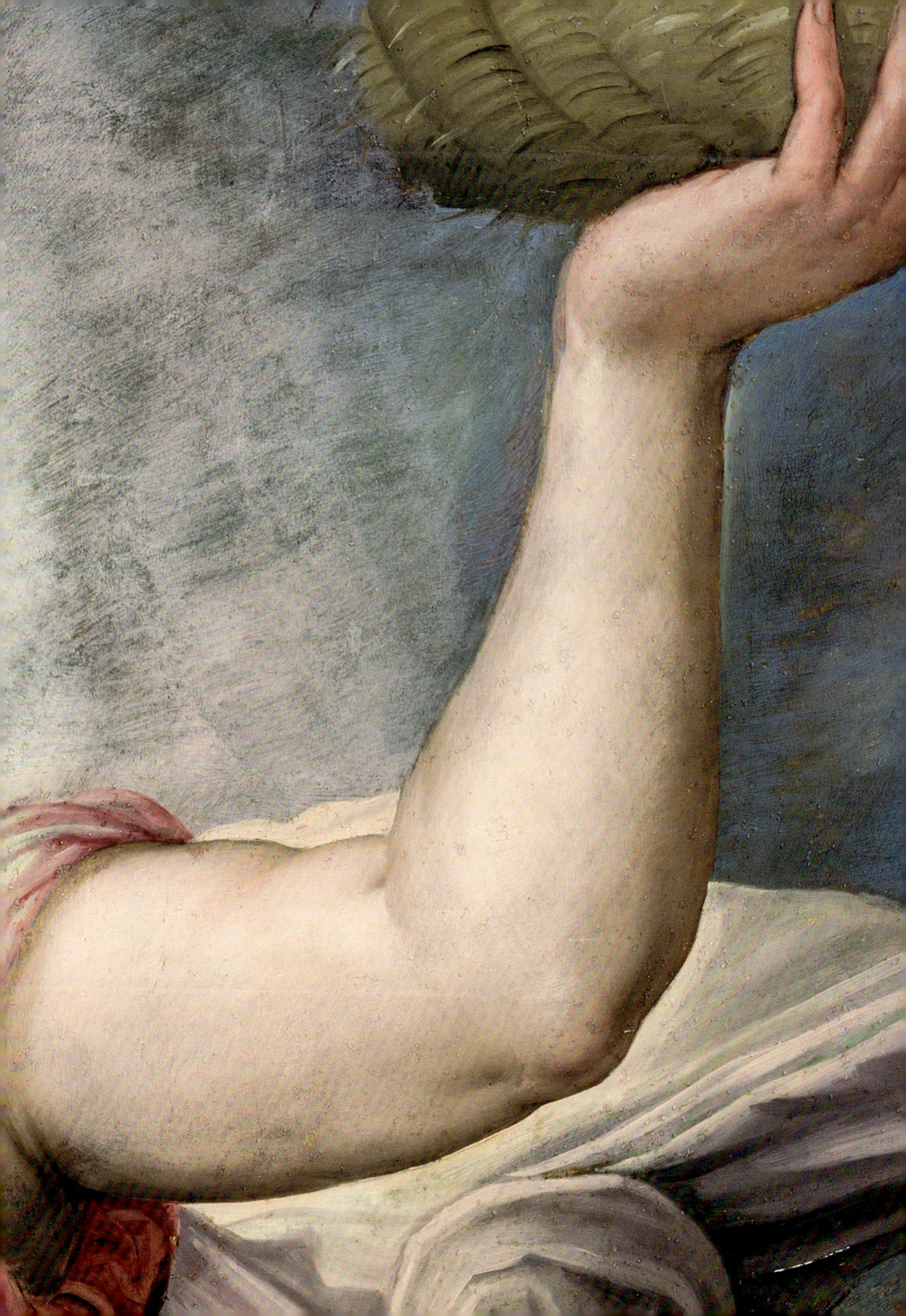

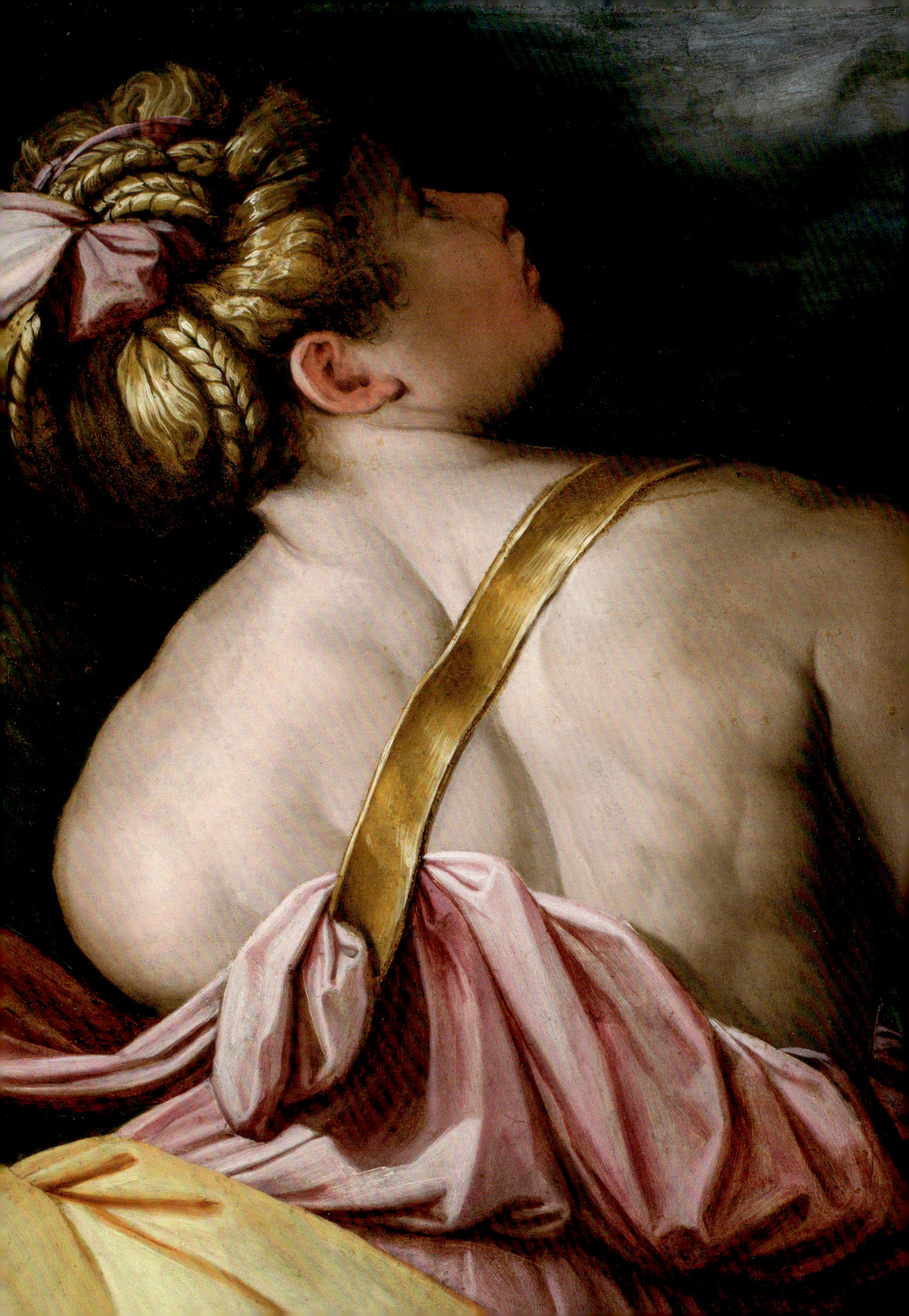

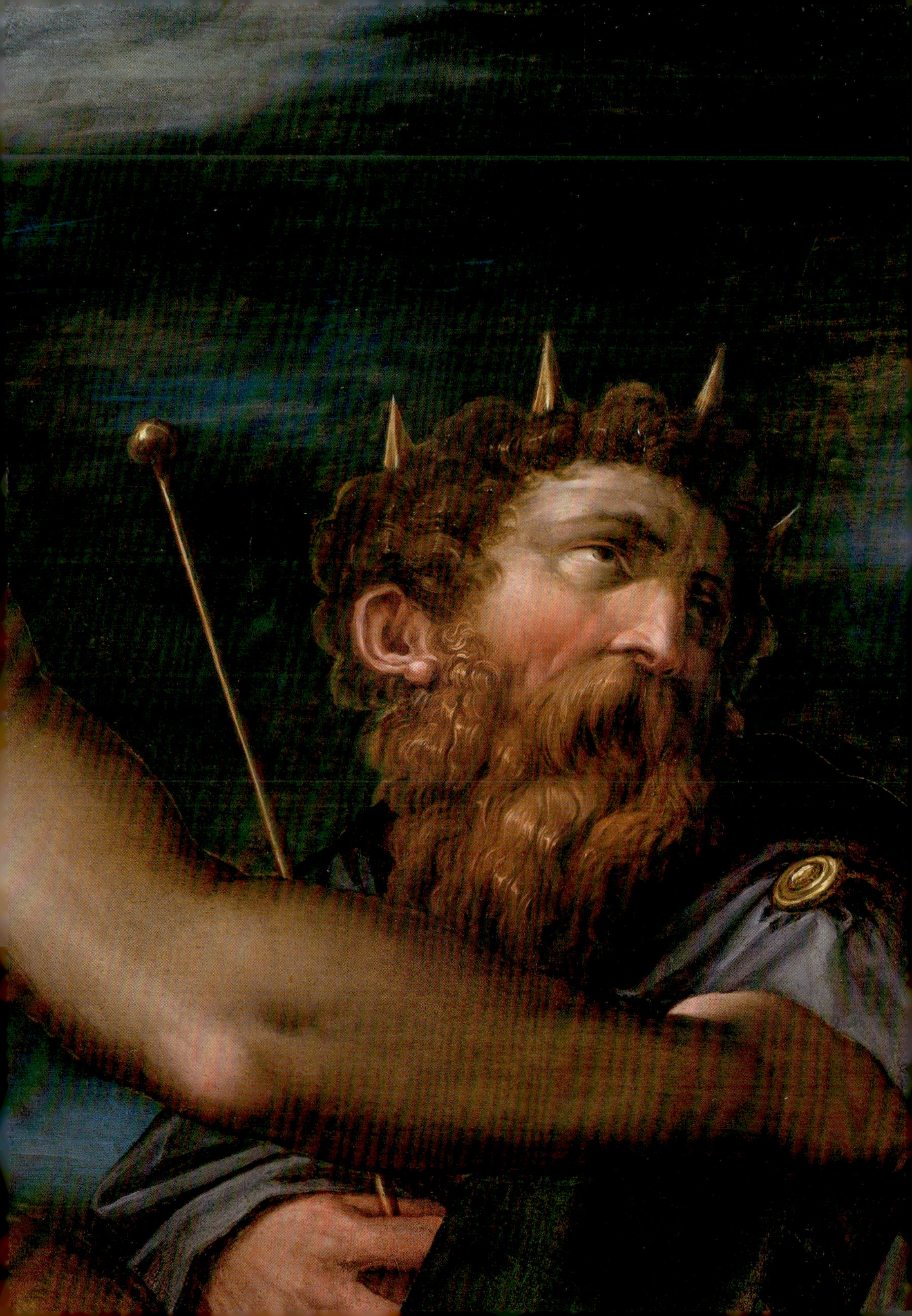

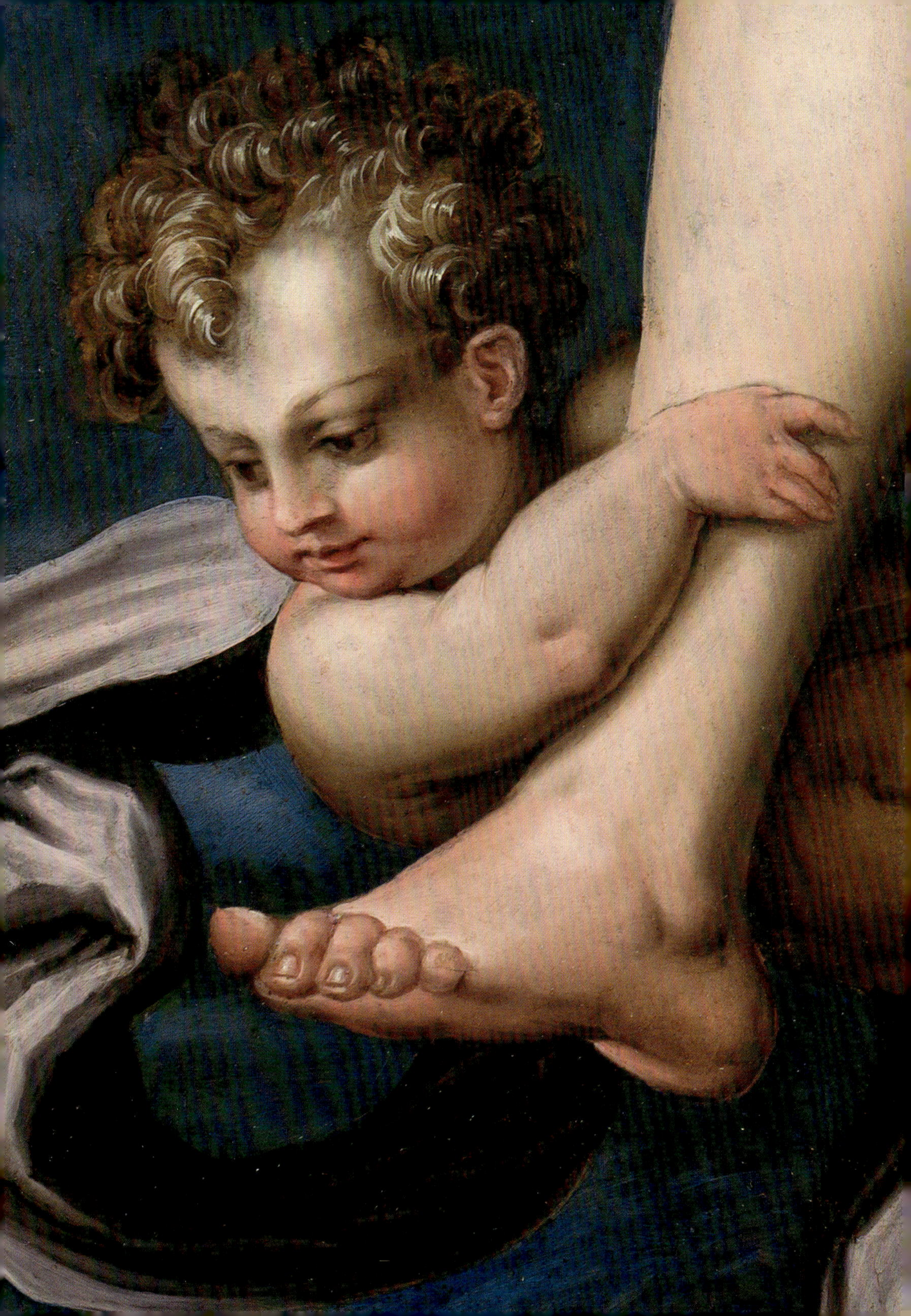

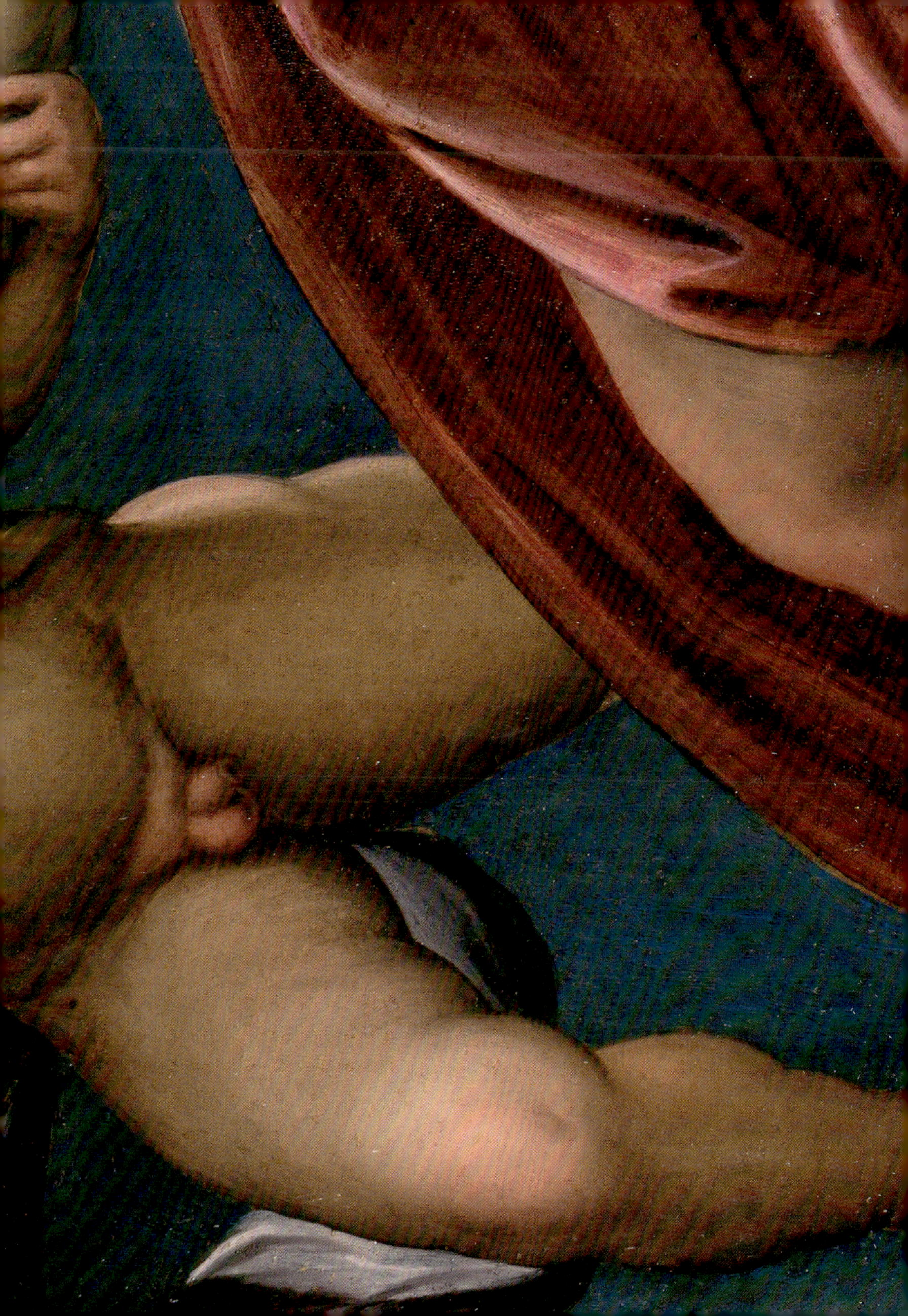

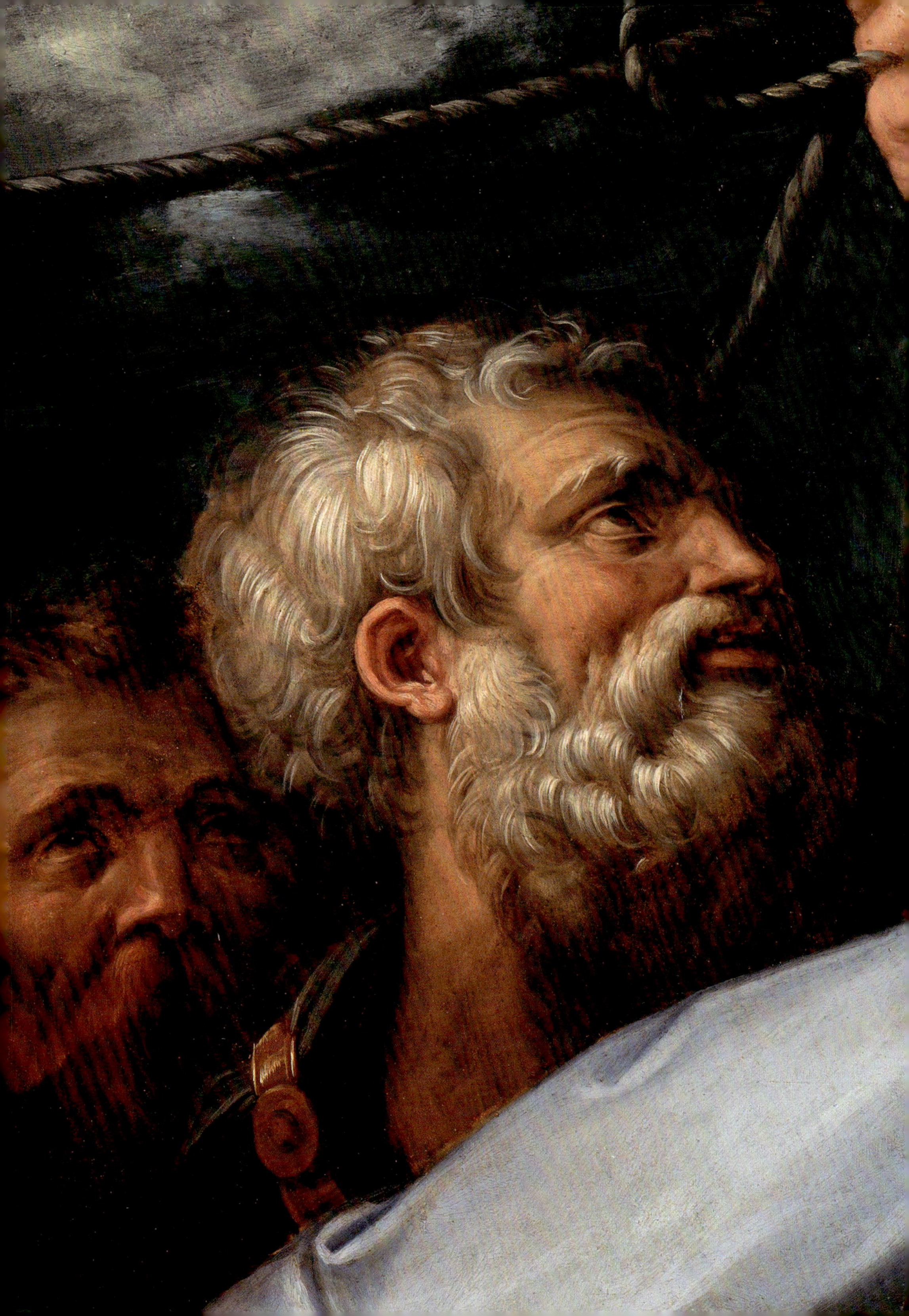